STUDIES IN HIGHER EDUCATION
DISSERTATION SERIES

Edited by

Philip G. Altbach
Monan Professor of Higher Education
Lynch School of Education, Boston College

A ROUTLEDGEFALMER SERIES

STUDIES IN HIGHER EDUCATION
PHILIP G. ALTBACH, *General Editor*

THE VIRTUAL DELIVERY AND VIRTUAL ORGANIZATION OF POSTSECONDARY EDUCATION

Daniel M. Carchidi

RoutledgeFalmer
New York & London

Published in 2002 by
RoutledgeFalmer
29 West 35th Street
New York, NY 10001

Published in Great Britain by
RoutledgeFalmer
11 New Fetter Lane
London EC4P 4EE

RoutledgeFalmer is an imprint of the Taylor & Francis Group
Printed in the United States of America on acid-free paper.

10 9 8 7 6 5 4 3 2 1

Library of Congress Cataloging-in-Publication Data
Carchidi, Daniel, 1964–
   Virtual delivery and virtual organization of post secondary education / Daniel
M. Carchidi.
      p. cm. — (Higher education)
   Includes bibliographical references and index.
   ISBN 0-415-93088-X
   1. Distance educaion—United States—Computer-assisted instruction—Case
studies. I. Title. II. Higher education (London, England)
LC5803.C65 C37 2002
378.1'758—dc21   2001048299

For Lisa

Contents

Acknowledgments

I AM DEEPLY GRATEFUL TO THE MANY ADMINISTRATORS, FACULTY AND STU-
dents from the Network for Information and Technology Services,
National Technological University, University of California
Extension, Center for Media and Independent Learning, Colorado
Electronic Community College and Penn State University World Campus,
who gave of their time to participate in this study. Because I promised them
anonymity, I am not able to acknowledge each by name; however, I wish to
thank them all for their accessibility, candor and feedback during all phases of this research project.

There are also many others who through their support and teaching
have provided the elements that made this study possible. Marv Peterson
was and continues to be a model of rigorous scholarship and a thoughtful
reviewer of and advocate for my research. Barb Nanzig and Doug Van
Houweling offered the support and work experience that nurtured the
ideas represented in this book. Elaine Didier was an advocate of this
research and provided useful comments about applications of these findings. Were it not for Gil Whitaker, I would not have been able to secure
funding for this study from the Andrew W. Mellon Foundation. Peggy
Plawchan's administrative support was invaluable in keeping track of the
numerous expenses associated with this study. I am grateful to the members of my dissertation committee—Michael Cohen, Eric Dey and Judy
Olson—each of whom offered insight that helped to push my thinking to
the next level. I also wish to thank friends from my time at Teachers
College, Columbia University, especially Bob Furno and Sharon McDade,
whose guidance in forming my interests in postsecondary education has
been invaluable. I am particularly indebted to my colleagues while I was a

student at the University of Michigan. In particular, I would like to thank Gerti Arnold, Jack Bernard, Matt Brown, Greg Cascione, Marlene Coles, Mike Cross, Marne Einerson, Phil Knutel, Michael McLendon, Kay Millett, Chris Navia, Scott Rosevear, Sally Sharp, David Siegel and Jim Vander Putten for their encouragement and good humor. I am also indebted to Philip Altbach, Farideh Kamali, and John Shea for their thoughtful review, comments, and production assistance on earlier versions of the manuscript.

The Knowledge Age and the Organization of Postsecondary Education

S PECULATION ABOUT THE FUTURE OF COLLEGES AND UNIVERSITIES IN THE knowledge age abounds. In the future what will the learning experience consist of and how will higher learning be organized? On one side are those who believe that institutions of postsecondary education must change radically to accommodate the inexhaustible supply and circumstantiated demand for information and knowledge that the knowledge age itself represents. On the other side are those who object to the actions taken by educational leaders in response to a knowledge age environment; at times protesting vociferously the lack of careful forethought in incorporating new technologies, challenging established patterns of governance or redesigning educational experiences to satisfy the student as customer. This debate is still in its infancy, yet much is already at stake for those who seek learning as well as for those who facilitate it.

The innumerable constituencies of postsecondary education, while diverse, are united if only in seeking a learning experience that is of high quality, reasonable cost and sufficient individuality. Clearly, mass education is giving way to the demand for flexibility and responsiveness in the educational process. These demands are creating intensified competition that is palpable to educational leaders. Environmental forces inspired by the knowledge age are propelling postsecondary education toward what has been described as a "Knowledge Industry" model (Ives and Jarvenpaa, 1996) or "Postsecondary Knowledge Industry" model (Peterson and Dill, 1997). These models are predicated on predicted and emerging changes taking place in the postsecondary educational environment. The models illustrate an environment in which the core technologies (e.g., development, transmission and dissemination of knowledge), new organizational entrants (e.g., new public, private and proprietary institutions), customers (e.g., non-traditional students), and suppliers (e.g., software and entertainment firms) are reshaping the organization, expectations and competitive nature of what postsecondary education is and what it should accomplish (Peterson and Dill, 1997).

How are these changes taking shape? These changes in the environment of postsecondary education have not always been grounded in intellectual or philosophical concerns, but rather, quite practical ones. It is evident in the increasing demands on educational institutions to provide lifelong education that can advance one's career and generate upward economic mobility. It has been noted that many students, especially graduate students, will seek professional development and degree programs at teleconferencing sites that are conveniently located in lieu of face to face interaction with an instructor. For adult students, convenience and quality of courses have become more significant than the campus experience itself (NRENAISSANCE Committee, et al., 1994). At the same time, the technology to deliver and manage educational services has become more powerful. The growth of the Internet and the increasing sophistication of other information technologies, such as CD-ROMs, interactive television, video conferencing, groupware and wireless communication devices are providing organizations with more varied options for content delivery and organizational management. Many believe that information technology will create far-reaching changes in approaches to teaching, research, service and administration of postsecondary institutions than had ever been available in previous periods in our history (Keller, 1993; March, 1987; Ward, 1994).

The inchoate Knowledge Industry has begun to demonstrate these changes through the organizational forms and delivery mechanisms supporting teaching and learning. These new and redesigned extant organizations have taken on a more prominent and controversial role in the educational landscape. Some of these new institutions, popularly called "virtual universities", "virtual colleges" or "cybercolleges", offer the promise of highly relevant educational content delivered to one's home or workplace. In 1993, Peterson's guide to distance education referenced 93 "cybercolleges." By 1997, that number had grown to over 760. As these institutions develop, there is concern being expressed over their organization, mission, value and long-term viability.

Dolence and Norris (1995) contended that on-line education offered by some new organizations is merely transactional, not transformational - implying that these organizations and their educational products are not as groundbreaking as some would suggest. Schank (1998) scrutinized technology-based learning as well, but in a slightly different vein. He argued that online education replicates the deficiencies found in traditional teaching methods. He calls for a learning experience that maximizes the use of technology and proposes goal-based scenarios in which artificial time constraints and activities embodied in the classroom metaphor give way to learning that is based upon the actual experience and tasks that a student must accomplish in order to be successful within his or her discipline.

For many people, this new paradigm of education means turning away from residential and face-to-face forms of knowledge based activities toward a more uncertain, but perhaps more efficient and market responsive kind of educational experience, from which students may gain greater satisfaction (Kauffman, 1996). Clearly, interest in these organizational forms that deliver technology-mediated education at a distance and organize in innovative ways is on the rise. The literature dedicated to virtual organizational forms, alliance-based organizations, joint educational ventures and educational organizations that provide distance learning is growing as well. That literature base has focused primarily on refining descriptions of virtual organizations, educational or otherwise, and examining management issues associated with new, distributed forms of organization. In the main, however, the literature base is not empirically derived and is essentially prescriptive in its orientation.

ORIGINS OF THIS STUDY

My interest in researching virtual postsecondary education organizations began in the mid-1990s through my work within and study of organizations that were wrestling with the demands of the knowledge intensive economy. At that time, leaders of many higher and postsecondary education organizations were viewing technology-based education as a new imperative if they were to be perceived as truly vital institutions. Others saw the possibility of improving the learning experience. Still others felt they had few choices since the market or their state legislatures demanded that they expand educational opportunities and technology-based education seemed the logical choice. The willingness of venture capital firms to invest in education companies also created interesting new possibilities that raised the bar for technology use in higher and postsecondary education. For many leaders, technology offered an obvious approach for achieving several of their goals.

Teamed with the growth of technology usage was also the realization that the organizations providing education were changing as well. I was continually struck by how uncritically terms such as "virtual university" were being presented. The term often reflected an emphasis on the virtual delivery of education, that is technology-based delivery, but little attention was given to the organizational meaning of virtual. Organizations were indeed forming and restructuring themselves in ways that spanned geographical, hierarchical and for and non-profit status boundaries, for example. These virtual or network organization forms revealed the other element of what had been missing in the discussion of "virtual universities" in higher and postsecondary education.

The goal of this study was to explain how virtual postsecondary education organizations function by taking into account the extraorganizational, intraorganizational and interorganizational forces that continually shape the strategy, structures and processes of each organization as well as their observable administrative patterns. In other words, how do environmental, collaborative, internal management and historical conditions shape the organizational form and administrative patterns that are demonstrated by these organizations? I was particularly interested in four sub-areas related to the operation of these organizations: The relationship of the organization's educational products and services to the manner in which the organizations function; What the organization's values reveal about the manner in which they function; What the organization's purpose reveals about the manner in which these organizations function; And do differentiations in the manner in which these organizations function provide clues to successful virtual postsecondary educational organizations in a Knowledge Industry environment?

This study began in 1996 when I was a doctoral student at the University of Michigan's Center for the Study of Higher and Postsecondary Education. The Andrew W. Mellon Foundation was the principal sponsor for this study. The University Continuing Education Association also provided financial support. Because the literature on virtual postsecondary educational organizations yielded no specific organizationally related typology to guide the site selection for this study, I developed a classification scheme to distinguish the various organizational types observed within the United States, from which five institutions were selected. During the course of the study, I visited each of the institutions. In order to understand the organizational form and administrative patterns of these organizations, it was necessary to select case sites that provided both compelling intrinsic interest (Stake, 1994) and a level of maturity worthy of study. For this reason I considered only those virtual postsecondary educational organizations that have been developing educational products and services at a distance for approximately two years or more. The principal informants for this study consisted of the management team as determined by the institutional representative (gatekeeper) and a review of organization documents and organization charts. Just as the organizational form of these various organizations are clearly different, I found that what constitutes the "management team" in each organization differed as well. In order to assure a comprehensive approach to identifying the management team, I used a referral or snowball sampling technique (Weiss, 1994) to identify other members of the management team who had been identified through docu-ment analysis or interaction with the institutional representative.

To construct a richer description and capture the historical elements contributing to the organizational form and administrative patterns of each organization, I extended the list of informants beyond the management team. For organizations who had experienced turn-over in their manage-ment team or whose communication structure was more distributed, this meant contacting former managers or persons not directly within the exist-ing organizational structure. When appropriate, I spoke with current staff, students and faculty, which provided additional insights essential for a clearer understanding of organizational dynamics. In total, I conducted seventy-two interviews ranging from twenty minutes to over three hours in length. The typical interview lasted for over an hour. From the interviews, document analysis and observation, I was able to construct an organiza-tional overview and history, a profile of the educational community and an analysis of the extra, inter and intra organizational conditions influencing the organizational form and administrative patterns of each organization. With these data, I developed an adaptation model for virtual postsecondary education organizations that reflects the products/services, values and pur-poses of these organization types.

The findings from this study confirm that these organizations are experimental and adaptive in their orientation. It also emphasizes their importance as organizational entities in an emerging industry that has yet to establish rules of leadership. I hope that the case studies and findings contained in this book will be useful to leaders from traditional colleges and universities as well as other postsecondary education institutions that are considering or currently managing virtual postsecondary educational organizations. Also, my hope is that the information presented in this book lends clarity to the notion of a "virtual university" and provides researchers and educational leaders with authentic accounts and insights for furthering their own research agendas and administrative practices. In chapter 1, I present a review of current views of virtual postsecondary organizations. Chapter 2 presents the research context for the study. In chapters 3-7, I provide case studies of five virtual postsecondary education organizations within the United States in which I highlight their structure and history and analyze how their extra, inter and intraorganizational characteristics influence their organizational form and administrative pat-terns. In Chapter 8, I conduct cross case analyzes consistent with the research framework and questions proposed in this study. And in chapters 9 and 10, I offer a model of organizational adaptation and offer several observations on effective administration of these institutions.

The Virtual Delivery and Virtual Organization of Postsecondary Education

CHAPTER 1

The Integration of Virtual Delivery and Virtual Organization

MOVING FROM INDUSTRY TO ORGANIZATIONS: THE EMERGING ORGANIZATIONAL LANDSCAPE OF POSTSECONDARY EDUCATION

THE TERM "VIRTUAL UNIVERSITY" OR "CYBERCOLLEGE," WHILE USEful shorthand for describing a current phenomenon in postsecondary education, is not very illustrative in a research context. Few would argue that the organizational complexity exhibited in a university or college is present in its virtual incarnation, nor is such a term capable of capturing the organizational variety that exists within postsecondary education. Additionally, these terms tend to gloss over the fact that truly new organizational forms are emerging that rely on network forms of organization to carry out their organizational objectives, since the popular terms rely only on established educational metaphors. Taking the assertions of Dolence and Norris (1995) seriously, is there something new to be found in studying a variety of organizations that deliver education to learners at a distance through the use of technology and organize in increasingly innovative ways? Clearly there is, but to do so, a better way of defining the unique nature of these organizational types is needed if they are to be studied effectively. The term used through out this book in referring to these organizations is virtual postsecondary educational organization. In using this term, "virtual" refers to the virtual delivery of education found in technology-mediated distance education, which frees the teacher and learner from the constraints of time and place. Yet, "virtual" also applies to an organization in which units are horizontally, vertically and spatially integrated across multiple geographic locations. These organizations are becoming more prevalent, yet are often misunderstood since their forms are

3

highly experimental. Before delving into the specifics of these organizations, it is important to see their place within the larger context of organizational types in postsecondary education.

Competition and its Consequences

Along with utilizing new technology to deliver educational services, postsecondary educational organizations may need to radically reevaluate their processes, strategies, structures and administrative patterns in order to survive (Drucker, as cited in Lenzner and Johnson, 1997; Perrin, 1997). If the characterizations of industry emergence suggested by Peterson and Dill (1997) are indeed underway, then the nature of organizations in postsecondary education is likely to change as a result. The emerging competitive marketplace is placing greater emphasis on the application of new technologies to extend the teaching/learning environment. It is also stressing organizational structures that are more flexible and respond more quickly and effectively to market forces. A starting point for understanding the emerging organizational landscape of postsecondary education lies in differentiating organizations according to their educational delivery and organizational structure characteristics (see Figure 1.1).

Figure 1.1: An Integrated Framework of Educational Delivery and Organizational Structure

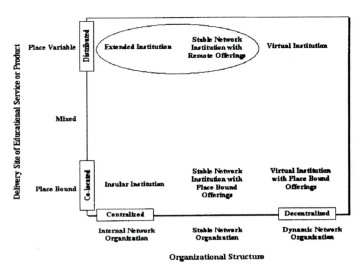

The first dimension of the Integrated Framework of Educational Delivery and Organizational Structure, educational delivery, recognizes that delivery extends from a face-to-face learning environment in which student and teacher are co-located to a more remote and distributed approach to teacher-student interaction in which each resides in a different place. Gradations of educational delivery may extend from a completely remote or distributed experience for student and instructor to those experiences involving solely face-to-face, co-located delivery. Understandably, some organizations will choose to develop both distributed and co-located educational delivery capacity in order to make a wider variety of learning experiences available to students.

The notion of educational content delivery that is based on connecting learners and instructors through an electronically mediated delivery mechanism is not new to postsecondary education. Technologies such as educational television and audio/videotape have been used as educational delivery tools for decades. More recent educational delivery methods such as Internet-based cooperative learning spaces account for many advances in remote delivery technologies connecting students and instructors. What is new is the growing emphasis that postsecondary educational institutions are placing upon remote delivery technologies. The use of technology for remote delivery constitutes the virtuality of educational delivery as embodied by an evolving class of organizations that leverage these new technologies to create learning environments that are free from the restrictions of physical place. Another nuance of technology-enhanced delivery, often linked to the notion of place, is that of time. Typically phased in terms of synchronous (real-time interaction) and asynchronous (non-real-time interaction), many new technologies free the learner and instructor from the same time and same place constraints that are evident in traditional educational delivery methods.

The second dimension of Figure 1.1, organizational structure, consists of a range of institutional types extending from a hierarchical approach to organization (in which decision making is more centralized) to more decentralized approaches (in which multiple partners engage in short-term, focused, projects). Here, the notion of an organization as a network of social ties may be particularly illustrative since the structural implications of organizations as networks provide rather distinct categories for considering a wide variety of extant and emerging organizational types. It is important to note that the notion of networks does have other connotations outside of the social—organizational context. For example, technologists often speak of networks in terms of a group of connected computers. Here, I use network in its organizational sense. As Baker (1992) has asserted, all organizations are networks of some type. Networks may be hierarchical or flexible and decentralized. What is clear is that the network organization is one that is integrated across organizational boundaries "of multiple types of socially important relations" (p. 400). Miles and Snow (1986) and Snow, Miles and Coleman (1992) believe structural models of these social relations exist in three forms; internal networks, stable networks and dynamic networks.

An internal network organization possesses most or all of the assets needed to carry out its business objectives. Managers within internal network organizations are encouraged, and often expected, to subject the assets of their organization to the conditions of the market. The rationale is that if internal units are forced to operate with prices set by the market instead of artificially fixed through transfer prices, then they will seek innovative practices to improve their performance. Little, if any, outsourcing arrangements take place in internal networks since the resources the organization needs are assumed to exist somewhere within the larger organizing structure. Most postsecondary education institutions do not operate in this manner, although there are applications of this concept. Consider an institution's effort to lower its costs by having academic or administrative units operate in a more entrepreneurial fashion (the phrases "responsibility-centered-management" or "every-tub-on-its-own-bottom" are often used to describe this type of financial management system). Such a structure may be used in order to drive innovation into the system.

Stable networks use partial outsourcing arrangements as a means to create more flexibility within its organizational processes and better serve its customers. In this type of network organization, the assets are owned by several entities, each providing some component or function of what is needed by the organization. Typically, a group of vendors are clustered around a core firm. Increasingly, postsecondary education institutions are recognizing that all of the resources needed to create innovative educational products may not be available within their organization (e.g., an internal network). Such institutions may intentionally create partnerships with the express purpose of assembling the resources necessary to offer a new and distinctive educational product. In stable networks individuals and units collaborate and often share the risk in order to achieve a particular outcome of mutual benefit to each partner.

The dynamic network, the third type of network organization, represents the most flexible form of network organization. Miles and Snow (1986) outline several characteristics of dynamic network organizations. These include: 1.) Vertical desegregation, as individual organizations perform specific functions within the network; 2.) The use of brokers to structure and assemble members of the network. A single broker may take the leadership role in assembling services and subcontractors, partnerships between equal partners may be established by several brokers who have competencies in a specific area, or one member of the network may use a broker for expertise in other needed functions. 3.) Incorporation of market mechanisms to serve as guiding forces holding the functions within the network together. Contracts and result-based compensation are most often used as administrative controls, rather than supervision or individual progress reports. And 4.) Installation of full disclosure information systems that may serve as proxies for trust building processes that take time and experience to develop. Members of the network negotiate the payment for the value that they add to the network then connect to a continuously updated information system, allowing each member to verify the contribution of other members and supply information on their own progress. The application of this network form in the realm of postsecondary education may be emerging, often in response to the limitations of existing organizational structures. Its use, given an increasing competitive environment, is likely to become more widespread.

The integration of distributed, technology-mediated education and distributed, network organizational structures is having profound effects on the potential organization and management structures of postsecondary education. The evolution and development of alliances between new entrants to the Knowledge Industry and more mature members from colleges, universities and training organizations, for example, is resulting in transformations in how leaders must think about managing within their institutions. However, leaders must also sort through opportunities brought to the fore by potential new external partners. As institutions consider extending their teaching and learning environments with instructional technology and seek support from organizations outside of their institution in order to accomplish this, a new framework for understanding the emerging environment of postsecondary education is needed to make sense of the shifting landscape. Figure 1.1 illustrates the six organizational archetypes that emerge from the integration of the educational delivery and organizational structure dimensions. While not all of these institutional types are the subject of this book (I will deal with those that are demarcated by the ellipse in Figure 1.1), a broader understanding of these organization types is important in order to put into context those organizations that are the subject of this study. These institutional types include:

The Insular Institution: Insular institutions possess centralized organizational structures in which decision making authority resides in the senior administration. The most traditional of the six archetypes, these institutions instruct students using a residential, face-to-face educational model. They also rely upon internal institutional resources to provide instruction to students. Examples of this type of organization include many postsecondary education institutions that offer only residential education utilizing their own faculty and staff.

The Extended Institution: Extended institutions have redesigned their instructional delivery systems to take advantage of distance learning technologies in order to extend the resources of the institution to new constituencies of learners. Such institutions rely on an internal network of relationships within the boundaries of the organization to deliver new educational services. Examples include the University of Phoenix Online Campus, the New School for Social Research DIAL program, and Penn State World Campus.

The Stable Network Organization with Place-bound Offerings: This type of organization utilizes multi-partner outsourcing agreements with a stable group of partners to deliver its co-located, face-to-face educational products and services. Prior to the advent of distance learning, many universities such as Columbia or Harvard provided educational services in concert with sister institutions within their larger organizing context. For Columbia this included Barnard College or Teachers College, at Harvard, Radcliffe.

The Stable Network Organization with Remote Offerings: This organizational type combines stable outsourcing relationships with technology-mediated remote delivery. These organizations have formed partnerships with vendors and/or individuals who are able to provide key functions for the organization. The organization's products and services are entirely dependent upon technology for their transmission. Examples include Colorado Electronic Community College and National Technological University.

The Virtual Organization with Place-bound Offerings: This organizational type appears most often in corporate settings in which training expertise is primarily outsourced to consultants and corporate trainers. Such organizations may lack the technological sophistication or resources to take advantage of computer-based training (CBT) or other educational technologies. To achieve their training and educational goals, these organizations rely on place-bound educational experiences for their employees, typically using a fluid combination of outside expertise provided by consultants and internal expertise possessed by the firm's managers. A popular example is The Learning Annex, an adult learning organization offering short, inexpensive courses on personal growth, business and career opportunities, health and healing, spirituality, relationships and high technology issues. It uses a wide variety of instructors to teach its students. It can therefore respond to market demands for new workshops and seminars quite easily. A majority of classes are held at learning centers in major metropolitan areas, although a few classes are now available via the World Wide Web.

The Virtual Institution: This model reflects an organizational archetype that is emerging within postsecondary education and has been the subject of great interest. Numerous organizations, particularly corporate universities at firms such as Dell and Oracle, are making advances in this form of education organization. A virtual organization relies almost entirely on outsourcing to achieve its organizational goals. Technology facilitates this by linking disparate groups and allowing them to collaborate in a manner that is free from the constraints of time and place. Each entity in the partnership, be it individual or group, brings unique expertise to the virtual organization in order to provide the educational service or support that service. But unlike more stable organizational alliances, virtual organizations form to achieve particular organizational goals then disband or take a new shape depending on the task at hand. This fluid, decentralized approach to organizing allows educational partners to move more quickly to meet marketplace needs than would a single partner be able to accomplish if acting unilaterally.

USING THE INTEGRATION OF VIRTUAL EDUCATIONAL DELIVERY AND NETWORK ORGANIZATION AS A STARTING POINT FOR CONSIDERING VIRTUAL POSTSECONDARY EDUCATIONAL ORGANIZATIONS

The first forms of remote delivery, correspondence and independent study offered by colleges and universities, have a long tradition in the United States dating back to the late 1800s. This form of distributed education has allowed students to take courses without having to set foot on a college or university campus. This method is hardly radical. However, new technologies have both reinforced and extended individual, distributed learning and also expanded the possibilities for students to collaborate and interact with classmates who may be located in physically separated locations. Once the domain of less distinctive institutions, distance education is entering the mainstream. Niche programs at elite institutions such as Stanford, Duke, and Johns-Hopkins are causing many in higher education to take notice. The growth of institutions that provide only distance learning courses and cater to adult students such as International University in Colorado and Magellan University in Arizona are also a subject of interest. A recent study completed by the National Center for Education Statistics found that a third of 2 and 4-year higher education institutions sampled offered distance education courses in the fall of 1995, while another quarter planned to offer distance learning courses by 1998. Distance education is moving from the periphery of postsecondary education to the mainstream. The remote delivery of educational products and services is on the rise within postsecondary education.

The popularity of distance education is being matched by innovations in organizational structures. Organizational structures of internal, stable, and dynamic organizations may yield new perspectives on the organization of postsecondary education in the knowledge age. It is hardly surprising that advances in instructional technology that allow learners to participate virtually would not have organizational implications. As students are educated remotely they are coming to expect remote, technology-based administrative support. As instructors teach remote students, the faculty support services that accompany residential instruction should logically follow in a technology-mediated, remote medium. Such a distributed medium is certain to affect the administrative patterns within the organizations. What are those influences? And what can these influences reveal about the workings of new organizational forms in postsecondary education? While dynamic network organizations are not yet evident in a form to be studied, numerous examples exist of organizations that are either internal networks or stable networks and which provide technology-mediated delivery of educational products and services.

THE VIRTUAL POSTSECONDARY EDUCATIONAL ORGANIZATION: EXPERIMENTAL, CONTROVERSIAL AND BECOMING MORE WIDESPREAD

Of the six archetypes presented in Figure 1.1, three may be identified as virtual postsecondary educational organizations—those occupying the upper most sections of the diagram—extended institutions, stable network organizations with remote offerings, and virtual institutions. Each of these virtual postsecondary educational organizations offers technology-mediated products and services remotely but does so by organizing in varied network organization forms. The combination of delivery and structure provided a starting point for this study by identifying a known population of postsecondary education organizations generally, and a group of virtual postsecondary educational organizations specifically. Upon further examination, it became clear that the virtual institution archetype was entirely too immature a postsecondary education form to consider for inclusion within this study. Even for those more mature organization types that are represented in extended and stable network organizations with remote offerings, much experimentation and controversy were present. Extended and stable network organizations with remote offerings have also been the focus of much attention from educational leaders and policy makers, which have made them the recipients of substantial investments of time and money. Understanding the risks and benefits of these organizations has become incredibly important. The success of these organizations, whether one wishes them well or ill, is rarely an insouciant endeavor.

CHAPTER 2

Research Context

WHILE THE MAIN TOPIC OF THIS STUDY EXAMINES HOW VIRTUAL postsecondary educational organizations function, issues regarding the environment of postsecondary organizations and means by which organizations adapt to that environment inform the framework for this study. In the research context of this book, I begin by providing an overview of the limited literature base on virtual organization and virtual delivery of educational services and products. Next, I advance a framework based on open systems, institutional and resource dependence theories of organizational adaptation. These approaches to organizational behavior were used as starting points for structuring investigation within the research settings, rather than an immutable approach to understanding organizational-environment interaction. Next, I present the research settings and scope this study. In the final section, I provide an overview of the eight types of virtual postsecondary education organizations and those specific institutions that are included in this study.

LITERATURE RELATED TO THE VIRTUAL ORGANIZATION AND VIRTUAL DELIVERY OF EDUCATIONAL SERVICES AND PRODUCTS

Interest in virtual organizational forms surfaced in the early 1990s as business and industry sought innovative ways to satisfy their customers and compete more effectively amidst new challenges in their external environments. The new business environment, as described by Tapscott and Caston (1993), challenges organizations to react rapidly to changing market conditions, competitive threats and customer demands by increasing

11

knowledge and service worker productivity, improving quality, meeting customers' needs quickly and in more customized ways, emphasizing global implications, outsourcing organizational functions, increasing organizational partnering, and acting in more socially and environmentally responsible ways. The appropriate application of information technology in this formidable business environment was seen as a critical element for generating success. The literature on virtual organizations reflects these business concerns. Moreover, similar concerns as expressed by businesses about competition, partnerships, information technology and quality have influenced thinking in the educational realm. With the precipitous growth of organizations that fit the virtual postsecondary educational organization parameters has come a literature base that is perspective, not particularly scholarly in its orientation, but clearly of interest to authors in fields as diverse as business, higher education and information technology. The diversity of perspectives makes finding commonalities among these strains difficult because the contexts for application of virtual forms of organization and delivery are so different.

Authors writing from a business perspective have concentrated on describing the organizational qualities of virtual organizations and explaining managerial implications of working virtually. For example, writers have discussed re-engineering organizational processes and structures to create virtual work environments (Alexander, 1997; Davidow and Malone, 1992; Davis and Darling, 1995; Grenier and Metes, 1995; O'Leary, Kuokka and Plant, 1997); the key characteristics of virtual organizations (Voss, 1996); the theoretical implications of virtual organization as a goal-oriented approach to matching satisfiers to tasks (Mowshowitz, 1997); and the philosophical and psychological underpinnings of virtual means of organizing (Faucheux, 1997). Other authors writing in a business bent have been focused principally on operational concerns from a managerial perspective. For instance, Handy (1995) emphasized trust as a key component of effective management in virtual organizations, while Chesbrough and Teece (1996) accentuated the use of virtual organization designs to enhance managers' approaches to innovation.

The work of Davidow and Malone (1992) has been particularly influential in developing an understanding of the concept of virtual operations in business, the strategic application of information technology to construct a virtual organization, and the management environment in which multiple partners create shared values (co-destiny) to serve their customers. These authors argue that the virtual corporation, synonymous with virtual organization, may actually be a more stable organizational form as compared with its physical counterpart. Virtual organizations aim to give customers ultimate control over the products and services that they seek. One way that virtual organizations may meet customer needs according to the authors is through "mass customization," a process used to denote an organization's ability to provide personalized products and services to a wide array of customers. Trust and cooperation among partners in the virtual organization and their agreement to focus on customer needs are the keys to delivering what the customer wants. While highly complex, the partnership also creates enduring ties based on recognition of each partner's mutual destiny, which may result in a more stable organizational form.

For scholars and practitioners writing from a higher education perspective, the concept of virtual organization and virtual delivery of educational services and products have tended to cluster around issues of educational reform, the influences of technology, issues of access, quality and certification of distance education services and products, and various organizational models and governance structures for delivering educational services and products. For example, a wide variety of reform issues such as total quality management, research, teaching and service revisions, and new and modified federal and state policies are addressed under the virtual campus rubric (Van Dusen, 1997). The virtual university concept has been examined in terms of its technology components and vision as an integrated campus network (Baker and Gloster, 1994). Issues of access, quality and certification of distance education services and products have been addressed in terms of principles of good practice for virtual universities (Johnstone and Krauth, 1996); competency-based assessment practices (Jones, 1995); and online accreditation considerations (Rucker, 1998).

The largest area of the literature deals with the subject of virtual university organization models. Several authors, writing in varied contexts, have attempted to capture the nature of virtual university organization. Some focus on distance education (Holmberg, 1989; Verdin and Clark, 1991), collaboration and technology-mediated interactions (Acker, 1995; Rossman, 1992) or the governance structure of the organization (Hurst, 1998). Of these models, Verdin and Clark's is the most comprehensive as it identifies six types of distance learning organizations. However, Hurst's explanation of governance model scenarios has the closest adherence to the virtual postsecondary educational organization parameters established in this study. Hurst (1998) suggests six scenarios for governance structures of a virtual university:

> "*Open University*: The governor or the legislature decides that the state's traditional public postsecondary education institutions should focus on their current missions rather than trying to meet the needs of new learners. Therefore the policymakers create an Open University (OU), independent and charged with responding to the needs of students and businesses.

Governor's University: The academic content is brokered from other institutions and the degrees awarded by the GU. The content will be brokered from the public and private institutions in the state, with courses brokered from institutions outside the state when in-state courses are not available.

Virtual Community College and University: The courses and academic content will be offered by—and the degrees and certificates will be awarded by—existing institutions.

Institutional Competition and Consumer Advocacy: This scenario embraces free market, open competition among all institutions in the state. This requires the creation of a centralized neutral student and employer advocacy organization to provide information, marketing, needs assessment, and standards for academic and student services.

Coordinated Collaboration: Public higher education systems will each choose institutions to be primarily responsible for the provision of distance learning degrees.

Current Structure: Institutions will continue to develop distance-learning courses within their current structure. The largest universities will prosper by taking the cream of the crop of residential students and by developing distance learning for specific high-volume and high-profit markets" (pp. 1, 4-8).

Another group of writers appear critical of the changes that the virtual organization and virtual delivery of education present. For example, Brown and Duguid (1995) offer a critique of Rossman's concept of the worldwide electronic university. While these authors provide no particular definition of the virtual university, they are suspect of Rossman's notion of the universality of knowledge. They also point to the tentative relationship between pedagogy, credentialing, and control of degree granting that is largely unexamined in Rossman's vision of the new university paradigm. The authors contend that new institutional arrangements are necessary and are not a function of technological transformation alone. They assert that leading institutions toward a virtual university is wrong-headed since distance teaching (the core activity of the virtual university) focuses only on delivery, rather than the development of communities of practice—the core competency of traditional universities. They do believe, however, that technology can play a pivotal role in fostering notions of learning communities. Brand (1995) offers criticism of the virtual university as a preeminent mode of higher education in the United States. He describes the virtual university as a "highly sophisticated communication network housed in a broadcast (not ivory) tower" (p. 40). His criticism centers on the integration of learning, research and service that is fully developed in the traditional university but which is fragmented or nonexistent in the virtual university. He argues in favor of distance education as a supplement to traditional campus arrangements.

SUMMARY OF THE LITERATURE

The literature pertaining to virtual organizations is largely anecdotal and is not theoretically derived. While some organizational typologies exist in the literature on "virtual universities" or distance education organizations, these characterizations have not possessed a theoretical perspective focusing on environment-organization interaction, nor the resulting organizational forms and administrative patterns. Rather, as an emerging phenomenon, the literature on virtual forms of organization has dealt with the pragmatic issues of import to practitioners and managers of such organizations. Beyond the anecdotal explanations of the dynamics of virtual organizations in business or speculative models of virtual universities in higher education, a great need exists for an understanding of how virtual postsecondary educational organizations function that blends theoretical rigor with comprehensive description and analysis. Clearly, a conceptual model would advance our understanding of these organizations as well as suggest strategic actions for developing successful virtual postsecondary educational organization ventures. The next section provides a theoretically derived approach to studying virtual postsecondary educational organizations, which is an operational starting point for addressing this gap in the growing literature base.

OPERATIONAL FRAMEWORK

A review of the extant literature suggests that influences on the organizational form and administrative patterns of virtual postsecondary educational organizations may be divided into three distinct areas vis-à-vis the organization's relationship to its environment (environment denoted here by the Knowledge Industry and the organizations of which it is comprised). These areas include: extra-organizational conditions faced by the organization, pertaining to a broad class of environmental variables regarding the organization's ability to make sense of environmental uncertainty, secure needed resources and receive the legitimacy and support needed to operate effectively; inter-organizational conditions, a specific set of environmental variables examining the collaborative influences that affect the virtual postsecondary educational organization. (These variables examine relationships that the organization maintains with other organizations within its environment, which may influence organizational form and administrative patterns—collaboration, as the business literature reveals, is a critical characteristic of any virtual organization); finally, intra-organizational conditions, although not an environmental concept *per se*, incorporate a set of variables meant to examine the internal dynamics of people in time and those influences more emblematic of the emerging culture of the organization. (Intra-organizational conditions are viewed as a third potential group of variables capable of influencing organizational form and administrative patterns.)

The basis for these three sets of variables comprising the operational framework derives from specific theoretical perspectives within open systems theory (Katz and Kahn, 1978). Operational variables pertaining to extra-organizational conditions and inter-organizational conditions were developed using both institutional and resource dependence theories as a lens through which to view organizational adaptation processes. Those variables relating to intra-organizational influences are based upon conceptions of internal organizational dynamics tied to organizational culture perspectives of organizations and the influences of an organization's history on its organizational form and administrative patterns. More detailed explanation of the theoretical traditions comprising the operational framework, the environment of virtual postsecondary educational organizations, and the assumptions underlying the specific variables are contained in the following sections and accompanying appendices.

Open Systems Theory and the Organizational Adaptation Perspective

Virtual postsecondary educational organizations may be viewed as open systems. Katz and Kahn (1978) have described open systems theory as one that

> emphasizes the close relationship between a structure and its supporting environment. It begins with the concept of entropy, the assumption that without continued inputs any system soon runs down. . . . The other major emphasis.
> . . .is on throughput: the processing of production inputs to yield some outcome that is then used by an outside group or system . . . another aspect of open systems theory is its inclusion of different systems and their interrelationships. A pattern of collective behavior with a limited specific function may tie into other patterns to achieve a more general outcome, as in the case of work groups whose cooperative relationship insures a final product (p. 3).

Building on the premise posited by open systems theory, the nature of relations between an organization and its environment may be characterized in terms of an organization's ability to adapt to its environment. Organizational adaptation is a complex term that is difficult to define because it may be operationalized in terms of its outcome (in the case of this study organizational form and administrative patterns) or as a process occurring over time (Singh, House & Tucker, 1986). Because of this, scholars examining theoretical approaches to organizational adaptation have tended to conceptualize it in different ways. Categorizations of organizational theory relating to organizational adaptation have been well documented in the organizational behavior literature (see for example, Lee,

1993, in a non-United States context and Singh, House and Tucker, 1986) and have been given only limited treatment in the higher education literature (Cameron, 1991). Since virtual postsecondary educational organizations are assumed to be highly adaptable organizational models with strong institutional characteristics and environmental dependencies, institutional theory (DiMaggio and Powell, 1983; Meyer and Rowan, 1977; Meyer and Scott, 1983; Zucker, 1977), and resource dependence theory (Child, 1972; Pfeffer and Salancik, 1978) provided the initial theoretical grounding for the operational framework.

Institutional Theory

Institutional theory emphasizes the symbolic aspects of an organization's environment or organizational field. In this approach, the environment is assumed to be one that consists of cultural elements or commonly accepted beliefs and rules that serve as patterns for organizing and which define similar organizations (DiMaggio and Powell, 1983). The directives of external forces shape the internal attributes of modern organizations— positions, policies, programs, and procedures. These forces may be laws, public opinion, significant constituents of the organization, the need for social prestige, pronouncements of the court system or the base of knowledge created by the educational system (Meyer and Rowan, 1977).

DiMaggio and Powell (1983) point out that there are three mechanisms by which organizations change or adapt within their organizational field. They argue that isomorphic change is engendered through coercive, mimetic and normative processes. Coercive isomorphism refers to the pressures, both formal and informal, which one organization may exert over another or the cultural exceptions that society places on an organization. Mimetic processes concern the modeling of one organization after another. Such processes may occur when an organization's goals are not clear or when symbolic uncertainty is present in the environment. Normative pressures involve the organization's need to conform to professional principles or standards in order to be seen as legitimate within their organizational field. Meyer and Rowan (1977) suggest that institutional researchers see the organizational structures, patterns and policies present within an organization as playing a role in influencing the nature of the organizational field. Operating as myths, structures and practices become accepted and legitimated through key constituents and social systems, which ultimately lie beyond the control of individuals or single organizational entities to affect in a meaningful way. When organizations adopt the rationalized conditions of their organizational field, greater stability, legitimacy and resources are likely to result.

Institutional theory provides a valuable lens for examining virtual postsecondary educational organizations. First, because these are educational organizations, institutional theory provides a systematic way to examine how organizational form and administrative patterns become institutionalized in environments guided by socially pervasive practices and policies. Next, virtual postsecondary educational organizations represent innovative new structures in postsecondary education (some might suggest radically new structures). Institutional theory may help to explain how such organizations that are under pressure to adhere to the structural expectations existing within their environment adapt in order to be viewed as legitimate organizations capable of obtaining needed financial, social and expertise support. Finally, institutional theory is a useful perspective for comparing organizations within the same industry that manifest differing organizational forms and patterns. It provides a way to understand commonalities in patterns and structural features that may be institutionalized due to isomorphic tendencies created by adaptation to the environment.

Resource Dependence Theory

Resource dependence theory is based on an open systems perspective and focuses upon the exchange relationships in which a focal organization engages. The most extensive treatment of resource dependence theory is advanced in Pfeffer and Salancik's (1978) work, *The External Control of Organizations*. In their rendering, resource dependence theory views organizations as coalitions that adapt their "purposes and domains to accommodate new interests, sloughing off parts of themselves to avoid some interests, and when necessary, becoming involved in activities far afield from their stated central purposes" (Pfeffer and Salancik, 1978, p. 24). Organizational actors are seen as actively constructing relationships that will bring favorable results and beneficial exchanges to the organization. Management aspires to obtain the resources that the organization requires without creating dependencies that will ultimately affect the survivability of the organization.

The resource dependence approach suggests that in the process of adapting to environmental conditions, organizational managers will develop strategies to ensure the organization's success and long-term viability. These strategies may focus on intraorganizational techniques (Pfeffer and Salancik, 1978; Thompson, 1967) such as those meant to buffer the organization from external threats; or interorganizational strategies (Pfeffer and Salancik, 1978) designed to respond to increasing interorganizational dependence through bridging techniques aimed at facilitating greater coordination between organizations. In each strategy, organizations attempt to limit the uncertainty present in their environment, which may affect the core of their operations or vital resource exchange relationships.

Virtual postsecondary educational organizations are comprised of multiple partners, each of whom controls resources that are of value to the organization as a whole. As network organizations, virtual postsecondary educational organizations depend on their environment for the resources they need because the focal organization is not capable of delivering the educational product or service in its entirety. The resource dependence perspective provides insight because it focuses on the transactions that occur between and among partners for necessary resources. Further, resource dependence theory provides a lens for evaluating the nature of control and power present in interorganizational relations (Pfeffer and Salancik, 1978), which may be reflected in the organizational patterns and form of the organization. Strategies resulting from the virtual postsecondary educational organization's environmental response may illustrate important similarities and differences across organizations within the emerging Knowledge Industry.

Operational Framework Variables

Several premises guide the structure of this study and the resulting operational framework (see Figure 2.1). First, I assumed that institutional theory and resource dependence theory provide appropriate theoretical lenses for understanding why the organizational forms and administrative patterns of virtual postsecondary educational organizations differ within the Knowledge Industry. Tolbert's (1985) study of how nontraditional sources of support influence administrative differentiation and Blau et al.'s (1994) study of two-year college expansion between 1942 and 1979 each suggest that institutional theory and resource dependence theory are complementary theories for understanding the relationship of environment and organization and the differences in organizational form and administrative patterns that result from organizational adaptation.

Second, based on an open systems perspective of organizations (Katz and Kahn, 1978), I assumed that extra-organizational conditions, particularly the influences within an organization's external environment, will influence organization managers to shape the organizational form and administrative patterns of their organization in ways that embody certain assumptions they have made about their environment. My framework draws on Scott's (1991, 1992) conceptions of environment emphasizing uncertainty/dependence and normative/cognitive distinctions as central environmental constructs. Dimensions of the environment consistent with Scott's (1991, 1992) characterization include complexity (Dill, 1958; Thompson, 1967); stability-variability (Lawrence and Lorsch, 1967;

Thompson, 1967); degree of threat or security perceived by the organization (McKelvey, 1982); munificence-scarcity (Aldrich, 1979; Pfeffer and Salancik, 1978); authorization of structural features (DiMaggio and Powell, 1983; Singh, Tucker and House, 1986); acquisition (Tolbert and Zucker, 1983); imprinting (Kimberly, 1975; Stinchcombe, 1965); incorporation (Scott and Meyer, 1988); legitimation (Dowling and Pfeffer, 1975; Pfeffer and Salancik, 1978); and institutionally shared beliefs (Meyer, Scott and Deal, 1981).

The third premise is based upon the assumption that institutional theory and resource dependence theory stress the importance of inter-organizational conditions, particularly the collaborative influences of organizational interaction on internal organization dynamics. Because virtual postsecondary educational organizations are conceived to be highly collaborative organizational forms, the framework emphasized collaborative dimensions suggested by resource dependence and institutional perspectives. The six basic dimensions of the framework include: interconnectedness-isolation (Pfeffer and Salancik, 1978); coordination-noncoordination (Jurkovich, 1974); concentration-dispersion (Pfeffer and Salancik, 1978); degree of interorganizational power (Pfeffer and Salancik, 1978); inducement strategies (DiMaggio, 1983; Meyer and Scott, 1983); and imposition of organizational form (DiMaggio and Powell, 1983).

My fourth premise assumes that an organization's external factors will influence its form and administrative patterns, internal factors may play a role as well. Historical influences such as the collective understanding present within an organization based on the creation of an organizational saga (Clark, 1991) or the myths (Kamens, 1977) by which an organization may establish patterns or organizational forms, are assumed to be key determinants.

Fifth, I assumed that the nature of the organization might be described in terms of its organizational form and administrative patterns. Organizational form refers to strategy dimensions, intra and interorganizational (Pfeffer and Salancik, 1978; Thompson, 1967); structural dimensions, centralization, formalization, complexity, and configuration (Miles, 1980); and process dimensions, design and management of core technologies and tasks (Scott, 1992) and political processes (Pfeffer and Salancik, 1978).

Finally, I assumed that the administrative patterns of the virtual postsecondary educational organization (the formation of consistent, standardized activities concerned with the management of virtual postsecondary educational organizations, which are formally or informally developed within the organization) might be operationalized in terms of the social structure of the organization. Scott (1992) differentiates two aspects of social structure—normative structure and behavioral structure. Normative structure consists of the values, norms and role expectations of the organization's members. The behavioral structure focuses on the collective activities, interactions and sentiments of individuals in the organization (Homans, 1950).

Figure 2.1: Operational Framework: Influences on Virtual Postsecondary Educational Organization Form and Administrative Patterns

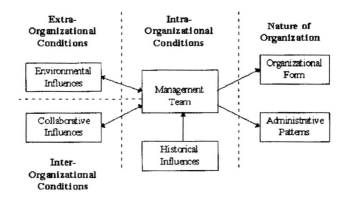

Summary of Operational Framework

This operational framework was used as a guide to structure the field research and develop a protocol. The framework relied on aspects of institutional theory and resource dependence theory to provide a context that is lacking in the research base on virtual organizations. The framework should not be considered a comprehensive treatment of organizational-environment interaction, covering every possible dimension influencing organizational form or administrative patterns, nor a theoretical framework in which constructs and relationships between constructs are delineated with precision. Because virtual postsecondary educational organizations have not been the focus of theoretical explication, the framework was used as a starting point for exploration of a new organizational form and should be viewed as an adaptable tool. Indeed, my expectation was that the conceptual framework emerging from this study would in all likelihood look very different from the operational framework outlined in this section. The dimensions I used to shape the protocol and structure the case chapters are summarized in Table 2.1.

Table 2.1: Delineation of Variables in Operational Framework

Extra-Organizational Conditions	Intra-Organizational Conditions	Nature of Organization
Environmental Influences	*Management Team*	*Organizational Form*
Uncertainty	• Role of Management Team	Strategy
• Complexity	*Historical Influences*	• Intraorganizational
• Stability-Variability	• Organizational Saga	• Interorganizational
• Threat-Security	• Organizational Myths	• Resource
Dependence		Structure
• Munificence-Scarcity		• Centralization
Normative		• Formalization
• Authorization of structural features		• Complexity
• Acquisition		• Configuration
• Imprinting		Process
• Incorporation		• Design and management
Cognitive		of technologies and tasks
• Legitimation		
• Institutionally shared beliefs		*Administrative Patterns*
		Normative Structure
Inter-Organizational		• Values
Conditions		• Norms
		Behavioral Structure
Collaborative Influences		• Activities
Uncertainty		• Interactions
• Interconnectedness-Isolation		• Sentiment
• Dependence		
• Coordination-Non-coordination		
• Concentration-Dispersion		
• Interorganizational power		
Normative		
• Inducement strategies		
• Imposition of organizational form		

RESEARCH SETTINGS AND SCOPE OF THE STUDY

Because the literature on virtual postsecondary educational organizations yielded no specific organizationally related typology to guide the site selection for this study, I developed a classification scheme to distinguish the various organizational types observed within the United States. The organizational types are identified based on dimensions of delivery of educational service or product and organizational structure. However, a more detailed typology was needed in order to move from theoretical organizational types to actual organizations within postsecondary education that demonstrated the desired characteristics of remote educational delivery across the organizational archetypes presented in Figure 1.1.

Eight Types of Virtual Postsecondary Educational Organizations

In order to construct a typology of virtual postsecondary educational organizations, I examined descriptions of virtual educational organizations from three sources. The major source of information was provided through comprehensive searches of the World Wide Web. My rationale was that organizations of this type would create a Web presence since the World Wide Web provides an inexpensive and wide ranging outlet for marketing educational services. I began by using the Metacrawler Search Engine, which combines the searching capabilities of several individual search engines. I also used the Infoseek and Magellan search engines, which combined with Metacrawler, yielded several thousand occurrences of the phrases virtual, virtual organization, virtual university, distance learning, and distance education. The second source of data for this paper was selected from the following local and national databases: Education Resources Information Center (ERIC), Public Affairs Information System (PAIS), Wilson Indexes to Journal Articles (WILS), American Business Index (ABI), Book Abstracts International (DAI), the University of Michigan Library Catalog (MCAT), and the Kresge Business School Catalog (BUSI). The final source of data for site selection was collected through conversations with practitioners and researchers whom I encountered at conferences and through telephone and email contacts. These conversations proved invaluable for placing a finer point on institutional types considered for site selection.

Based on this survey of web sites, literature sources and personal conversations, eight distinct types of virtual postsecondary education organizations are advanced. The eight approaches (see Appendix A) provide an alternative view of virtual educational organizations to complement the models offered by other researchers that do not emphasize organizational structure and educational delivery dimensions.

The typology of virtual postsecondary educational organizations presented in Appendix A assumed that educational services are exchanged within a Knowledge Industry context in which educational/knowledge providers face increasing competition for their services, this makes the definition of an organization's purpose in providing educational services extremely important; therefore, non-traditional education providers (e.g., corporations) as suggested by a postsecondary Knowledge Industry perspective (Peterson and Dill, 1997) are included. The following institutions were included in this study:

University of Maine System Network for Education and Technology Services—Formerly The Education Network of Maine (UNET)

Established: Education Network of Maine established in 1989. Merged with Computing and Data Processing Services (CAPS) in 1997 to form UNET.

Description: UNET offers access to university, technical college and Maine Maritime Academy education at dozens of community locations throughout Maine.

Audience/Enrollment: Programs are primarily for working adults in the State of Maine. UNET serves approximately 2,600 students per semester.

Instructional technology-Delivery technology: Primarily one-way instructional television with two-way audio (telephone) connections. Video conferencing is used for some graduate programs. 2-3 computer-based (Web) courses are offered each term with more in development.

Educational product/service: UNET provides access for campus-sponsored degree, certificate and individual courses for students in Maine. Consultation, development and production services are available for system faculty. With the merger of CAPS, enhanced help-desk and emerging technology support services for students and faculty are available.

National Technological University (NTU)

Established: National Technological University was established in 1984.

Description: NTU's programs are broadcast from over 45 different universities and reach over 860 sites at companies, laboratories and agencies. NTU maintains a brokering arrangement with its partnering universities and offers master's level engineering programs and special purpose short courses to engineers, scientists and technical specialists. NTU announced recently that it would re-incorporate all but its academic functions from non-profit to for-profit status.

Audience/Enrollment: Master's level engineering programs and special-purpose short programs are offered to engineers, scientists and technical specialists. NTU admitted approximately 1,300 students to degree programs in 1996-97. During the last school year, enrollment for NTU short courses exceeded 110,000.

Instructional technology-Delivery technology: NTU uses satellite-delivered multi-channel compressed video to deliver courses, which originate on member university campuses (which may also distribute them locally via cable television). There are direct phone lines from receive sites to the originating classrooms. Interaction among students, and between students and faculty, is conducted by email, fax, phone, and mail. WWW home pages for courses, posting assignments, syllabi, and other pertinent information are being developed by many professors.

Educational product/service: NTU offers 13 Master's programs. It also offers approximately 500 non-credit short programs and research symposia each year.

University of California Extension—Center for Media and Independent Learning (CMIL)

Established: University of California Extension was established in 1913.

Description: CMIL is a statewide division of the University of California Extension. It offers more than 180 high school, university, and professional development courses online, and by mail, electronic mail, and fax. CMIL is the distance learning division of UC-Extension.

Audience/Enrollment: CMIL serves over 3,000 students each year. Over half are between the ages of 27-45. CMIL attracts a local, national and international audience. 67% of CMIL students live in California, 28% live elsewhere in the U.S., and 5% live abroad.

Instructional technology-Delivery technology: CMIL offers independent study and distance learning courses in which students send and receive written assignments by regular mail, electronic mail, and/or fax. Courses offered via the Web and through America Online contain special online for group activities and for research: bulletin boards, chat rooms, electronic libraries containing files and software for downloading, and links to electronic sites.

Educational product/service: CMIL offers a full online certificate program in Hazardous Materials Management. Students may also complete University of California Berkeley Extension's Certificate in Computer Information Systems through CMIL. CMIL also offers instructional development and production services for the approximately 125 instructors, including University of California faculty members, which participate in extension programs.

Colorado Electronic Community College (CECC)

Established: Colorado Electronic Community College was created in 1995 by the Colorado Community College and Occupational Educational System.

Description: CECC is a partnership between the Colorado Community College System (a public entity) and Jones Education Company (a private company). The institution awards an Associate of Arts degree under the auspices of Arapahoe Community College, which also serves as the supporting college. A video and multimedia training facility is co-operated by the community college system and Jones Education Company. It is housed at the former Lowry Air Force Base. Jones Education Company is CECC's technology delivery and course production partner. Colorado Community College Online (CCC Online), offers courses and degree programs via the World Wide Web in partnership with Web content developer and publisher Real Education, Inc.

Audience/Enrollment: CECC has an open door policy of admitting anyone over the age of 16. A majority of their enrollees are working adults.

Instructional technology-Delivery technology: Cable television supplemented by telephone/computer-based interaction. WWW courses are also available through CCC Online.

Educational product/service: CECC offers the Associate of Arts degree through Arapahoe Community College and Web-based courses through CCC Online. It also coordinates the use of course production facilities for community college system faculty.

The Pennsylvania State University—World Campus (World Campus)

Established: First correspondence study offered by Penn State in 1892. In 1994 the Department of Distance Education was established. In 1997, the World Campus was initiated with a $1.3 million grant from the Sloan Foundation.

Description: The World Campus is the virtual campus of Penn State University (a Research I university) established to respond to the needs of adult learners by establishing lifelong educational relationships facilitated by a wide range of instructional technologies.

Audience/Enrollment: Adult learners in Pennsylvania, the U.S. and globally.

Instructional technology-Delivery technology: World Wide Web, computer conferencing, video, and other media.

Educational product/service: Undergraduate and graduate certificates in Penn State's signature programs.

SUMMARY—ASSURING VALIDITY AND RELIABILITY

The research context of this study takes place amid a larger industry context that is evolving at a rapid pace. Therefore, it is natural for concerns to be raised regarding the validity and reliability of the data and findings in such an environment. I used two techniques to ensure that I have provided a precise rendering of the data presented in this research study, had interpreted the cases accurately and came to legitimate judgments about my observations, interviews and analysis of documents. To do so, I conducted member checks at two points in the research process: the first was informally during the course of observations and interviews by paraphrasing informants' responses and my own observations to organization members as to ensure validity; the second was by rechecking with informants who figure most prominently in the case report. Data were gathered using interviews (semi-structured and informal), observation, and document analysis. Since case studies, like experiments, are generalizable to theoretical propositions not populations as in the case of quantitative research, I relied upon the experience of the first case study to clarify the operationalized constructs in my interview protocol and to ensure generalizability. Reliability refers to the researcher's ability to demonstrate that the procedures of a study may be successfully repeated with consistent results. This is especially important in a multiple case study like this one since comparative analysis is based on replicable results. In order to assure that this study was performed reliably, I used the same case study protocol for each case and developed a case study database during the data collection phase.

In order to understand how virtual postsecondary education organizations function, it is essential to understand the extra, inter and intra organizational conditions that shape the organizational form and administrative patterns of these entities. In chapters 3 – 7, I examine each organization in more depth and offer analysis based on the theoretically derived framework that guided the field research.

CHAPTER 3

The Network for Education and Technology Services: The Utility of the University of Maine System

After I had worked all day at what I earn my living,
I was tired. Now my own work has lost another day,
I thought, but began slowly,
and slowly my strength came back to me.
Surely, the tide comes in twice a day.

–Charles Reznikoff
After I Had Worked All Day

ORGANIZATIONAL OVERVIEW

UNET, THE NETWORK FOR EDUCATION AND TECHNOLOGY SERVICES, IS AN organization that extends throughout the State of Maine. It is a young organization with roots in the Education Network of Maine (ENM) and the Computing and Data Processing Services (CAPS) group of the University of Maine System. The Education Network of Maine was once characterized by the Wall Street Journal (September, 1991) as a liberator of sorts:

The University of Maine's venture was designed to pull the state out of an educational morass. In 1985, Maine ranked dead last among the states in adult education, and 47th in the percentage of high-school graduates who continue their schooling. Two-thirds of the population also lived beyond a reasonable commuting distance from any of the seven university campuses. So the university decided to go where the students were.

CAPS developed a reputation for strong community relationships seen in projects connecting higher education institutions, schools, libraries and other community and non-profit institutions to the Internet, as well as providing

29

research and administrative support for campuses in the Maine system. UNET's founding was in the estimation of some meant to have a calming effect after a controversial period in the history of the Maine System and ENM. To others, UNET is a natural and logical outcome of technological integration and an orientation meant to place the leadership of distance learning programs in the hands of the University of Maine System campuses.

Through the organization's instructional television system, cable television and increasingly, Internet offerings, professors from one of the seven regional campuses in the University of Maine System conduct classes for students around the state. The organization serves over 3000 students each year and broadcasts classes at 131 locations within the state. Students may take individual courses (about 125 are offered) or enroll in Associate's, Bachelor's or Master's degree programs in a variety of concentrations. Students may also enroll in specialized degree completion and certificate programs. UNET describes its students as disciplined and eager to learn, but also savvy consumers. Many students use UNET programs to improve their marketable job skills or train for a second career. A majority of the students are adults. Registration for courses may be done by phone or through a community-based University Center or System campus. At these centers, students are able to access the online network of library catalogs, databases, email services, and computer conferencing tools. These centers are also places for students to order books and receive placement testing and admission and financial aid counseling.

For many students, the learning experience revolves around the University Center or other community-based site, such as a local high school. There, the learner has access to classrooms with instructional television and phone bridges. Students watch lectures prepared by instructors from one of the regional campuses and interact with the instructor by phone. A student may be alone in the classroom or share it with several other students from the area. Exams are mailed directly to instructors and returned via the central academic logistics office in Augusta. For students who are enrolled in Web-based courses, the experience is somewhat different. The asynchronous delivery allows students access to their course from any point with an Internet connection. This includes their local University Center or, if accessible, their home. While each Web course is slightly different, many use chat or bulletin board features to foster interaction among students and between student and instructor. Exams are proctored through University Centers or high school sites.

The organizational structure of UNET is divided into four functional areas, each headed by directors who report to an Executive Director (a post that was vacant during the time of this study). The entire organization reports to the Vice Chancellor for Academic Affairs, the senior academic post in the University of Maine Higher Education System. The largest of the four units, Education Services, is responsible for academic and student support services and all instructional development and faculty support associated with the creation and maintenance of the educational programs. The Education Services unit also oversees the vast statewide network of community based educational centers and instructional television and computer sites. The technology services unit has responsibility for all of the technology within the system. It is responsible for maintaining the infrastructure for the instructional television (microwave) network, video conferencing network, as well as UNET's data networks. The Finance and Administration Office provides administrative support and oversees budget and financial planning for UNET. The Public Information Office is responsible for creating informational materials and presents the face of UNET to the public.

The UNET Steering Committee, a body responsible for making policy recommendations on the use of information and instructional technologies for the University of Maine System, exists to assist the leaders of the state system. The group serves in an advisory role to the Executive Director of UNET, who is an ex officio member of the Committee. The Steering Committee may organize itself into standing or ad hoc sub-committees as specific needs are identified.

The merger of the Education Network of Maine and the Computing and Data Processing Services organization, which occurred in early 1997, shaped the organizational purpose of UNET. The new organization was established to "provide Maine people with improved access to quality education, emerging technologies and personal support." (Summer Course Catalog, 1998.) Prior to the merger, CAPS, an organization supporting the research, instruction and public service missions and administrative needs of the University System in computing and data communication, was already serving a utility function for the Maine system. ENM, on the other hand, has undergone significant reorientation culturally and symbolically. While the structural characteristics of the ENM within the UNET utility approach have not been altered substantially, its independence and prominence as evidenced in its reporting structure have been reduced. One staff member summarized the creation of UNET by contrasting how the word "utility" was perceived among the organization's members. He pointed out, "The notion of the utility was to "serve all"—it was perceived to be student and faculty oriented. But, the notion of a "utility" is offensive to some in the organization, it is seen as an important political statement." One senior administrator emphasized a technological orientation based on the notion of service:

> We are now a merged entity that is a system service organization so that we exist kind of like a public utility. . .providing technological pathways for all of the aspects, for the University of Maine's system mission, including administration, public service, and instruction.

Uncertainty over the purpose of UNET was also expressed as an unspoken agenda on the part of the system campuses, which UNET was created to serve. Because the purpose of the organization has shifted from one where the unit was more self-directed to one that is now intended to be more campus-directed, the effectiveness of any central unit has become dependent on understanding the needs of the campuses, while also communicating the capabilities that the central unit possesses.

ORIGINS AND HISTORY OF THE NETWORK FOR EDUCATION AND TECHNOLOGY SERVICES

Today's Network for Education and Technology Services has grown from a rather singular mission—to serve the communities of Maine. In the early 1970s, several years before the application of instructional technology, access to education was created through off-campus extension centers. Supported by the University of Southern Maine, the Saco and Sanford community centers, some of the first extension centers in the state, offered academic opportunities to students in southern Maine. Knowing their students and understanding their educational needs was expressed as a "one-stop shopping model" as early as the mid-70s when each center served its own geographic region by offering courses from the regional campus.

By 1983, the role that telecommunications could play in higher education was beginning to be demonstrated in efforts throughout the country. It was during this period that a senior administrator at the University of Southern Maine took notice of the emerging technology and sought to expand educational access through the application of instructional television funded by a Title III grant. The grant provided the University of Southern Maine with the resources to link their Saco and Sanford extension centers to the Portland and Gorham campuses. The experience of grant writing and setting up an interactive television network would prove valuable in subsequent years, as resources and expertise were needed to scale technological access to educational resources throughout Maine. It was during this period that the senior administrator associated with launching the instructional television project at the University of Southern Maine assumed the leadership of the University of Maine at Augusta (UMA).

By January of 1985, the Board of Trustees of the Maine higher education system had approved a revised mission statement for the UMA campus. The change in mission for UMA included responsibility for the community college function within the University of Maine System and the subsequent reformation as the Community College of Maine. What was evident following the change was the realization that the UMA campus faced obstacles in achieving its mission on a statewide basis. Technology was critical for expanding access. Between July 1988 and September 1989, new campus centers were established, distance education gained emphasis at UMA and the instructional television network and related telecommunication technologies were constructed. These actions sought to augment existing levels of access by providing educational opportunities to a wider range of communities throughout Maine. The Community College of Maine was officially inaugurated on September 4, 1989. In the fall of 1989, with the fiber optic network in place and microwave technology extending the broadcast signal, the Community College of Maine began airing courses at 54 locations throughout the state to 1,400 students. Its offerings were modest—an associate degree in General Studies and 37 courses.

In July of 1992, the Board of Trustees approved a request submitted by the Ad hoc Committee on Community College Education that the Community College of Maine be renamed the Educational Network of Maine, owing in part to its growth in serving lifelong learners. In August 1992, the Education Network of Maine Progress Report was issued. The Report made clear that implementation and discussion of instructional technology were linked to budgetary concerns. An implied message in the report is that technology possesses the potential to be a cost-effective approach for reaching students in isolated areas. The Report champions technological innovation. What the Report also makes evident is that the project's scope was extensive, involving both public and private sector cooperation in order to make the instructional technology operational throughout the State of Maine. It also made clear the necessity of coordination and consistency among campus units and the need for policies that would address shortcomings in student services, curriculum and testing and assessment.

In 1994, at the prompting of the Chancellor, a taskforce was formed to examine the creation of a new organization that would be charged with developing, coordinating, supporting and delivering "telemediated education and training to a diverse, geographically dispersed population of students and organizations" (Telecommunications and Technology for the University of Maine System: Preliminary Recommendations, 1994). The taskforce advocated separating the Educational Network of Maine from the University of Maine at Augusta. The taskforce also intended to create an organization that possessed a collaborative structure that could maximize the System's limited resources. Productivity and responsiveness to change were also highly sought values for this organization. In its report, the taskforce emphasized collaboration among campus units but also struck what would later prove to be a controversial tone:

> Its [the new organization's] ability to meet the state's educational needs and promote innovation in teaching and learning will be limited if its responsibilities are restricted to course brokering and delivery. . .In the event that the System campuses and other providers (within Maine and outside) choose not to develop a particular program for which there is assessed a clear statewide need, the new organization should also be charged with that responsibility. As an academic unit, the new entity would be eligible to compete for federal and state funds to expand capacity, help campuses develop new programs and services and to create expanded partnerships on behalf of all its constituencies.

In July 1994, a planning group was formed and controversy regarding the new organization soon followed. The Portland Press Herald reported on a pending vote by the trustees of the University of Maine System to make the Education

Network of Maine the eighth campus of the system. The newspaper found that some faculty members in the University of Maine System were upset that instructors had "no clear role and the network does not a have a full-time, tenured faculty." The Maine Sunday Telegram noted the comments of one top administrator who pointed out that the initiative was actually the start of a virtual institution and that Maine must hurry or potentially be left behind as institutions from outside the state began to offer courses via distance learning to Maine students. The newspaper also captured the opinion of a department chair that expressed the need for a slow down in the process and a thorough review. She contended that technology had been the driving force behind the initiative, not academic priorities. Despite objections, in January 1995 the Chancellor moved ahead with plans to accredit the Education Network of Maine as a separate campus of the University System with the ability to award degrees.

Notwithstanding the explanations and assurances of cooperation offered by ENM's officials, opposition to the initiative (in particular the Chancellor's handling of the new organization) became quite vociferous. By mid-March, faculty at the System campuses were mounting a petition drive "to force a vote of no-confidence" in the Chancellor (Kennebec Journal, March 14, 1995). The petition circulated by the faculty accused the chancellor of a

> lack of leadership, failure to consult with faculty about key decisions, arbitrary decisions and wasting money on interactive television technology when the campuses need funds. . . . [He] arrogantly disregarded the rights, interests and welfare of faculty and other university workers. . . . He violates due process, refuses to bargain in good faith and shows an unwillingness to listen to legitimate concerns of his colleagues.

The reaction by officials of the Chancellor's office was dismissive, which was probably a natural reaction since many of the people raising objections had never taught on the network. A spokesman for the Chancellor linked the negative reaction by faculty to what he termed a "continuation of tensions that arose because of failed salary negotiations. Salary talks have stopped, and the issue has gone to mediation. . . . It's just one more tool, like picketing, to exert pressure to get across contract demands" (Kennebec Journal, March 14, 1995). One faculty member quoted in the same article noted that "In spite of the fact that faculty has not had a raise for four years. . .that is not really an issue in the petition" (Kennebec Journal, March 14, 1995).

About a week later, the Kennebec Journal reported that one of the campus presidents had spoken out against the Chancellor's plans noting that, "[the Chancellor] is running rough-shod over a plan supported by trustees in 1992" (Kennebec Journal, March 22, 1995). A day later, faculty voted on the petition of no confidence, fewer than two dozen of the 1150 full-time faculty members in the Maine System supported the Chancellor. In an interesting turn, given the vote of no confidence by the faculty just a few days prior, the Maine System trustees threw their support behind the Chancellor. Attacks on the Chancellor's plan continued. These included charges of creating an expensive bureaucracy, lack of justification for accreditation, and an inability to demonstrate that ENM would ever be cost effective.

In April 1995, the Chancellor resigned. By May 1995, the Board of Trustees decided to halt any plan to seek accreditation for the Education Network of Maine, make it a separate, virtual campus, or allow the network to award degrees. The Education Network of Maine continued on for over a year following the resignation of the Chancellor, essentially as it had done in the past. But by January 1997, the notion that ENM would become simply a delivery system, not unlike the system wide computing organization that reported to the Chancellor's office, was gaining credence. In February 1997, consultants hired by the University of Maine System, under the operation of a special taskforce, concluded that the television system used by ENM should be replaced gradually by newer technologies. By spring 1997, the Board of Trustees recommended that the Computing and Data Processing Services operation merge with the Education Network of Maine to form UNET—the Network for Education and Technology Services. A convincing case for integrated technology systems was made through a scenario called "Educating Amy." It highlighted the difficulties that a typical student might face when making her way through the system as a non-residential student and revealed how technology could overcome those difficulties. In the summer of 1997, the merger was approved, which united ENM and CAPS.

Concurrently, the Committee on Quality Assurance in Distance Learning was established. The Committee made recommendations that were intended to guide the application of distance education initiatives within the state. The UNET Steering Committee was established during this period as well. It is to provide policy recommendations on the use of information and instructional technologies for the Maine system. UNET's current configuration and advisory committees are intended to collect system-wide input and advance system-wide goals for distance education. These goals, as articulated in such reports as the Chancellor's 1998 Report to the Maine State Legislature, emphasize the role of higher education in advancing the economic productivity of the State by enhancing the skills and talents of its citizens. Distance education and technological integration are viewed as critical components for realizing the Chancellor's vision. The unit's history is certain to continue to shape how distance education and technological integration inform that vision as well.

In the next section, I examine UNET based on the dimensions of the operational framework discussed in chapter 2.

ANALYSIS OF THE NETWORK FOR EDUCATION AND TECHNOLOGY SERVICES

Extraorganizational Conditions Influencing the Organizational Form and Administrative Patterns of the Network for Education and Technology Services

Examination of broad extraorganizational conditions faced by UNET focused on four distinct variable groups (uncertainty, dependence, normative and cognitive factors) deemed important for understanding the influences of both competitive and institutional environments on the form and administrative patterns of the organization. A vast majority of the sub-factors within these categories were evident as influences upon the organizational form and administrative patterns of the organization. Incorporation (from the normative category) did not seem to emerge as a major theme in this analysis.

Uncertainty

Complexity: The nature of complexity experienced within UNET's educational environment reflects decreasing as opposed to increasing levels that are defined by the organization's interaction with similar and varied types of organizations within its environment. In the current stage of the organization's development, UNET has been restricted through the organizational mission and reporting structure to relate to the campuses as its principal service group. In earlier periods, especially those in which grants and private partnerships were needed to build the network infrastructure, the variety of organizations with which the unit interacted were more diverse. One exception is within the technology policy function of the organization. During my visit, the organization was in the process of preparing a grant to extend the technology infrastructure school districts within the state. Rapid changes in the telecommunications industry are certain to shape the relationships in which UNET will find itself, as it seeks to increase its current level of technological sophistication.

   Stability-Variability: The management team of UNET perceives organizations within its environment to be undergoing tremendous change. This was documented particularly in demand by students for technology-mediated curriculum. A manager explained:

> Outside of Maine, there is a great openness to begin to look at alternatives to the traditional campus—especially for busy adult students. I do get a lot of requests from people outside of Maine for Internet courses and full Internet degrees, and I think that people are beginning to take that kind of access for granted. Within Maine, it's a little bit more traditional. I think that people still view education as campus based, that is also changing, but I think Maine is a little bit behind the rest of the country.

According to a different manager from the technology side of UNET, rapid transition in this arena, particularly in policies created through the Federal Telecommunications Act, could bring about new partnering opportunities with Maine school districts. The E-RATE section of the Act, a subsidy to increase connectivity and telecommunications use, could push UNET in new directions. Clearly, the new technologies that UNET is embracing, such as Asynchronous Transfer Mode and Internet-based applications, are responses to perceived changes taking place within the environment of the organization.

Threat—Security: While organization members are keenly aware of the nature of changes taking place in the environment of higher education, many are convinced that UNET is ill prepared to respond in a timely manner to the opportunities available in the educational marketplace. Several managers and staff cited the realignment of UNET from a potential separate campus to its current configuration as a utility of the system as the source of this trepidation. Responsiveness to campus needs places the burden of perceiving and responding to environmental stimuli upon individual campus leaders, rather than the central unit. Speed of response, especially to student needs, was an area that several managers found to be unsatisfactory in the current configuration. Funding within the System as a whole has increased modestly in the past two academic years. UNET, however, has not been the beneficiary. Future funding cuts would place increased pressure to cut costs internally and potentially retard technological innovation. Central units, like UNET, are also vulnerable to campus demands for funding reallocations that can draw money away from central service units. Similarly, the unwillingness of school districts to fund portions of adult education budgets within their communities could have a detrimental effect on UNET's ability to support local ITV receive sites.

Conversely, the management team was generally very supportive of the merger of CAPS and ENM due to the enhancements that integration of technology might create for enhancing the student experience and the pool of technological expertise. Convincing scenario pieces such as "Educating Amy" enforce the value of such a structural reconfiguration. UNET's pervasiveness within the communities of Maine also affords it some security from environmental threats. The statewide centers and receive sites, potentially the unit's most demonstrated strength, are seen as effective and in some cases indispensable community resources. Community partnerships, cultivated over a period of years, have the potential to provide valuable sources of information for shaping UNET's student services policies.

Dependence

Munificence—Scarcity: The resources that UNET requires to sustain its operation were most often spoken of by managers and staff as consisting of three types: technology resources, financial resources and human resources. Because many within UNET see the organization's mission as keeping the University of Maine System as technologically sophisticated as possible, technology resources and funding for those resources are very much on the minds of UNET managers. The constant tension to maximize the expertise, funding and partnership arrangements for developing and maintaining the technology infrastructure was voiced as a concern by various managers. This was often manifested in weighing the relative strengths and weaknesses of outsourcing and partnerships.

Human resource staffing in the technology areas was also a cause for concern. The availability of qualified information technology professionals is a national problem. Within the university System, lower pay scales were viewed as detrimental to attracting and maintaining sufficient staffing levels to operate the organization most effectively. Perhaps the area of greatest concern when analyzing the degree to which essential resources were available within UNET's environment is the stability of financial resources for meeting the mission. The munificence or scarcity of financial resources has been shaped by historical changes in funding allocations between campus units and UNET and political maneuvering among units for central system funding. The gradual shift of course revenue to the campus units and away from UNET has been a major concern. One manager described the shift in this manner:

> Initially the campuses didn't want to share revenue. They didn't want risk; they wanted some guarantees, so the initial arrangement with the campuses when the ITV system was started was that they got $4,000 per broadcast course. So, every course they broadcast they got $4,000 and they could use that to compensate faculty. They could use that to hire graduate assistants, graders, whatever they wanted to use it for. . . . They got it regardless of whether there were 100 students in the class or 10. . . . When we split off as a separate unit, the proposal at that time was to share the revenue 50/50. 50 percent to the campuses, 50 percent to what was then ENM, Education Network of Maine. That 50 percent never really materialized. By the time discussions were done, it was 60 percent. . .and it's now 80/20. We get 20 percent. And all that migration from the campuses getting $4,000 per course and UNET getting everything else, to sharing revenue 50/50 has been accomplished without any additional funding. We've had to reallocate and rearrange our resources in order to accommodate that.

Normative

Authorization of Structural Features: UNET is an organization whose organizational form and administrative patterns are controlled to a large degree by the system level administrators and campus level leaders. While some flexibility is afforded the organization on the basis of its expertise in recommending technology policies or understanding the needs of the community because of its extension centers, a good deal of that flexibility appears to be mediated by the UNET

Steering Committee. The attempt to create a separate organization is clearly pivotal in determining the current organizational configuration and decision-making structure. The views of one manager sum it up best:

> The campuses' missions, they all have a different mission, the plan for the University of Maine's system . . . that is really what we have to follow. That's sort of the key we have to go by. . .Because what they want to do, what kinds of technologies they want to use, what kinds of programming they want to produce and what kind of access they want to give out there, is really . . . the key . . . I think that they're the major players in what we do.

When I asked if it had always been this way, she answered:

> No. Not in the early days, we really didn't see the campuses. They were part of who we served, but they weren't as primary as they are today. We really began to see ourselves as providing access to students, distant students. That is still our mission . . . we had listened to the center directors, who were out there in the communities listening to businesses, and we developed a list of the most pressing programs needed out there. This way it's happening through the steering committee.

Acquisition: The selection of structural models or practices that are presumed by the management team to be more appropriate, rational or modern appear to be a fundamental purpose in creating the organizations that were forerunners to UNET. As a former senior administrator described,

> The end result that lead to this idea [creation of the Community College of Maine]—let's look outside of education for some models. How to build this and that's what lead to our discussions about use of technology because technology was certainly what was creating change and driving change in the business sector in government and other areas . . . military, healthcare, and so on. . . . Build it as though that consumer out there has to have everything at a distance and so think creatively. Look at business models. Look at L.L. Bean. Look at Lands End. We also had, or at least I did, a basic view that whenever institutions are faced with a problem, they throw people at it. I said before you come to me with any plan that calls for people, tell me how our technologies can help address that plan.

While elements of this outlook on organizing and innovating survive today in some of the original managers, it is unlikely that practices considered more modern, for example, will be incorporated within the organizational form in the near term. Uses of new technology to deliver educational content more effectively and efficiently is a notable exception. The reliance that UNET has on the campuses and system office for direction is certain to slow the introduction of organizational innovations. This is the case, not because the campuses are far less modern or rational in their thinking (some would argue that they are far more traditional, however), but rather because the level of consensus needed to initiate change is much more complex under this organizational decision-making structure than the model proposed during the mid-1990s. New models of organization, according to one former administrator, look nothing like the current UNET model. He pointed out that "the ones that are moving the quickest, the ones that are really having an impact of what's going on across the country are organizations that are totally separate from existing organizations."

Imprinting: Two salient characteristics retained from the organization's founding are clearly evident after reviewing the history of UNET. The extension center model, considered by many to be the centerpiece of the organization's structure, has evolved to cover large portions of the state. These centers have provided community outreach and cultural extension since their inception in the early 1980s. The second structural characteristic, the instructional television technology, offers four channels for delivery of courses. ITV remains the workhorse of UNET's content delivery system. This technology is likely to recede in the coming years as Internet-based and compressed video technology are delivered via an Asynchronous Transfer Mode protocol.

Cognitive

Legitimation: For UNET, the nature of legitimation in its organizational form and administrative patterns has changed over time. The organization's ability to attract grant funding (principally during the Community College of Maine and ENM years) provided a source of legitimacy for the unit. The funding established an impression of leadership that seemed, at the time, to be unparalleled in the nation in terms of the organization's scope and innovation in applying technology to create new academic programs. In the current organizational configuration, legitimacy is also tied to technology innovation. The control that UNET exercises in gaining legitimacy appears constricted since the organization will find validation externally largely through its ability to innovate technologically. In the past, it could have exercised greater control over the academic aspects of legitimacy. The campus units, to whom UNET must respond, carry a greater responsibility for generating external legitimacy in academic programming since innovation must start with them. It is unlikely that this legitimacy de-coupling between the two organizations will be at all apparent to the students. Since student enrollment may be considered the ultimate arbitrator of legitimacy, UNET may face problems in portraying the value of their products and services to students when they have reduced control over academic product selection for the educational marketplace.

Institutionally Shared Beliefs: Institutionally shared beliefs originating from externally defined beliefs, rules and roles were found to be a problematic area for UNET. The internalization of expectations about competition and structural autonomy were held by some to be sources of conflict between UNET and the campuses. One manager felt that holding up external models to the campuses actually precipitated some of the conflict that emerged in the mid-1990s. The attempts to internalize some of those external beliefs were perceived as antagonistic, as one manager pointed out:

> I think that one of the things that got us in trouble with the campuses was pointing out what the competition was doing. . . . And that's not what they wanted to hear because it made it sound like we were saying you're not good enough, you don't care enough, you're not doing enough.

In technical areas, for example, like the use of Web-based tools for students' registration, UNET and the system were perceived as behind. One manager described this as a structural and political problem in getting the campuses to coordinate around common student service processes. Another felt that lack of staffing, particularly since technical staff were dedicated to the resolution of Year 2000 issues, slowed this effort. Beliefs about student expectations in a distance learning environment were not considered high priorities in the view of several managers.

Interorganizational Conditions Influencing the Organizational Form and Administrative Patterns of the Network for Education and Technology Services

Interorganizational conditions emphasize collaborative influences among and between specific organizations within UNET's external environment that may shape its organizational form and administrative patterns. The analysis derived from the conceptual framework focused on elements of the competitive and institutional environments reflected in three broad categories—uncertainty, dependence and normative factors. What became readily apparent following the analysis of this section was the influence that UNET's reorientation toward a campus-centric approach had in subordinating external, collaborative interactions. Again, technology areas are an exception to this trend. Due to the organization's internal focus on serving the campuses and the intermediation provided by the UNET Steering Committee, fluidity in dealing with external entities and individual organizations, at least on the academic side, appeared to be stalled. This is not surprising given that many UNET managers believe that such decisions are now clearly the responsibility of the campuses. Three sub-variables, notably those dealing with the unit's interaction with coordinated entities, the concentration or dispersion of needed resources and inducement strategies for changing organizational characteristics did not emerge within the analysis, due in part I sense, to the organization's stated focus of serving campuses and faculty.

Uncertainty

Interconnectedness—Isolation: UNET's connection to other entities within its environment are at once long-standing and shifting. Long standing connections exist between UNET's community extension centers and students, and educational, community and business leaders. These ties have been critical for shaping the educational services strategy, as well as enriching the cultural milieu of many Maine communities. One manager captured the nature of these enduring relationships, when she noted:

> From the perspective of the centers and the sites, which is the closest unit to the students, we have very strong partnerships in the community with adult education programs. We work with all the social service agencies in the region. We have very strong business partnerships. We have community advisory boards at each of our centers and the centers really are an integral part of the community.

One might suspect that the cost of remaining on the cutting edge technologically would be quite a financial burden in light of the budget cuts the unit has endured over the past few years.

More transitory relationships and connections are found under the technology infrastructure rubric. Rapid technological changes occurring with the organization's environment have caused UNET's management team to constantly reevaluate their technology partnerships, grant submissions and pilot partners. For example, overtures from wireless firms and cable companies for pilot partnerships have raised questions about scalability and equity of access to all service regions.

Dependence

Interorganizational Power: UNET's exertion of influence over other organizations in order to control resources may best be described as a negotiated, rather than a control relationship with external partners. This was most evident in the community interactions that take place between community extension center leaders and local community and business leaders, leaders who often possess resources of value to the centers. An extension center manager described her strategy for achieving organizational goals and obtaining needed resources. She explained:

> Lots of times I'll seek resources out in our community. For instance, for internships and practica and trying to give students the opportunity to have some job experience. . . . That's something that's taken a lot of time and then the way that I do that is I serve on a lot of boards. . . . I do that because I represent the university's system in this community. I also represent more students, so I am on economic development committees and domestic violence

boards and the hospital board and different boards and committees. That has allowed me over the years to develop relationships where I can go to people and I can say I have a student who really needs the opportunity to practice what their learning in a well supervised environment, can you help? So that's another way of getting resources.

As the previous quote suggests, the importance of community participation creates opportunities for resource flows into the organization. Yet, representation on various boards by a community center manager also lends valuable insight and validation to activities and policies proposed by the boards.

Normative

Imposition of Organizational Form: External agents appeared to have only a minor influence on UNET's organizational form and administrative patterns, particularly in areas of strategy, structure and organizational processes. The organization perceived very few coercive factors that would cause them to alter their established patterns of operation. A brief mention was made of one regional agency, the New England Association of School and Colleges, but its effect on the organization was perceived to be limited. Legislators, another external group that UNET is sensitive to, were perceived as being satisfied with the unit's progress to date. I asked several administrators if any external agents such as accreditation agencies or state/local government bodies had a noticeable role in shaping the manner in which UNET operated; this answer was typical:

> The New England Association of School and Colleges just adopted some new guidelines for distance learning programs, but despite the fact that we got out front so quickly, we still only have 12 percent of the total student population enrolled in our distance learning activities, so we're nowhere near approaching the 50 percent mark that the federal government uses with regard to questioning financial aid.

The 50% enrollment mark for distance education courses is an important figure, although one obviously that is not likely to affect UNET in the short term. Federal student aid funding is withheld to students within institutions that have over 50% (full-time equivalent) of their students enrolled in distance education courses. The 1998 Higher Education Authorization Act upheld this requirement, but did leave provisions for pilot testing of less than 50% enrollment models.

Intraorganizational Conditions Influencing the Organizational Form and Administrative Patterns of the Network for Education and Technology Services

The portion of the conceptual framework examining intraorganizational conditions emphasizes the influence of the management team, as well as historical influences deemed important in shaping the organization's form and administrative patterns. Admittedly the most exploratory of the three major variable groupings, the majority of findings are not related to specific constructs contained within the conceptual framework. Interviews, documentary analysis and observation were focused on influential individuals within the management team and historical influences such as the sagas and myths that developed within the organization. The analysis was drawn heavily from the history and origins of UNET presented earlier in this chapter.

Leadership/Management Team: One of the key themes to emerge in analyzing UNET's history is the pivotal role that the Community College of Maine and the Education Network of Maine's leaders had in shaping the organizational form and administrative patterns of what is today's organization. The process of evolution has been heavily influenced by the vision of a single champion, the former president of the organization, whose great passion for distance education, technology and accessibility has so undeniably influenced the thinking of the current management team, the values of the organization and the services that UNET provides. The resignation of this leader has created a symbolic void in the culture of the organization. Several members of the management team and other staff expressed a sense of ambiguity or "leaderlessness" in the wake of his departure. References to this leader conjure up images of the familial role that he held as head of the organization. One staff member summed up the feelings of many whom I interviewed when she stated her perception of the leadership void created by their leader's resignation and the reduction in status that the organization suffered as a result:

> So with [the former head of the organization] resigning it became an opportunity to take this new virtual campus and push it back a bit and have it be...not be a campus any longer, no longer be represented in that decision-making level. . . . [The former head of the organization] would go to those [high level] meetings, come back, share anything that he felt that his staff needed to be aware of that was happening in the state of Maine at other campuses that we needed to be aware of so that we could either partner or direct students to these resources and now we don't have that, and it's a real loss.

Technology Selection: The broadcast system, which has been in place for many years, appears to be a central force in shaping the organizational structure and processes. The instructional television system brings with it an entire set of support structure personnel and procedures that would have been organized quite differently had the organization selected a different type of technology. Additionally, the community extension centers and receive sites are linked quite closely to the processes and structure established by the architecture of the instructional television system. The unit's increasing use of Internet-based technologies and desire to embrace statewide infrastructure changes, such as ATM, are likely to bring distinct organizational changes in the next few years.

Geographic Context and Service Area: UNET's geographic service area, technology selection and organizational structure is profoundly influenced by Maine's geographic and demographic context. Because Maine is a fairly large state with a sparse population, UNET is faced with a service area that is distributed over many thousands of miles with few established cultural and educational anchors from which to draw its resources. The establishment of extension centers is a direct response to address the issues of geography and small population concentrations. The technology as well is shaped to match this context. The pre-Internet technologies still in use by UNET, with their elaborate series of linkages and rebroadcast stations, artfully weave the broadcast signal over mountain tops and through valleys within the state. Maine's geographic context generates staffing considerations and procedures for maintaining the network that are particular to rural areas. One technology manager explained:

> if we have an outage that happens to our microwave system . . . we've got to dispatch from here to the top of that mountain. . . . We've hedged it a little bit by having technicians that don't all live in Augusta, but that we don't have technicians that live in the far you know, far north Aroostook County area. So if we've got an outage that occurs up there and we've got to dispatch them, you've got longer outage times. You also have all those sundry expenses that a lot of people in the telecommunications world aren't used to, and we have leases with—it might be a paging company, a TV broadcast company, or the person that owns the tallest hill in the area so that we can put out our repeater on top of that. . .we have so many different locations and so many different unique problems with each one of them.

The structural configuration of the organization is tied closely to the technological architecture of the system. Distinct technical support functions are evident within the organization, which are comprised of staff with specialized skills for maintaining the broadcast infrastructure.

Students, Faculty and Campuses: It seems axiomatic that characteristics particular to the students, faculty and campuses within the Maine system are critical influences on the organizational structure and administrative processes of UNET. Following the controversy of the mid-1990s, UNET administrators have gained a keen appreciation of the intentions and clout of the system faculty. Similarly, the controversy has resulted in new structures, such as the UNET Steering Committee, which have been constituted as a mediating body between UNET and the campuses.

Despite the belief by some senior leaders that UNET's purpose is to serve the campuses and the campuses' purpose to serve the students, the student service ethic is deeply coded within the culture of UNET. The student is a key strand of UNET's DNA and it is unlikely that that view will be soon changed. Comments such as this one were typical of UNET member's affinity for and pride in students that they served:

> I was at a meeting one day, out of seven I counted five who either directly or indirectly had connected with the university system because of distance education, and when I see clam diggers coming in and fishermen and laborers, migrant laborers. . .come in and start to pick away at degrees that change their lives, they don't just change their life. They change their kids lives.

It is highly unlikely that the symbolic attachment that members of the organization share in serving and advocating for distant students will be very easily turned over to campus units.

The Nature of the Organization

In this section, the organizational form and administrative patterns of UNET are analyzed. Attention is given to describing the issues pertinent to the strategy, structure and processes of the organization—its organizational form—and the normative and behavioral structure of the organization—its administrative patterns.

The Organizational Form of the Network for Education and Technology Services

Strategy

Intraorganizational Strategy: UNET's strategy vis-à-vis other units within the University system appears to be reactive as opposed to strategic. Several organization members noted that, due to recent changes in the structure and management philosophy of the organization, they were to be responsive to the needs of the campuses, which placed them in the position of reactor rather than initiator. Several members of the management team voiced concern over their inability to initiate change on behalf of the organization, since they felt it would jeopardize the welfare of students. For several managers and staff, the reactor role was viewed as a strategic move on the part of the senior leadership in the system to calm the unrest that had surfaced on the campuses during the mid-1990s. However, the technology functions of the organization looked to operate under a slightly different approach. This group seemed to be called upon to initiate policy for the system, so in some sense played a very important strategic. This is not too surprising since the CAPS organization had traditionally performed this function and since the negative reaction from the campus faculty had not been directed toward that group, they seemed to address many of the same types of issues as they had prior to the merger.

Interorganizational Strategy: UNET's interorganizational strategy is best understood as existing at two levels. At the strategic or policy setting level, UNET has only limited interorganizational discretion in setting policies. Its intra-organizational approach, focused on reacting to campus needs, ensures that the autonomy once sought by the organization remains in check. The decision-making structure embodied in the UNET Steering Committee also tends to mediate the decision-making power of UNET to act unilaterally with external entities. The organization's previous strategy was summed up by one manager as more entrepreneurial and risk taking:

> And that was the reason why that organization idea was put forth. This would be a part of the university system that would be quick, you know, sort of like a new product division in a company who would have the sort of permission to go for it and really just try to do something new, maybe fail at some things.

At the strategic level, this sort of experimental approach to educational product development is today the responsibility of the campuses to initiate. Many managers and staff within UNET feel that the introduction of innovative ideas will likely suffer as a result.

At the second level of interorganizational policy, the tactical or operational level, UNET is highly engaged in interorganizational relationships, yet it is unclear if there is indeed a strategy in place for working with partners at the operational level. The lack of a defined strategic approach creates an autonomous working environment for extension center personnel, for example. The lack of a clearly defined strategy may actually trade on the talents for community building that as least some center supervisors possess: One center supervisor explained:

> Recently when we all knew that Eastern Maine Technical College was going to be moving into the area, they made it clear to me that as business people and tax payers, that they would be very upset if there was duplication of services and there wasn't cooperation or collaboration between the two institutions, so I met with the President up at Eastern Maine Technical College and some of the people who are on my advisory committee actually ended up being on some of the advisory committees up there. Some university folks say, aren't you concerned about competition? No. I'm not. There'll be some competition, but ultimately they only offer associate degrees. We offer baccalaureate degrees. They will feed our programs.

Resource Strategy: As a utility organization, UNET is principally dependent on the Maine System office for an annual allocation. The unit has a strong history of grant funding, which has aided its ability to enhance its technology systems and develop innovative new programming.

Structure

Centralization: The notion of centralization that I examined within this study focused on the degree to which persons in lower levels of the organization participated in the decision-making process. UNET's decision-making process is complex. It is moderated by the UNET Steering Committee, a recently created structure, which many members of the organization feel constrains the input to decisions that they once had experienced. One supervisor summed up her feelings about the decision-making process in this way:

> I don't sit on the steering committee . . . but my fear is that when people come to the table basically representing whatever their narrow constituents see, as to make decisions about a resource that really is a system wide resource, I'm fearful that things will be dismantled that shouldn't, that there's this constant pressure between as I'm sure you know, centralization, and decentralization.

Members of the management team and the staff of the organization also expressed other notions of centralization. One manager discussed what she believed was the value of a centralized and autonomous unit that had the ability to act unilaterally on behalf of the entire system when only limited financial resources were available. She noted:

> If you were to say, well, lets take the $.5 million budget that supports this and divide it up and give everybody a chunk, then nobody's going to have enough to have any kind of significant impact and then of course the smaller campuses would be severely disadvantaged in that process. So . . . we used to have the authority and the independence to basically. . .move ahead with initiatives and to say okay, here's an idea, let's do it and six months later it would be done.

The internal decision-making environment of UNET appears to be moving toward a more centralized decision-making style, albeit a rather informal and collegial approach. Following the merger of ENM and CAPS, it appears some of the cross-functional teams that were sources of input for decision-making had dissipated. Although staff have described the atmosphere as collegial, it is also more departmental than in the past, owing in part to the absence of an executive director. In some instances, however, the reorganization of the unit has created pockets of autonomy and highly decentralized decision-making opportunities on the part of the management team. The responsibilities of senior officials at the system-level place UNET as one of several organizations for which the senior leadership is responsible. The competition from other areas creates decision-making patterns that quite naturally (and appropriately) fall to lower levels of the organization.

Formalization: My observations and conversations with UNET managers and staff reveal that the organization's managers tend to make expectations about the means by which work should be accomplished and performance level explicit, but do so without introducing a good deal of structure or hierarchical levels. Work performance goals and procedures for accomplishing a particular project appear to be negotiated among relevant parties with only a minimal number of formal deadlines or meetings. Communication patterns tend to be informal and frequent. When asked if the work environment was one that tended to be very structured, a manager stated:

> No, not at all. Not at all. That's one of the things that I like about working here. It's informal, it's college you know, it's collegial, and it just works better that way and in fact . . . I think in this organization, there's a mistrust of anybody who works in a hierarchical kind of manner.

Coordination mechanisms do exist that connect means to ends in the work process. These devices for formalizing the work environment tend to be reflected in policy and procedure manuals, job descriptions and trouble-shooting checklists. Yet, such explicit guides are also intended to provide orientation and back-up support to staff members, like those employed in the community centers throughout the state, who are somewhat disconnected physically from the main office in Augusta.

Complexity: The recent merger of ENM and CAPS has resulted in an organizational configuration with greater differentiation and organizational capacity to deliver services within the system. The merger appears to influence operations on the technology side of UNET more so than in the student service, financial or public information areas. The integration of computing support (provided by CAPS) and instructional infrastructure and support (provided by ENM) has both expanded and differentiated the technical expertise available within UNET. However, as one manager pointed out, with increased differentiation spawned by the merger comes the task of integrating two very different cultures and decision-making styles, which in and of itself, leads to added organizational complexity.

Configuration: UNET is a highly distributed organization with organizational components located throughout the state of Maine. UNET is not a virtual university in an organizational sense, but rather a central organization whose functional areas provide support to campuses, students and faculty to free these constituents from the constraints of physical location . The unit is configured into four broad areas reporting to an executive director. The education services group, the largest of the four, is made up of two sub-groups: student and academic support services and instructional development and faculty support. This functional area is responsible for the extension center sites, student services administration and faculty development. The second major group, the Public Information

Office, coordinates marketing and promotional areas for the organization. The Finance and Administration group monitors the budget, conducts financial planning, and is responsible for personnel services and other financial activities. Finally, the technology services group is responsible for maintenance of the system's academic data networks, instructional television, compressed video and internal administrative computer systems.

Process

Design and Management of Technology and Tasks: Analysis of processes within UNET began with an examination of how materials, operations and knowledge are combined to yield the educational services and products the unit offers. Since UNET focuses primarily on services, with the initiative for product development coming from the campuses, only some aspects of this critical sub-process are discussed in this section. One of the first characteristics I observed regarding how work was designed and supervised was how the purposeful application of technology was creating significant changes in the work processes at UNET and throughout the system. UNET's role as the distance learning service organization and advocate for distant students was having ripple effects throughout the system. One manager explained:

> It's interesting that distance learning is definitely pushing this issue. . . . They would never bother having the discussions [unified student services system] without the context of distance learning, all the issues that that brings up and also the fact that we're getting a new computer system, every student in the state will have only one record. . . . They wouldn't bother without the distance learning component. I don't think the discussion would have ever come up.

For the education services area of the organization, particularly Student and Academic Support Services, the distributed nature of the organization makes design and supervision of work a more local concern and more technology-mediated as well. Center directors, using guidelines they and their staffs develop with the main office in Augusta, appear to possess the freedom to create partnerships and engage the community on behalf of UNET. The instructional television network has been used to communicate to members of the organization located throughout the state.

I was not made aware of any flow charts or documentation on the steps for creating distance education courses. The process, partly influenced I suspect by the varied media used, appears to be a individually crafted rather than standardized product. Instructional television courses seem to be more standardized since the development team's experience is far greater for this medium. The process is moving toward one in which a team of designers, technologists and student support specialists, along with the faculty member, create the course. The general process for creating a course was described in detail by a manager I spoke with. She noted:

> Basically it starts with a faculty member who has an idea, comes to us with an idea of how they want to do something differently. And the first thing you have to do is sit down and try to figure out what it is they want to do and then help them understand how they have to think about what they're doing in a different way, because if they want to move out of this sort of one-on-one . . . you basically walk in and lecture . . . I think it's because we have such limited resources and we really do, it's very important to try to get a handle on—does it make sense to do it that way? Will the faculty member have the time to really put into it, cause they never have enough time, plus they never really understand how much work it's going to be. . . . We try to kind of get it all just on paper at first. And then make a timeline. Once you have it on paper you can kind of figure out what it is you're talking about and then make these guesses about this will take this long and try to basically apportion resources whether they're human or physical, cause it's a combination of the above. . . . So that you're able to meet all of those deadlines and the deadlines in our case tend to be semester driven. . . . Then of course, you're wrong because you never can figure those things out. For whatever the reason is, half of the projects fizzle out, for again, whatever the reasons, so it's a constant sort of balancing act and shifting. We've tried to move to a sort of project team management sort of model.

Political Process: The focus of the political process in this case centered on the nature of conflict—its sources and means of resolution. Conflict within the organization tended to emerge from differences between persons in dissimilar parts of the organization whose positions did not allow for frequent contact and for whom ownership of particular functions could be quite strong. While the conflict was typically rather minor, one manager described a source of it in this way:

> Centers are so student oriented. We spend so much time, we have this tendency to think that we're the only one that covets that student and then we connect with the technicians and the technical people. And we have this tendency to think that they don't know what students need or want or should have.

Another source of conflict stemmed from the expectations some members of the organization had about how higher education institutions *should* work and in fact how they *actually* did work. These sources of conflict tended to bridge intra and interorganizational areas. Some members of the organization whose previous careers had exposed them to non-academic settings expressed comments about the lack of accountability in the work process and among the campuses.

Conflict resolution for matters within the organization tended to be handled between the disagreeing parties or occasionally aired in larger meetings. Sources of resolution for interorganizational matters (e.g., conflict between UNET and a campus) are mediated through the UNET Steering Committee. This body provides the mechanism for raising and solving problems among campus units and between UNET and the campus units. A senior administrator explained:

> I think . . . it's showing itself to begin to be a very useful vehicle for adjudicating disputes, resolving some difficulties. In some cases, bringing issues up that require an administrative decision, you know? Where you just really can't get all the sides on board so you listen to them and come up with what you think is the best approach.

Members of the organization who discussed the Steering Committee expressed a "wait and see" attitude, since their experience as participants had been limited to only a few months.

The Administrative Patterns of the Network for Education and Technology Services

Normative Structure

Values: The values expressed by members of UNET, system-level administrators and others with close ties to the organization reflect an abiding commitment to service, particularly as that service influences the student learning experience. The value of service to faculty and the system as a whole were also expressed as key values by many of the persons I interviewed. Members of the management team voiced concerns over priorities, the new reporting structure and UNET's intraorganizational strategy that emphasized the desire to serve students indirectly by serving the needs of the campuses. One senior administrator described the organization's values as "collaborative and service oriented." The senior officials stressed collaboration as a critical value that they hoped to incorporate through the new reporting structure. A faculty member offered a subtle perspective on the connections between values, structure and functions that UNET performs. He pointed out:

> Some of the people in the organization, many of them I think are very committed to their jobs, which is important. I don't think the organization is important, I think that the functions that the organization performs are important . . . it doesn't have to be an independent body, it could be associated with the university, it doesn't have to be independent, it could be employees of the university instead of independent.

While collaboration and service were values several members of the organization discussed with some pride, other values, such as technological leadership seemed to be a source of disappointment for many organization members. Several mentioned the bold course that the previous leader had set in the application of new learning technologies within the state and the sense of loss that they felt in realizing that being at the leading edge of technological change was no longer a core organizational value. Being a technologically leading edge organization was a former value that brought prominence to the system and the unit. A senior administrator expressed her conception of how that focus would be reinterpreted within the new organization:

> I still tend to think that if we're successful in doing what we're trying to do, we will be nationally known because of that success. Not because the technology will be startling, but because our success in using it to ensure the economic future of the state and the educational access of people in the state. I'm hoping that we're going to be remarkably successful.

Role Expectations: Specific role expectations for staff and members of the management team are typically set under the system's employment policies. UNET's working environment is highly unionized. Classified employees and professional employees are unionized. Essentially, any staff member who is not supervising someone is part of a unionized bargaining unit. As one non-unionized manager pointed out, "I've never seen a professional bargaining unit before I came into this environment and I think it's partially because there's a bargaining unit for the faculty." These classifications are used to assess the performance of the organization's members. The classifications also provide guidelines for behavior and social position within the unit.

Norms: UNET seems to exhibit a blurring of values and role expectations in setting out the generalized rules of behavior for the organization. Attention to the classified, professional and supervisory classifications in the system tends to form the explicit behavioral guidelines or norms of the organization. Procedure manuals, such as those used by the community extension centers, convey both the rules of operating the sites and also serve as a symbol of commitment to bottom-up input for improving the operation. Implicit expectations (not in writing) about behavior are captured in the value statements members of the organization make about serving students, working with faculty, and committing themselves to serving the communities of Maine. However much these explicit and implicit norms of the organization guide members' behavior, the message conveyed to many in the organization following the controversy of the mid-1990s has been one of restraint and care in dealing with the campuses of the system.

Behavioral Structure

Activities: The activities of UNET members are diverse. The management team is responsible for coordinating the activities of an organization that is distributed throughout the state of Maine. Technicians maintain the broadcast towers and ensure that the internal infrastructure is working appropriately. Courses are produced and broadcast. Faculty members are taught how to make use of instructional technologies and create Internet based courses and educational materials. Students receive advice on course selections and careers. Promotional materials are prepared and mailed. Tests are mailed, graded and returned. Questions are raised on a host of topics and answers are given to a host of questions. Fax machines operate through the night to deliver course updates and registration information. Videotapes are produced, edited, duplicated and mailed. The cycle of activities seem to defy such constraints as semesters, geography and time of day.

Within the last year from the reorganization, UNET's organizational activities have become increasingly less bifurcated between academic issues and administrative issues. Those administrative activities most closely related to student service functions and faculty development continue to be the principal focus of organization members, as has exploration of new technology infrastructure. During the period in which the organization was being considered for separate status within the system, greater energy was focused on addressing academic questions such as locating degree programs beyond the state. However, more recently this has been given decidedly less attention. The management reporting structure and activities have been redesigned and in some instances behaviorally reinforced to be responsive to campus initiatives. The distributed nature of the organization makes coordination of activities reliant upon technology for effective communication. Group facsimiles, email and instructional television are used to keep organization members at multiple locations abreast of changes within the organization and to coordinate activities among locations and between the central office in Augusta and extension centers and receive sites.

Interactions: Interactions among members of the management team appear to be familiar, frequent and generally unstructured, due in some measure to the length of time each has been with the organization and common experiences they have shared with each other. Due to the distance between the system office and UNET's main office in Augusta, personal interaction between senior administrators and lower level managers is intermittent and more formally structured. Despite what appears on paper to be a hierarchical structure, there seem to be few recognizable social distinctions made regarding interaction. As one manager remarked sarcastically, "I think that people who fail to communicate in this organization, it's not out of a power trip, I think it's just ignorance."

The mixture of talents and expertise needed to deliver UNET's educational services can at times be a source of misunderstanding, as persons from different backgrounds and with expectations about the process of developing courses and serving students and faculty work together to carry out their objectives. Something as simple as setting completion dates for a project can be a source of controversy, as this recollection by one manger makes evident:

To be able to say to somebody well, tell me how long you think it's going to take you to do X, and if you say that to somebody who comes out of academia, if it's an instructional designer, it seems to me that they're insulted that you would even ask. [feigning an instructional designer's response] I don't know? I mean, it will be done when it's done. But, can't you just guess? [feigning an instructional designer's response] Well, no, because what if I'm wrong. Well, it doesn't matter if you're wrong, you know, it could be you're going to be wrong. It's either going to go faster or it's going to take longer. That's not the point, but to be able to figure out how to get from here to here, we've got to have some rough idea of what it's going take and it's like no, I can't do it. What do you mean you can't do it?

For some staff members, decision-making and problem solving seemed weighed down by consensus and committee actions—procedures that often seem intolerable to many observers of higher education organizations. Again, expectations about how organizations "ought" to interact to accomplish goals varied noticeably by the background of the staff member and his or her relative comfort with academe's culture of consensus. One staff member characterized interactions surrounding decision-making and problem solving with some frustration: "Oh, everything is by committee. You form a committee for a problem, and then you go to the committee meeting and you form another committee to look at the problem. . . It's practiced here pretty actively—if you ignore a problem, eventually it will go away."

Sentiment: The feelings and attitudes that managers and staff have about their work were far more consistent than I might have otherwise guessed prior to the site visit. Commitment, expressed through numerous stories and anecdotes, was consistently and overwhelmingly focused on addressing student needs. For many, low pay (compared with other professions) was justified by the sense of satisfaction derived from seeing students reach their potential and sharing work tasks with colleagues who are similarly motivated to serve students. Day to day struggles not withstanding, mangers and staff in all areas of the organization find value in their work as measured by the importance of serving communities in Maine. It is this attitudinal quality that underscores this organization.

Yet, a very dissimilar theme also exists regarding feelings and attitudes toward work. The frustrations brought about by the organization's change in direction and reduction in stature has many of the staff confused about the contribution of their work within UNET. The following passage captures a sense of the cultural strife many members of the organization conveyed during the interviews. The comments seem to capture a sense of the familial.

It's been a hard thing for this organization [the reorganization]. I think to make the shift from this sort of out in front organization that was seeing itself as a leader in the nation really, in doing some of these things, and excited and energized, by a very dynamic leader, who was a visionary in may ways. . . .

> Then having to be pushed . . . sort of pushed back and said no, no, we can't
> do this anymore, and culturally that was tough. . . . People that work here,
> are still reeling from that shift of identity.

Another manager voiced a sense of pessimism in recent changes and reflected upon how it might ultimately affect students and the community at large. The passage emphasizes violation of a fundamental organizational value—continuing improvement in service to students.

> You see and I think that always before and I've gone through actually several changes . . . originally when I opened this center as part of the University of Maine at the Orono campus and then in '92 we became part of the University of Maine at Augusta, and then in '94 or '95, we became the Education Network of Maine. We were our own entity and now we're merged with CAPS under the Chancellor's Office. Up until this last change, I had always felt movement forward. . . . Now, I'm not sure of that. . . . I don't know that anybody's listening.

CONCLUSION

UNET, the organization resulting from the merger of the Education Network of Maine and Computing and Data Processing Services, enjoys national recognition for its technology mediated educational services. The organization represents a public higher education system utility model for the delivery of distance education. Formed in the wake of controversy over an attempt to create a separate, virtual campus within the Maine System, it is an organization that is coming to terms with its less prominent status within the system. The system provides a personal presence within Maine communities through a series of local centers where students receive academic counseling, program resources and instructional television broadcasts of course content. It has a dedicated staff that believes deeply in the type of educational services they provide to the State of Maine and beyond. It is however, first and foremost, an advocate for the non-residential student.

UNET offers several lessons for leaders of virtual postsecondary education organizations or other distance learning ventures. First, the creation of an organization with characteristics of a virtual postsecondary education organization can generate controversy. In a climate where relations between faculty and the administration are strained, for example, a controversial decision can often become attached to other issues, which can create greater ambiguity around the focal decision itself. One need only consider the climate during the introduction of ENM's "virtual university" plan to understand how other issues that had been simmering below the surface within the Maine System became attached to the virtual university idea. Second, UNET's organizational structure and educational delivery approach illustrates the value that community-based centers and technology mediated learning, when joined together, have for Maine students. The positive cultural influence on Maine's communities is clear. There is a personal nature to UNET's approach that students seem to appreciate. Third, virtual post-secondary education organizations that operate within traditional university or system structures may see their ability to innovate restricted due to the nature of existing policies and decision-making structures. Last, the geographic composition of State of Maine gives UNET a unique challenge and underscores the value of technology mediated education delivery. Because the rather sparse population of Maine is geographically distributed, educational leaders are under pressure to serve remote communities. Ubiquitous technologies like the World Wide Web should make educational opportunities for Maine's learners more accessible; however it may also attract other educational service providers who will compete for UNET students.

CHAPTER 4

The National Technological University: The First Truly Virtual University?

> He does not show himself, and so is conspicuous;
> He does not consider himself right, and so is illustrious;
> He does not brag, and so has merit;
> He does not boast, and so endures.
>
> – Lao Tzu
> Tao Te Ching, Book 1, XXII

ORGANIZATIONAL OVERVIEW

THE NATIONAL TECHNOLOGICAL UNIVERSITY (NTU) AND THE NATIONAL Technological University Corporation (NTUC) are respectively the non-profit and for-profit arms of a unique virtual postsecondary education organization. The organization is a collaborative effort among 51 universities and numerous content providers to deliver continuing education and academic certificate and master's degree programs to "engineers, technical professionals and managers using advanced educational and telecommunications technology" (National Technological University Bulletin, 1998, p. 4). Participating universities are connected by satellite telecommunications and compressed video technology to over 1162 work sites around the globe and by inter-connections to regional networks that provide access to an additional 428 sites in North America. NTU has the largest digital telecast network in the world. It offers master's degree programs in fourteen areas and broadcasts non-credit short courses to approximately 105,000 participants each year. Its customers include technology-based corporations and government agencies such as "AT&T, IBM, 3M, Hewlett-Packard, Lucent Technologies, Motorola, Texas

Instruments, Boeing and the U.S. Departments of Defense and Energy" (National Technological University Corporation Business Plan, July 2, 1997).

Students who enroll in NTU programs participate through the sponsorship of their employers. This usually means participating in satellite broadcast classes in their workplace, although plans have been underway to extend satellite service to the home. Typically, students may join colleagues who are enrolled in the same course or view the broadcast alone in a company-sponsored classroom or viewing area. Videotapes of the classes are available for students who are unable to attend the original airing of the class. Exams are proctored by the company's site coordinator and are mailed to the faculty member. The central office in Fort Collins then tracks students' grades.

NTU's structure may be described as hybridization within postsecondary education organizations. The organization is divided into two separate units. The academic functions, including the curricula of the master's degree programs and related support, which are subject to accreditation review, remain non-profit entities with a board of trustees. The non-academic functions, which include marketing, recruitment, student services, technology support and development and delivery of NTU's non-credit short courses, are under the for-profit entity with a three-member board of directors (the membership of this board had not been finalized at the time of my visit). The principal advantage of this manner of organizing is the ability of the for-profit wing to attract capital to finance the entire operation. Indeed soon after drawing up the business plan, NTUC moved quickly to attract new capital. The NTUC venture was valued at $45 million. Olympus Partners, a private-equity firm that invests in growing companies, supplied half that amount in return for one-third ownership of the for-profit company. The infusion of capital permits the University to promote its programs and short courses more aggressively throughout the world. Some expect that NTUC will go public in a few years, thus giving investors a potentially lucrative return and NTU the possibility of building an endowment from the stock shares owned in the for-profit venture.

The organization structure is divided into two sectors. The non-profit side is headed by the President who reports to a fifteen-member board comprised of executives from major corporations and senior engineering school administrators. Board members serve a three-year term. The President oversees an academic vice president. The Academic Vice President is responsible for the academic coordinators and support staff (admissions, records, and evaluation) and the chairs of the respective academic departments. The Academic Vice President also chairs the academic executive committee. The academic departmental structure of NTU is the most distinctive aspect of the organization and is what gives rise to its virtual nature in an organizational sense. Faculty members from participating universities deliver synchronous (satellite and compressed video) and asynchronous (videotape) courses from their home institutions to students around the world. Chairs and faculty members (referred to as consultants) from these institutions comprise a "virtual department," that is, they are geographically distributed, connecting with students and colleagues through email, phone and fax, in addition to the satellite and compressed video network. The Academic Vice President appoints department chairs. Approximately every two years, chairs and faculty members meet in person to discuss revisions in curriculum, admission policies, advising polices and degree requirements for their programs.

The for-profit side of the organization was under development during my site visit. Guided by a board of directors, the organization will be headed by a former member of the board of trustees of NTU, who has extensive experience in marketing and organization building for higher education markets, having come from a senior position at International Business Machines. All of the other support functions that are critical to the marketing and delivery of NTU degree programs and its non-credit short courses (called the Advanced Technology and Management Program—ATMP) will be handled by the for-profit organization. Emphasis on international markets and marketing and sales are the key functional areas that the new corporation will add within the NTU structure by virtue of the venture capital it has received.

The organization's mission is articulated clearly in informational and promotional documents. It is also highly consistent with the perception of mission that members of the management team elaborated on during the interviews. The NTU Bulletin describes the mission as one intended to:

> 1.) Serve the advanced educational needs of graduate engineers, technical professionals and managers; 2.) Award degrees and certificates at the master's level; 3.) Explore, develop and use advanced educational and telecommunications technologies to deliver instructional programs to students at their employment locations; and 4.) Provide a satellite network infrastructure linking technical professionals and managers nationally and internationally in research seminars, technology transfer activities and related technical exchanges.

One senior administrator noted that unlike units that are focused solely on training, often found in corporations, "we're trying to promote the career path of these people, not just training." In this way NTU/NTUC is an organization whose services address professional and academic development and through their ATMP programs, student training needs as well. One of NTU's basic principles is that the participating university or producers of non-credit short courses must own and copyright the intellectual property that NTU broadcasts. The non-exclusive license policy assures that students and their corporations, which pay the tuition, have up-to-date content at the most reasonable price.

ORIGINS AND HISTORY OF NATIONAL TECHNOLOGICAL UNIVERSITY

The origins of NTU and watershed points in its history are tied very closely to the vision of its founder. As one member of the board of trustees pointed out: "He put together the NTU concept from the beginning. . .He is well ahead of his time. He set the norm for distance education." A core concept of the organization has been its desire to lead technologically – to be a test bed for new ideas and applications of instructional technology. The history of NTU is filled with such examples. While these events are telling, they are not surprising given the field that NTU occupies. Degree programs and short courses are intended for persons and companies whose engineering and technology approaches are considered to be leading edge and who would expect nothing less. The combination of educational vision and technological experimentation define NTU's origins and history.

It is important to note that NTU is accredited by the Commission on Institutions of Higher Education of the North Central Association of Colleges and Schools. This point is not trivial. As this section will reveal, the history of NTU is marked by numerous "firsts." Accreditation for a virtual university anticipates the accreditation issue of other virtual or alliance-based institutions within the field of postsecondary education within several years. The question of educational quality raised by any accreditation review is answered by NTU through its synergistic approach to technology-mediated content delivery. As analysis later in this chapter will reveal, the accreditation issue is critical to NTU's standing and legitimacy among its customers and participating universities.

In 1984, NTU was launched as a private non-profit university with one degree program – computer engineering – that was delivered via videotape. When NTU began it had eight university partners. Initially, NTU was part of a co-venture between the Association for Media-based Continuing Education for Engineers, Inc. (AMCEE), a non-profit consortium of engineering schools that has provided video continuing education courses since 1976. AMCEE was to offer non-credit short courses, while NTU would be responsible for master's degree programs. By 1985, NTU's place as a technological leader was beginning to take shape. In that year it became the first university to offer educational services via a telecommunications satellite. The influential role of a member of the board of trustees and the growth of satellite capacity figured prominently in the organization's early years as the comments of this senior administrator illustrate:

> We started offering courses in fall of '84 . . . we intended to be on satellite, but we didn't have a satellite contract. . . . We had a satellite technical consultant as we put it, so I had one of my trustees intervene on our behalf with GTE Space Net in 1985 so that in August of '85, we went on satellite on a regular basis. It was clearly a make or break [situation]. We couldn't have prospered in videotape. . .So we were very fortunate both to have the trustee

as personal contacts, but also at the time new satellites were coming on-line in a surplus capacity.

Grants also played a major role in providing a source of revenue for operating the organization, especially in the early years. It is important to point out, however, that external grants, according to one estimate, only totaled about 2-3% of revenue in any given year. Grants such as those provided by the National Telecommunications and Information Administration (NTIA), an agency of the U.S. Department of Commerce, were very important. The manner in which at least some portion of the grant money was secured explains a great deal about NTU's management strategy. Collaboration, a hallmark of NTU's approach, is clearly evident in the recollections of one senior administrator. The relationship he describes refers to a matching grants program administered by NTIA, which required matching funds from institutions in order to secure funding from the government. One senior leader recalled:

> We got the first of what later became six or more grants from the Department of Commerce in a program that I was totally unfamiliar with until, a few months before. Those matching grants were enough to entice the schools to make the rest of the investment so that we came on-line quickly. . . . We didn't have any funds and this was very expensive. Georgia Tech, being in Georgia got Scientific Atlanta to donate . . . equipment. Georgia Tech promptly, at my request, put a lien on their equipment so that we could use it as matching funds in the government process . . . everybody pitched in to help us.

The division of labor between AMCEE and NTU over credit and non-credit offerings was not to be long standing, however. As one senior administrator pointed out:

> Initially, the parent consortium AMCEE, was to do the non-credit on the network that is operated by NTU. . . . That confused people. They didn't do it well and ultimately passed it back to us in 1987 so then we added the non-credit agenda to our mission statement, but originally we were to be credit only.

NTU's approach to educational services, at least in the case of non-credit short courses, appears to be more opportunistic than strategically predetermined. This is in contrast to the master's degree program offerings that were planned from the organization's inception and which by 1986, had yielded its first graduate. The decision to offer non-credit short courses had observable structural implications for NTU. The nature of the content (timely topics within the engineering and management fields) provided an opportunity for the newly formed organization to establish partnerships with additional participating universities.

Moreover, the short courses became a venue for interaction with varied course providers from the non-profit and for-profit sectors as well. Today those relationships include the Oracle Corporation, the Public Broadcasting Business Channel, Prentice Hall and others. What leaders of the organization learned quickly was that this new opportunity was not so easily managed, despite what appeared to be a lucrative market for non-credit courses and the realization that short-courses were critical to their organizational objectives.

By the late 1980s, NTU's operation was becoming more complex both in terms of partnerships and experience in handling those partnerships. For its degree programs, NTU's partner university contacts totaled 29 and customer sites numbered 242. By this time, the organization's service area was also growing. In 1989, NTU expanded from two to four satellite channels allowing it to offer more educational programming. In 1990, NTU expanded its master's degree programs from five to seven. It connected its computer system to the Internet. It also graduated its 100th student.

A consistent objective in NTU's organizational strategy, as well as a value expressed uniformly by organization members was NTU's desire to be on the forefront of technological innovation for the delivery of educational content. It is an organization that is committed to discovering the latest technology and considering its value and appropriateness for delivering NTU programs. In 1990, as one member of the management team pointed out, new technology and the pressure to make a timely business decision coalesced. His enthusiasm over the technology is evident in these comments:

> In 1990, I attended a conference out in California and discovered Compression Labs. They said, "okay," you can take your big fat analog signals that are on this satellite and convert those to compressed digital video and they'll occupy 1/10th of the space. So, I said, "gee, this sounds exciting." So I came back and shared that with the boss. We had a quick meeting and it was decided on the spot we were going to [invest in this technology] because by 1990, '91 we were then faced with do we buy another million-dollar transponder to increase our offerings from four to six? Now we're getting to the point where we were able to make money at this venture, so when we converted to digital video we went from four channels on two transponders to twelve channels on one transponder and you know, this was a major breakthrough!

In 1991 the transfer to digital technology was initiated and the risks and advantages of being a technology leader were thrown into high relief. The recollections of one senior administrator portray the complexity and effects of the project.

> By that time [1991] we had two transponders and four channels with analog television and we were running around the clock . . . .Saturday/Sunday, all

the time. When the digital equipment came on the market, it was good quality—remarkable quality—we were the first adapter. In that '91 to '92 time-
frame, it didn't go well. The equipment worked some of the time, but not all
of the time. . . . We had to do analog and simultaneously do digital and as
people got their digital equipment in they would start broadcasting digital.
Well, that took six months longer than we had planned so we were stuck with
that second transponder's bill for six months, so we lost 1/2 million dollars
that year. The only time we had ever lost money. It was very stressful and
wasn't clear what the outcome was going to be, but it all shook out and we
were alive and happy to be on that equipment by the end of the day.

Since the organization did not have a financial cushion at that time, the stress
for the organization's leaders must have been quite high. Adding to the leadership team's uncertainty must have been the large task of convincing participating
universities that they should switch from a stable form of broadcast technology
(analog delivery) to a less stable form of delivery (digital), which was clearly the
case early in the process. As in the early years of NTU, the need to obtain external funding at critical points of transition was again evident. Relationship building and connections to influential funders buoyed this project, as did the cooperation of NTU's university partners and customers. One administrator explained:

I got a grant from DARPA (Defense Advanced Research Projects Agency—
the research and development arm of the Department of Defense), the only
time we had ever gotten any of what's in the trade press called pork. But I
had in fact gotten a few friends in the government and their friends, I had gotten $1.5 million grant to help with that transition, be an early adapter of dig-
ital television and a broadband network operated by universities . . . it was
adequate on the equipment side, and the universities pitched in, the customers bought their equipment. So it was once again enough to entice the
universities to invest the matching funds. This time the money flowed
through in a non-competitive way through DARPA.

By 1992, the conversion was largely complete and NTU could state that it
was the first university or broadcast network to convert its satellite network from
analog video to compressed digital video, thus pushing the boundaries of what
was possible in satellite transmission. Amid the technological changes, NTU's
participating universities had expanded to 45 by the end of 1992.

During the next four years, NTU made deliberate attempts to expand its market of learners. It did so by expanding the types of programs it offered and by
creating greater accessibility via satellite delivery. In 1993 NTU completed plans
for new service to employees of small and mid-sized companies (they had
focused almost exclusively on large corporations prior to that point). By 1994
NTU leadership was able to expand the number of participating universities to
47. NTU also moved to Telstar 401, a powerful new communications satellite,
which was at that time also the home to the Public Broadcasting System educa-

tional neighborhood. NTU initiated a satellite channel on the PanAmSat2 satellite to the Pacific Rim countries. By 1995, NTU had added 110 new sites to the Network bring the total to more than 800. In that same year, NTU also introduced its 13th master's degree program—transportation systems engineering—and awarded its 793rd degree. Around that same period, NTU moved strategically to develop offerings for Asian corporations and students. Asian programming started with three master's degree offerings and a full schedule of non-credit short courses. The expansion of NTU's programs into Asia signified a major new venture for the organization. The focus on an international audience brought with it unique challenges. Building relationships in Asia would prove to be difficult for NTU, but the experience taught members of the management team that new structural arrangements for the organization were possible and might be preferable to their current structure. A senior administrator discussed the opportunities in Asia and the results of the experience in this way:

> Let me say within the Asian Pacific, we didn't have the funds. We didn't want to take the risk, so we sought investors and we created a for-profit inner group to do the extension to into the Asian Pacific. We called it . . . NTU International. We got a Malaysian investor that was to put in 3 million dollars and would see us through the start up for 49 percent interest. . . . We knew it was going to be expensive and we didn't have the money, but when he, the investor withdrew . . . we were still stuck with neither wanting to withdraw . . . and so when we went to somebody who provided us an investor and pretty soon that fellow came back to us and said you know, why am I trying to get you an investor for the only part of the business that's losing money? Why try to get you an investor for the whole business? That's going to be a heck of a lot easier. . .Seems in retrospect that we should have thought of it, but in fact it. . .dawned on us when he came back with a comment which is of course exactly right. Why limit the investment opportunity to the Asian Pacific which everybody knows is going be hard . . . we've lost what? Two million dollars out there.

Creating new learning opportunities in the Asian Pacific was to become a much lower priority by 6:45am ET on January 11, 1997. At that moment, the core technology through which NTU delivered its educational content failed. Telstar 401, the satellite that allowed NTU to offer compressed digital satellite channels, stopped reflecting its signal. There was no back-up capacity due to the exorbitant cost of satellite transmission. As the President's letter in the Annual Report points out: "In the 1996-97 school year, there was the satellite failure...and there was everything else" (1996-97 Annual Report, p. 1). The failure brought an instant halt to NTU operations, but that halt in educational services was not to last for too long. Drawing on its standing and good relations with its customers, participating universities, producers, faculty and site coordinators, NTU immediately moved to deliver its programs by videotape. Participating universities offered to provide emergency aid whenever tape duplication machines were available. The cooperation among NTU's educational partners was outstanding according to several accounts. The virtual stoppage in delivery had no major impact as around the clock efforts averted what could have been certain disaster for students and NTU customers. Immediately following the failure NTU managers began efforts to find a new satellite, which was difficult since market capacity was limited. Approximately three weeks after the failure, NTU secured satellite capacity on the SBS-5, which allowed for support of eight digital channels during daytime hours and six channels during the evening. SBS-5, however, could "only support about half the number of channels NTU had been using before the outage, it was necessary to immediately search for a long-term solution" (1996-97 Annual Report, p. 10). The long-term solution came in the form of GE Americom's GE-3, a satellite capable of delivering 12 compressed digital channels, thus increasing NTU's capacity over any previous satellite contracts. The failure of Telstar 401 did take its toll financially. During 1996-97, NTU lost $318,000. Financial reports indicate that the loss could have been as much a $900,000 had internal cost controls not been put into place.

Despite what had been a rather shocking start to 1997, NTU moved boldly to reorient its organizational structure and future outlook based in part upon its experience in Asia. In July, 1998, the University formed the for-profit National Technological University Corporation. NTUC and the new sources of operating capital it was able to attract fueled plans for expansion. The $15 million raised by NTUC would be used to hire new staff, expand marketing efforts, enlarge its geographical reach and incorporate more leading-edge technology. The goals expressed in the January 1997 Long Range Plan reflect a continued emphasis on NTU's core competencies and strengths—accredited offerings with a clear focus and audience; organizational agility and flexibility; strong relationships with leading universities and course producers; and a commitment to leading-edge technological innovation.

In the next section, I examine NTU based on the dimensions of the operational framework discussed in chapter 2.

ANALYSIS OF THE NATIONAL TECHNOLOGICAL UNIVERSITY

Extraorganizational Conditions Influencing the Organizational Form and Administrative Patterns of the National Technological University

Extraorganizational conditions faced by NTU focused on the variable groups (uncertainty, dependence, normative and cognitive factors) developed previously in the conceptual framework. Numerous sub-variables within these categories were evident as influences on the organizational form and administrative patterns of the organization. However, authorization of structural features (normative category), which relates to determinations by a parent organization over a sub-unit were not observed since NTU is a stand-alone organization. Acquisition (cognitive category), defined as models or practices incorporated within the organization because they are deemed to be more modern or rational, also was not observed as a theme.

Uncertainty

Complexity: The creation of NTUC represents the principal mechanism for determining current and future organizational complexity. The relationships NTU has cultivated with its customer base, participating universities and short course producers have been relatively stable for some time and are not likely to lead to new interactions with entities that are dissimilar in nature to NTU's current partners. The organization's ability to attract venture capital and expand its marketing reach (particularly in the Asia Pacific region) will, if successful, lead to interactions that may expand not only its customer base, but also its sources of course content, capital investment and major gifts. Clearly, the organizations to which NTU relates are likely to be more dissimilar as its growth strategy is implemented.

Stability-Variability: Members of the organization are keenly aware of shifts taking place within particular aspects of their environment. Technological change, international markets and job force transition were often discussed as leading issues that were of concern to the management team. Technological change was internalized as a core value of the organization—this appears in NTU's literature and emerged repeatedly during interviews. As a core value, the management team was responsive to issues such as the creation of new hardware or software applications or the means by which current technologies could be extended. Most spoke of the pace of technological change as an external source of instability for the organization, but also spoke of it as an opportunity to expand programming to meet knowledge demands of its customers. International markets were discussed with both energy and caution as a key, but changing environmental determinant. Less than ideal past experiences in Asia Pacific markets offered lessons that could be applied to understand effective future marketing and program launch strategies for Asia and globally. The organization is, perhaps, most sensitive to the changes taking place within its customer organizations. The variability of continuing education policies in customer organizations—shifting focus toward individual responsibility for learning and away from firm responsibility—can create unstable relationships with some customers. The trends were summarized by one senior leader who pointed out:

> I think today with the tremendous increases in the speed of technological change, there's an ongoing need for continuing education. . . . Management principles are changing, everybody knows that the intellectual capital that their organization brings to the table is really their competitive advantage, because technology has become, by and large, a commodity. . . . And so companies are willing to invest more to attract people, retain them, and as nec-

essary, re-train them. However, the other side of that coin is. . .people don't have time and . . . corporations want to do it in the most efficient manner possible.

Threat—Security: The vulnerability that NTU faces vis-à-vis its environment is principally relationship based. Because NTU's organizational structure is one that is highly influenced by the quality of its relationships, the overall threat or security of the organization is determined by the strength of those relationships at any given point in time. It appears that the personal credibility of the leadership team has sustained the organization's relationships, particularly with participating universities. Support roles are critical to effective relationships and the perception that NTU is successful in achieving its mission. The site coordinator may be one of the most critical elements in the educational process, as the comments of one administrator indicate. He noted: "Where there's a strong site coordinator who really takes his or her job seriously and stays on top of what's available, and makes it available to the engineers that are there, it's very successful."

The degree to which NTU is vulnerable to its environment was also expressed in terms of a competitive threat, but understanding the sources of that threat were inherently more complex than is often the case of other organizations competing with similar services. Most members of the management team were confident that the service they provided was unique and saw no immediate threat by new competitors—ATMP short courses being an exception. Because of the reliance on participating universities for course content, competitive threats associated with partner institutions can become competition threats to NTU content. For example, some participating universities that offer little content see NTU as a competitor rather than a delivery conduit or market extender.

Quality perceptions of the NTU degree were also mentioned by some members of the leadership team as an ongoing threat to NTU's viability as a business. As one member of the board lamented:

> And so even though ten years later we've come a long way, there's really no reason why the NTU degree isn't valued higher than the Georgia Tech degree. No reason at all, because you've got the best faculty from the 48 schools, it's conceptual. It's not factual.

The organization's new emphasis on marketing may serve to reposition the NTU "brand" within the educational marketplace and change quality perceptions.

Dependence

Munificence—Scarcity: The resources that NTU needs to achieve its mission are primarily of three types. First, NTU needs monetary resources to meet its financial obligations and continue to grow. In the past, these have been obtained through grants and steady contract growth, but these revenue sources have given the organization few slack resources upon which to expand operations. The degree to which financial resources are available will depend in part on the success of NTUC. The for-profit subsidiary may help to identify and secure new and ongoing sources of revenue for the organization.

The second significant type of resource required by NTU is its course content. As a virtual organization reliant upon universities and other course producers, it is constrained to some extent by the offerings made available by its course suppliers. A department chair explained:

> And there's not a lot NTU in general can do . . . because we can only run courses that the universities are willing to put forward. NTU has never to my knowledge . . . required a university to offer a course. In fact, how could they? It's not possible.

Conversely, the organizational structure may also permit NTU greater flexibility to choose new courses, which is especially true in the non-credit short course area. While in theory the relationship that NTU negotiates with its course providers can make the organization quite dependent, in practice, the availability and variety of courses have been sufficient to serve NTU students. One senior administrator hoped, in fact, that no more institutions wanted to participate in the short-term since they had all of the courses they could handle.

Finally, NTU relies upon staff, technical coordinators and faculty with unique abilities and skills. The human capital that NTU requires and is apparent in its network of relationships provides specialized services that keep the network in operation, paper flowing and content available to students. Scarcity of support or perhaps better expressed as a lack of willingness on the part of participating institutions or customer site coordinators to value NTU services is a key area of dependence.

Normative

Imprinting: Organizational form and administrative patterns created during NTU's founding were largely retained by the organization up until it was reconfigured to for-profit status in the summer of 1998. As one administrator explained:

> There were never any major changes to the way we were organized or changes in the way we approached business decisions [or how] we actually got the job done. . . . We've gotten a little bit bigger in terms of head count, in terms of revenue, but I think through June 30 [1998] this structure has been pretty much the same.

While the structural changes are indeed a new direction for NTU and are likely to bring noticeable changes in aspects of administrative patterns such as staff roles, activities and interactions, these changes are not likely to bring sweeping changes in many aspects of NTU. The reason stems from the comments of several administrators who find the stability and longevity of the management team a distinct source of continuity. One administrator explained the notion of change in the organization in this way:

> [There are] just subtle discernible shifts. There is . . . low attrition in the upper ranks of NTU and there's a lot of people who have been involved for a long time and we're kind of a family . . . we've tried a lot of things to change our culture, and we found it very hard to change the way we do things by bringing up the new process and trying to put it in place . . . when there's times of . . . crises. . . . We boil it back down to our basic instincts and the way we work together, and there hasn't been the kind of management person or people in place that say hey, wait, you're starting to lose sight of this personnel review process or this issue or TQM or any of these things.

Operational changes, while subtle, have not changed the basic mission or vision of the organization since its founding.

Incorporation: The organizational structure and academic policies of NTU appear to replicate the key functional areas of more traditional universities. For example, departments conform to particular academic disciplines, while participatory faculty-led governance structures are the norm. Clearly, the means by which these functional areas operate is far from traditional, but their structure does seem to adhere to time honored notions of how academic departments should appear. It is likely that incorporation of these structural characteristics serves a number of purposes, foremost of which may be legitimizing the organization to external audiences such as participating universities and the North Central Accreditation body.

More recent changes in the financial status of the organization suggest that structural characteristics from business and industry, specifically marketing and sales functions, were incorporated to strengthen the organization. This is evident in the hiring patterns, new sales representatives will be added, and strategic outlook expressed by one member of the NTUC management team:

> It [NTU] was purely run as an academic institution. . . . There was very little marketing that went on . . . we are developing an end-to-end cohesive marketing and sales process that starts with market segmentation and analysis, selection of new markets to serve, product management which includes the development with new content with new strategic partners, as well as expanding the strategic partnerships with our universities and other partners.

Cognitive

Legitimation: Having secured accreditation on two occasions from the North Central Accreditation Association provides NTU with its most visible and arguably its most important form of legitimation. However, it is the quality of the organization's services, especially its ability to satisfy customer educational needs, which appears to provide its immediate measure of legitimation. NTU's marketplace orientation regarding educational services (for example its keen observation of new trends in ATMP short courses) seems to emphasize its reliance upon customer satisfaction (and associated learning outcomes) as the ultimate arbiter of its legitimacy as an organization. This is likely to intensify as marketing and sales functions within the organization assert added pressure to meet customer demands for educational services.

Institutionally Shared Beliefs: Externally defined beliefs, rules and roles tend to be afforded little serious consideration by members of the management team. This is not to say that the administration is insensitive to the environmental context in which the institution operates. Rather, the management team is concerned with leading -technologically and educationally—and thus tends to rely upon internally directed cues for how it will construct its organizational form and administrative patterns. It is unlikely, for example, to view other educational institutions as guides to how it should operate. However, NTU does listen very closely to its customer base and content providers. These groups are more likely to be viewed as existing within NTU structure as evidenced by representation on the board of trustees. NTU's partners, a broad group of organizations and individuals (customers, faculty, investors, alumni, etc.) with a interest in the institution, tend to have a constructive influence on the beliefs, rules and roles that shape the organizational form and administrative patterns. The recommendation to create a for-profit entity is a notable example of this externally defined influence operating within NTU's internal structure.

Interorganizational Conditions Influencing the Organizational Form and Administrative Patterns of the National Technological University

Variables discussed in this section examine NTU's relationship with organizations within the external environment that may shape its organizational form and administrative patterns. Consistent with the conceptual framework, the analysis examined aspects of the competitive and institutional environments reflected in three broad categories—uncertainty, dependence and normative factors. In addition to these categories, a cognitive category emerged (trust relationships), which I had not considered in the original model.

Uncertainty

Interconnectedness—Isolation: The distributed nature of NTU's organizational structure and its fundamental reliance on its educational partners, particularly content providers, illustrates the unique coexistence that NTU demonstrates between organizational interconnectedness and isolation. A distributed but highly interconnected structure is the *sine qua non* of the virtual organization. Yet, the course development and production functions are physically isolated from the main office in Fort Collins, Colorado. This creates a situation that makes NTU reliant on the site coordinators and local support staff and necessitates close working relationships as the comments of one senior staff member suggest:

> When you look at the whole thing and see how many pieces there are, it's amazing that the whole thing works . . . we rely on the site coordinators to give the students the courses. . . . The same thing with the universities. We are trusting that the instructors and the contacts are sending the handouts and the homeworks to the site coordinators so that the site coordinators can send those to the students. I mean, we're kind of out of the loop on that too.

For NTU, connectedness or integration is also highly contingent upon the responses of customer organizations. Constant feedback on the quality of their educational services tends to connect NTU with its customer organizations quite closely. The degree to which relationships with customer organizations will become more closely linked may be affected by the organizations shift to for-profit status and its increasing emphasis on sales and marketing services, since these functional areas promote dialogue and understanding of NTU's educational services to its customers.

Dependence

Coordination—Non-coordination: NTU faces a group of external entities whose actions are coordinated primarily by NTU itself. In that sense entities that make up its environment are tightly coordinated. The comments of one senior administrator explain just how much NTU is able to coordinate the actions of its partners and his comments also reveal the mechanisms by which they do so:

> We don't have a model . . . we're very well coordinated with what's going on with our customers. . . . We have the advisory committees that meet right here [Fort Collins] and are very open forums. People are very loyal to us and enjoy coming together because they talk to people in tech education from other companies that are competitors of theirs in a professional environment and we're the only forum that they have . . . with their peers and competitors, they don't often see sharing information, so I think we're very close to a pretty tight little community, where it works well. What doesn't work well is

where we haven't developed enough of a relationship or we're not represented well or the people that have brought us in have since left the scene.

Concentration—Dispersion: The resources that NTU requires to operate, primarily course content and satellite availability, are highly concentrated resources within the organizational environment. First, the course content that NTU needs to structure its degree program offerings is drawn from a selective group of engineering schools within the United States. Nearly all are well established research universities with a history of professional development and educational outreach to engineers and technical professionals. ATMP courses are less concentrated since more supplier options exist. Content may come from the engineering colleges as well as publishers or industry training groups. Second, as the failure of Telstar 401 demonstrated, the availability of satellite capacity is quite concentrated and not easily obtained in a timely manner. The movement of NTU courses to distinct, non-satellite based delivery systems such as Internet does not appear to be a major emphasis for the organization in the short term.

Interorganizational Power: The NTU management team described the relationship with its educational partners as one that provides them little direct control over their partner's actions. Most characterized the relationship as collaborative. While clearly there is some financial incentive for supplying a course to NTU, for example, the windfall is not so large as to shift the power balance to NTU. NTU administrators do have some "editorial control" over which courses will appear in a given semester, but those decisions are negotiated rather than controlled strictly by NTU.

Normative

Inducement Strategies: Because NTU is focused on providing degree program and short course content to a highly specialized audience, incentives for change within the organization are often influenced by its customer base. For example, the manner in which customer relations are organized and have been refined over time tend to be viewed as means to strengthen relationships with NTU customers. Specific incentives by the customer base are often not made explicit beyond that of continuing the business relationship. Grant funding may be viewed as another source of inducement for organizational change within NTU. Changes to the technological delivery infrastructure fostered by federal grants, for instance, appear to have had only marginal influences on the organizational structure or processes, primarily because the organization fully intended to move in directions that were consistent with the goals of the particular funder.

Imposition of Organizational Form: NTU's organizational structure, especially the academic side of NTU, seems to adhere quite closely to a traditional academic manner of organizing, although clearly issues such as lack of tenure and geographically distributed faculties are not traditional. It is very intentional that the academic structure of NTU retains the elements of university structure and is assuredly why the operation remained a non-profit and not a for-profit entity during the transition in July 1998. Many members of the management team were very cognizant of how NTU would appear to members of the site review team for the North Central Association (NTU has received accreditation following both of its reviews). Accreditation standards can restrict organizational alternatives if for no other reason than the standards established by these associations tend to reward that which is familiar and has stood the test of time.

Cognitive

Trust Relationships: Trust building may be best viewed as an antithetical notion to that of interorganizational power that develops in virtual organizations such as NTU. The nature of the trust relationship is both good business and good professional practice and has a noticeable influence on the administrative patterns of the organization. The point is made plain by a senior administrator:

> We have no content. So, we have other constraints and we have to have a little trust there. [The President] is very good at that. He started this business because all the Deans of Engineering knew him, I mean, they got together regularly. . . . They knew they could trust him, and he wouldn't do something that would embarrass them . . . we've run that way for 14 years. . . . They have confidence that we're not going to go out and do stupid things that are going to embarrass them as a participating university and they're going to have to go explain it to the president, cause he's going say you know, why on earth are you involved with these jerks?

The nature of the trust relationship between NTU and its partners is predicated on integrity of past relationships, presumably beginning with the current President long before NTU was created. That sense of trust is the glue of this organization and essentially the principal means by which it has been able to obtain the course content it requires. In the main, relationships with participating universities are stable, which supports the notion that trust building has been effective.

Intraorganizational Conditions Influencing the Organizational Form and Administrative Patterns of the National Technological University

The organizational form and administrative patterns of NTU were influenced by several factors derived from the organization's history and other non-environmentally related themes. The findings suggest that NTU has been influenced to a large degree by the vision of its founder. The themes also show strong connections to NTU's emerging emphasis on a market orientation, their planning and decision making approaches and their selection of and investment in specific technologies. These themes are the subject of this section.

Presence of an Organizational Champion: The organizational form and administrative patterns of NTU are driven to a large extent by the vision and personal energy of its president. It is not an overstatement to say that his foresight and credibility are the predominant characteristics that have shaped NTU's system of operation and interorganizational bonds. While day to day operations are delegated to members of the management team, his strategic outlook has influenced every aspect of the organization. The comments of this member of the management team express the sentiments of many of the informants with whom I spoke:

> [The president] is the driving force of NTU and he is the leader of NTU and it's been his culture that we've lived in—the way he likes to do things. The way he likes to work with his managers . . . he respects his managers and he likes the set up and he likes them to go out and do his bidding. . . . He doesn't really like TQM processes and he doesn't really like personnel review processes. He's not a business guy, he's an academic. And so we've went . . . at times, as we've grown, we've always turned back to his way or style.

Concern about Marketing and Sales: The realization that NTU has not had an adequate marketing and sales effort has been a major factor responsible for the bifurcated organizational structure that NTU now possesses. This issue has been a subject of concern by the board of trustees as well as members of the management team. In response to experiences in Asia and desire for growth domestically, NTU has created an organization that is capable of attracting venture capital, while keeping very careful control over its academic degree programs.

Planning Process: The planning process played a important role in surfacing issues that are helping to redefine the organizational structure, processes and strategies that NTU will use to shape its presence in the market place. As one senior administrator described it, the planning process was far from rational, rather it grew out of a sense of frustration by those who were involved in crafting the plan. He described the process and outcomes in this way:

> The first one [5 year strategic plan] was done by . . . a retired high senior official in IBM and he led us in learning how to do long range plans, and it took off since then. . . . So I don't know when the conflicts came to the fore, they just showed up as frustration. Nobody liked the plan. People who wrote the plan didn't like it. Trustees who read the plan didn't like it, and you know, we all . . . essentially what we were determining was we shouldn't be continuing to do it this way, there's got to be some other way to, to do what we're trying to do that's not just more of the same.

The frustration that developed as a result of the planning process and subsequent strategic plan raised very fundamental issues about how the organization should restructure itself to increase revenue, expand its markets and serve customers more effectively. The process brings together key members of the organization on an ongoing basis to review past practices and shape the direction that NTU will take in the future.

Decision Making Process: NTU is a small organization. As such, it possesses a flexibility and nimbleness that allows it to move quickly in response to environmental opportunities and threats. This is most evident in the informality of the decision making process. As the comments of this member of the management team illustrate, the ability to act quickly and decisively provides NTU with competitive advantages, but also may influence internal processes and administrative patterns quite quickly as well.

> When I came to a smaller organization like NTU, I lost an awful lot of the resources that I had in the big organization . . . but the flip-side of that is you can make decisions immediately—you don't make every decision immediately—but if you had a good idea in the shower, you come in and talk to the President at 8 o'clock, you could be implementing it at 8:30, and that's a decision that in a big company, or a big university, worst case, that could take not hours, not days, but months, or years to make. So, what I really think has been great for NTU is it's a very small organization, very agile, and very able to move quickly.

Maximizing Investment in Technology: One of the central organizational constraints that members of the management team work under is the ability to make appropriate decisions concerning the timing and longevity of new technologies, especially educational delivery technologies. The problem is one that challenges managers to balance their tendency to maximize an investment in existing technology (that which has already been purchased and tends to work well) with the organization's goal of being a technology leader (often meaning exploring more risky, but potentially superior technology). This tension is explained by a senior technical manager:

> Our problem is that we had 47 course providers and put a lot of money into this particular delivery technology [satellite] and then to just, as it keeps leapfrogging, we have to make the right decision of when to change. When that curve has gotten to the point where we've gotten our money's worth out of what we have and it's very compelling to move to new technology because we get X benefits. I see that as really changing, evolving, and improving, and it's a challenge to stay up with it and see what the right technologies are.

NTU leaders also must balance the willingness and ability of their participating universities to upgrade technology to match the pace of technology advancement that NTU itself seeks.

The selection of a particular type of technology (satellite in this case) to deliver NTU courses also creates organizational constraints. Unlike delivery by

Internet or even videotapes, for example, satellite transmission has relatively high up-front costs, although the costs over time may be lower than alternative delivery methods. Steep upfront costs can make switching the type of technology used to deliver educational services less likely. However, the stability of certain technologies and the expertise that develops around them can be a source of strength as the impressions of one of NTU's technical coordinators points out:

> Telstar 401 a year, a year and a half ago, blew a fuse. . . . It disappeared. That's probably the biggest problem with the satellite business is you've got all of these eggs in one basket. [However,] the deep, dark, dirty secret here about the satellite business that nobody wants to acknowledge, is if you are going to multiple sites it is absolutely the cheapest, most reliable, most versatile way to go.

The Nature of the Organization

The organizational form and administrative patterns of NTU are examined in the following sections, corresponding to the outline presented within the conceptual framework.

The Organizational Form of the National Technological University

Strategy

Intraorganizational Strategy: NTU has taken numerous steps to shield itself from events within its environment that might be detrimental to the organization. In the wake of the satellite failure, it had negotiated a better satellite contract to respond more quickly if another failure should occur. It had also explored Internet delivery of compressed video files as an alternate delivery means. To position itself as a technological leader, NTU leaders have, since its inception, been active grant writers and grant awardees. As one member of the management team explained, he felt that being on the leading edge of technology was a hedge against damaging events and that grant writing played a key role in this. He pointed out:

> NTU I think for a long time has been on the forefront. . . . A lot of times we've been the organization to stick our neck out and do it. Sometimes it's because of the help of the federal government because we're not-for-profit and [the President] been a prolific grant writer and he's known how to write the grants and he's known what the needs in the country are and that's been critical to get the money at the right time to do the right thing.

NTU also buffers itself is by creating alliances with traditional universities. This according to one NTU official provides a degree of safety. He noted:

One of the ways we've buffered ourselves is that we've aligned ourselves with the traditional university world. . . . And there are lots of programs that are being discussed in this country that don't do that. The Sylvan Learnings [sic] of the world and the Kaplan Learning Centers . . . and even the Western Governors by the way, are going to take higher education on point blank. . .They're not taking it on as an alliance, so we've bet that for the foreseeable future, education, higher education will remain in the hands of the traditional higher education providers.

Interorganizational Strategy: NTU's movement into the Asian Pacific market is viewed by some in the organization as a strategy to shift emphasis from what has become a more limited domestic market to that of a largely untapped global market. It is estimated that 20% of NTU's 250 member customer base provides upwards of 80% of its business. The creation of new educational services, the International Master of Business Administration degree for example, is an obvious attempt to shift the nature of NTU's external environment. NTU is also moving to establish better "brand recognition" for its educational services. The reorganization seems to bear this out, as venture capital funding is being used to expand marketing and sales activities. In addition, NTU has expanded its delivery options to include a "home learner" system that is capable of broadcasting to engineers and technical professionals at their homes, thus potentially creating a new niche in their well defined market.

Resource Strategy: Although the organization's resource strategy was not specifically addressed in the initial conceptual framework, such a perspective is useful for understanding important perspectives about NTU. NTU's key investments tend to center around new technologies for improving administrative operations or for reaching new customers or the same customers in new ways. The organization's revenues have been consistently tied to two principal sources—its tuition and fees and its professional development course fees. The creation of NTUC was a specific strategic move intended to contribute to revenue generation (expense reduction strategies were not heavily emphasized by the management team).

Structure

Centralization: Analysis of the degree of centralization within NTU focused on the degree to which all members of the organization, particularly those at lower levels, participated in decision making. Due to changes in the organizational structure prior to my site visit, I was not able to observe or discuss at length the decision making environment with persons associated with NTUC since some assumed that the decision making atmosphere might change to match the style of the new Chief Operating Officer. However, conversations with those on the academic side painted a picture of highly participatory arrangements in which faculty committees and faculty governance more generally, were encouraged. One chair spoke generically of a distrust of faculty governance as a self-fulfilling prophecy. He encouraged faculty to take the lead in shaping programs and policies within his department. Similar statements were made by other chairs, who felt that the politics associated with tenure (which NTU does not grant) helped to create a more focused and participatory working environment.

Formalization: The organizational structure of NTU tends to operate in an informal manner. Although there are regularly scheduled meetings in all areas of the organization, most of the interactions, particularly among the members of the management team, are inclined to be more casual and familiar. This is also true within the departments, but there is some variability depending upon the style of the department chair. The degree of formalization was expressed by one department chair who explained, "if you have an idea for some change in the academics of the program, there is no formal way, but there's all kinds of informal ways to bring forward an idea." Relationships between NTU and partner universities and site coordinators do have a more formal nature. Manuals and contracts are the means by which expectations about the working relationship are made explicit. Periodic meetings with members of NTU's customers base and distributed support staff are vehicles for improving procedures and ironing out differences between NTU and its partners.

Complexity: The differentiation of functions within NTU's organizational structure reflects nearly every function that would be found in a traditional university, as well as several functions that are more commonly associated with business settings. The academic departmental structure, finance and administration, and the satellite network function tend to replicate several functions that might be found within any university. Similarly, departments such as research and development, international operations, and marketing and sales are more typical of a business organization. NTU's ATMP short course programs tend to bridge the purely academic and the purely business areas. Some functions are not part of the organizational structure—and quite intentionally so. Since NTU does not offer financial aid, an office of this type does not exist. NTU also does not have course production facilities since this costly function is entirely the domain of the partner universities. The greater "departmentalization," as an administrator described it, was viewed as more necessary as NTU had grown, but has created somewhat more difficulty in communicating effectively between functional areas.

Configuration: NTU's structure possesses elements of both a physically distributed and centralized organizational configuration. NTUC, which controls all aspects of the organization except the academic departments, has a physically centralized structure (although some members of the NTUC sales force will most likely be more physically distributed as the organization grows). The academic side is highly distributed. Faculty form virtual departments while residing at their home institutions. The academic functions are more akin to a stable network configuration, while the other functions are primarily those of an internal network.

Process

Design and Management of Technology and Tasks: The manner in which work is designed within NTU conforms to the management style demonstrated by the institution's President, which emphasizes personal responsibility and initiative on the part of his managers. Most managers I spoke with saw the President as a visionary who left the business of management to them. Therefore, individual department heads typically handle daily operational decisions regarding how information, equipment and knowledge should be combined—this is generally consistent for both academic and non-academic departments. For example, there is a good deal of flexibility in the design of academic department processes since chairs are free to create committee structures and policies that they feel are most appropriate to their discipline. Because the institution seeks to be responsive to its customer base, the design of organizational processes also conforms to student needs such as scheduling courses so they may register for a course at almost any point during the calendar year.

The management and decision making atmosphere of the operation is decidedly ad hoc, with members of the management team coming together to address specific issues that are germane to their areas. One administrator described the manner in which management decisions are made in this way:

> I remember hardly any decisions where you had the entire organization together, or even department heads together and said okay, we've got to decide this, and you have eight people here to decide it. It's a pick up team of people who need to be involved. . . . They accept that and they like it. So you don't have anybody saying well hell, you know, when did that get decided and why didn't anybody ask my opinion about that, we don't get that.

The management of internal operations was undergoing revision with the implementation of a central, Web-based data management system that would be used to improve communication among and between NTU, its participating universities and its customers. This tool was viewed by one member of the management team as the result of "requests we couldn't fulfill" from its many constituents, which they hoped now would be addressed more effectively.

Political Process: Members of the organization appeared to down play areas of conflict. Process issues often followed a pragmatic problem solving approach, which was outcome oriented. For the management team at least, interactions seemed collegial, issue-oriented and involve a good deal of mutual trust. Among some department chairs, the issue of NTU's reconfiguration to include a for-profit organization was seen as a potential source of conflict. The chair of one department noted that he believed at some point he would receive a phone call asking to admit someone who he feels is not qualified, but because he or she (the student) has influence on the "for-profit" side, the expectation will be to admit. The organizational structure of NTU tends to limit the potential for conflict within the organization by removing some of the trigger points that are typically found in higher education organizations (e.g., tenure or budget allocations). Students and more particularly the firms they work for are all assumed to be the focal point for every organization member and this understanding tends to keep conflict low and cooperation high.

The Administrative Patterns of the National Technological University

Normative Structure

Values: It is often during times of stress that the values of an organization are most apparent. For NTU, the failure of Telstar 401 brought to the fore values of commitment and collaboration that were essential elements of its lean operating style. A review in aftermath of the failure suggests that collaboration between NTU and its participating universities was the key to stability during that troubled period. Commitment from the staff at Fort Collins and support staff at its many distributed sites made the situation bearable, it seems, for most students.

Quality and student responsiveness were also organizational values that many members of the organization felt were of central importance. The organization's structure may be viewed as an arrangement meant to encourage speed and market responsiveness. However, as one senior administrator emphasized:

> I would certainly not sacrifice an iota of quality to do something faster. We really hang our reputation . . . on the fact that we're going to try and provide you with the finest teaching, the finest classes that you can get anywhere in the world. I think if that began to slip away from us because we wanted to do something a little faster, that'd be a really bad thing to do.

Many felt that the structure of the organization afforded its students the finest quality engineering education in the world since it could "cherry pick" the finest courses and professors in the country. Offering high quality educational services is also linked to the value that organization members place on having leading edge technology. Risk taking associated with this value has, at times, placed NTU in tough financial straits. Yet, many see this fundamental organizational value as critical to its overall success despite the associated financial risks.

Norms: The general rules governing behavior in this organization were difficult to ascertain due in part to the informal nature of organizational interaction. Distinctions associated with social position, for example, are not easily observable. There is no employee union or other overt social structure below the management level. Daily meetings, such as those conducted by the satellite network group, offer occasions to direct the behavior of individual staff members.

However, such meetings are not characteristic of most NTU departments. Rules governing behavior tended to be expressed on a personal level as opposed to some generalized rules or policies of conduct.

Role Expectations: NTU had attempted to develop a formal personnel review procedure for assessing the performance of its employees. As one manager explained, NTU's informal operating style tends to make such practices difficult to sustain over a long period of time, particularly as seemingly more pressing issues confront the organization. Opportunities that inform the assessment of performance, such as the implementation of total quality management work groups, have been used as problem resolution applications (in this case to improve communication) as opposed to processes for examining performance.

Behavioral Structure

Activities: The activities of organization members are highly customer-focused and are perceived to be the activities that add the most value to the organization. The work that organization members do is often coordination oriented. For instance, the satellite network staff monitor very closely the quality of satellite transmissions and interact with their counterparts at participating institutions to ensure high quality transmissions. Research and Development projects are conducted in close collaboration with equipment manufacturers, participating universities and end users. And academic activities and associated administrative activities are migrating to more customer focused approaches such as Web and database technology, which are intended to be much more student and faculty accessible. Even with this new system, NTU staff will continue to focus on those activities that bring efficiency and customer satisfaction to the educational process.

An alternate perspective useful for understanding the activities that take place within NTU is to highlight the activities that it does not perform—some of which they choose to outsource. For example, it does not work with faculty to transform their courses to a technology mediated framework, nor does it provide faculty with on-going training in new technology tools. Since NTU students receive no financial aid, it does not assess student need or provide related financial aid counseling. While these activities are not part of the NTU operation, most other administrative and academic activities normally associated with the learning process are included. Many of them take place virtually, student advising, site coordination and the class room experience being the most prominent activities.

Interactions: The nature of interactions between participants within NTU can often transcend physical space and time. Because a significant portion of NTU interactions consist of coordination activities and educational experiences conducted in a geographically distributed environment, interactions tend to be stable, but not as highly personal as one might expect in face-to-face interactions.

Clearly, interactions are more personal in the headquarters at Fort Collins where the staff is co-located. Social barriers such as noticeable status differences among the headquarters staff appeared to be de-emphasized by the management team. Interactions seemed to be focused on responding to customer and student requests and solving problems associated with the technology for these customers.

Sentiment: For the management team of NTU, service to the engineering profession offered personal satisfaction regarding their work. For faculty this often meant interacting with high quality, mature students who were capable of "keeping them on their toes." Some found the chance to be on the leading edge of technology an exciting opportunity. The team atmosphere also provided a great deal of positive feelings about the organization, which one member of the management team described in this manner:

> The autonomy that we have as department heads to try things . . . and see if we sink or swim is really rewarding. As I'm sure you gather working with [the President] has been rewarding and working with the others here in the building. Working with a team attitude really.

Several members of the management team expressed enthusiasm over the additional revenue stream that the organization would have as a result of the reorganization. For many, this would be the first opportunity to move beyond the austere financial environment they were accustomed to and allow a bolder approach to marketing NTU's programs. Others admitted slight uneasiness, since this meant that there would be no excuses for flat or declining enrollments.

CONCLUSION

The National Technological University is a stand-alone proprietary institution that focuses on high quality master's degree programs and non-credit short courses for practicing engineers and technical professionals. Its origins are linked to the vision of its founder who saw a distinct market niche that could advance members of his profession. As a virtual organization, it relies heavily upon developing trust and collaborative relationships with the customers who purchase its educational services and the participating universities who provide NTU with its educational content. It is an organization that defines itself by being at the technological forefront. Yet, despite NTU's success, administrators and staff remain modest and focus on improving what they already do quite well. Their reorganization signals new opportunities for global expansion, which may portend future models of higher education—corporate cooperation.

NTU's organizational structure and operating model provide educational leaders with an early example of the issues involved in maintaining an enterprise that is comprised of both for and non-profit components. NTU was one of the first virtual postsecondary education organizations to form a for-profit arm and utilize venture capital funding as a lever to grow their organizational capacity and reach. As a stable network organization with remote offerings, it must continue to evaluate the viability and value of its educational suppliers in light of increasing demands to generate higher levels of net income. The melding of for and non-profit entities within NTU highlight the differences in values and expectations that can co-exist within a single organization. The strong relationships that NTU enjoys with its content suppliers may come under pressure as a result of its organizational design as there are now higher expectations placed on having academic programs generate more revenue and match market expectations more closely.

Organizational leaders may also find lessons in how NTU has constructed its management team. By bringing in a leader from the private sector while retaining its academic leadership structure in the non-profit areas, it tests whether the two may contradict or complement each other. The NTU case may illustrate a more advantageous model for institutional design in a turbulent educational marketplace.

CHAPTER 5

The University of California Extension Center for Media and Independent Learning: The Implications of Online Courses for the Organization

Whenever you drop a pebble in, when you make any change at all, it ripples everywhere and it's very easy to make a change and forget that you're going to see those ripples and then everybody's scrambling to try to deal with it. I'm really anxious to get to the point where everything isn't something new and different.

> \- A senior CMIL administrator

One could not pluck a flower without troubling a star.

> \- Loren Eiseley
> Anthropologist

ORGANIZATIONAL OVERVIEW

THE CENTER FOR MEDIA AND INDEPENDENT LEARNING (CMIL) IS A statewide service division of the University of California Extension. The organization was established in 1913 to extend the University of California's resources to the broader community, which has expanded to mean not only the local community but also a national and international community of learners. CMIL also distributes educational media such as videos and films. While it does not award degrees, it does offer over 180 high school, university and professional development courses in addition to several certificates. Courses are provided by mail, fax and electronic mail as well as via the Internet.

CMIL is part of one of the largest and most well regarded higher education institutions in the world. The University of California is the state's land-grant university and has nine campuses throughout the state. There are extension offices on each of the campuses. CMIL serves as the distance learning division of the University of California Extension. Although CMIL

87

is a statewide entity, it is administered through the University of California Berkeley Extension, which has administrative responsibility for CMIL operations and is accredited by the Western Association of Schools and Colleges.

CMIL serves more than 3,000 students per year. In 1996-97 it offered over 180 courses, sold over 600 and rented over 3,000 video and film titles. It offers a completely online certificate program in Hazardous Materials Management and, in conjunction with the University of California Berkeley Extension, provides a Certificate in Computer Information Systems. In partnership with America Online, over fifty courses are offered that feature bulletin boards, chat rooms and electronic library services. Although online courses are growing steadily, the majority of CMIL courses are of the non-Web based, independent study variety, which do not require classroom attendance. Instructors are drawn from the University of California faculty ranks, Extension instructors and faculty members from other colleges and universities.

For administrative purposes the director of CMIL reports to the dean of UC—Berkeley Extension. The dean of UC—Berkeley Extension reports to the Associate Provost of UC—Berkeley. The director of CMIL oversees an operation that combines media distribution, course development (both online and traditional independent study), customer service, online programming and marketing and public relations functions. In recent years, additional staff has been added to develop courses in accordance with the provisions of two succeeding Sloan Foundation grants, which are intended to be test beds for asynchronous course development and evaluation. The staff members reassigned or hired in response to the grant report to the director. Funding for the online projects came in the form of two grants, both made to University of California—Berkeley Extension. Money was then transferred to CMIL (initially $500,000) to develop a certificate in Hazardous Materials, and later additional courses and certificate programs. The courses developed were UC-Berkeley courses, which had to be approved by the Berkeley faculty. The project was co-directed by representatives from CMIL and UC-Berkeley Extension.

The purpose of CMIL is to extend the resources of the University of California through distance education and media to a wider community, not just in California, but nationally and internationally as well. The role it plays as a central office for extension among the University of California campuses is somewhat obscured by the organization's close association with UC-Berkeley Extension. Several members of the organization expressed a hope that the development of online courses would provide an opportunity for interaction or collaboration with all of the various campus extension units. The audience for UC Extension courses is primarily college-educated working adults who are seeking professional development, career change or personal enrichment. This is also true for online course participants—an area that has witnessed a greater growth percentage when compared to traditional independent study or correspondence courses. As a recent article about UC—Extension Online explains, "More than 1400 students have enrolled in UC Extension Online courses since the program's launch in January 1996. Currently, about two-thirds of the students enrolled in UC Extension Online are from California, with the remaining students from 46 states, the District of Columbia, Guam, and other countries such as s Russia, Mexico, Japan, and Canada. The number of students in a course can range from one or two, to more than fifty" (p. 6).

ORIGINS AND HISTORY OF THE CENTER FOR MEDIA AND INDEPENDENT LEARNING

The Center for Media and Independent Learning and University of California Extension has a long and important history. The history of extension services in California is well documented in Kathleen Rockhill's 1983 work, *Academic excellence and public policy: A history of university extension in California.* In it, she examines the development of extension—its links to the Morrill Act and the influence of the Wisconsin extension model upon extension in California—among other topics. She also analyzes (and does not hide her disappointment in) the modern extension organization in California with its increasing focus on markets and its desire to attract elite, professional students. She views this audience of means as a sign that extension has turned away from its core audience. Her findings about market orientation presage important themes about CMIL as an extension organization, which are obvious when one observes the introduction of online approaches to educational delivery and examines their influence on organizational form and administrative patterns.

As Rockhill (1983) points out, the decentralization of extension units and increasing self-support have been characteristic of the extension system's history in California since 1968. Decentralization from system to campus level units, and at a few of the larger campuses, to school and department level units has become the preferred approach to organizing. This has resulted in, Rockhill argues, "the gradual erosion of power in the Extension operation at the University wide level, and in some cases, at the campus level" (p. 180). She also suggests that increasing emphasis on self-support (1968 ended direct support from the State of California and 1982 saw an end to indirect support from campuses) has encouraged marketing objectives as a principal factor in continually redefining Extension's mission. Operational strategies may differ. More robust extension units, presumably those like UC—Berkeley Extension with which CMIL is allied, emphasize attracting students from more lucrative markets, while less stable extension programs attempt to reduce their margins by cutting staff or program support. Presumably, extension units might consider both strategic approaches. She contends that as an outcome of the trends toward decentralization and self-sufficiency, extension units have sought to appeal to an elite, more highly educated audience.

Decentralization and self-sufficiency provide a backdrop of broad environmental themes experienced by Extension leaders. While these themes inform the backdrop of extension in California, the changes and challenges involving the introduction of online instruction within CMIL reveal a more personal, purposeful and contemporary context. From its start in 1913, CMIL has been an organization focused primarily on creating and delivering correspondence courses. This has traditionally meant the creation of independent learning courses for delivery by mail. From 1913 until about 1992, traditional independent study was the hallmark of the organization. In late 1991, the program merged with another University of California Extension office, the Media Services department, which then formed the Center for Media Independent Learning. The reconstituted organization now had access to video collections and other media to support its independent study efforts.

Several members of the organization believe that the movement toward online delivery actually began in 1991 with the hiring of a new dean for University Extension at the University of California—Berkeley. When the dean was hired she brought with her an outlook on organizing that emphasized a strategic planning process, which had not been in place prior to her arrival. The dean sensed the importance of incorporating technology into extension programs. Further, her communication style tended to facilitate the introduction of new initiatives in which extension might play a role. Clearly, opportunities for growth that affected CMIL were a direct result of the dean's approach to educating others and marketing the strategic goals of Extension to internal campus units.

The most important outcome of the dean's efforts for CMIL came with the awarding of a grant from the Alfred P. Sloan Foundation for $500,000 to pilot a certificate program in Hazardous Materials Management. This occurred in 1994. The decision to select Hazardous Materials as the pilot was a pragmatic one in that initial marketing research suggested that the content would have wide appeal. Although the grant was provided to UC—Berkeley Extension, the money was transferred to CMIL since it was the unit with the capability to develop online courses. The grant supported the development of a completely online nine-course program; in addition CMIL contributed 16 more courses to bring to 25 the number that would be delivered online. What's more, the terms of the grant stipulated that Extension would partner with a commercial Internet provider in order to deliver the courses. The grant made UC—Berkeley the first major American research university to offer a variety of professional education courses via a commercial Internet Service Provider—America Online (AOL). The Sloan Foundation apparently had little interest in funding technology infrastructure.

The partnership with AOL (the organization viewed as having suitable interest and sufficient capability to deliver the courses in a high quality manner) became an immediate learning experience for members of CMIL and UC-Berkeley Extension. As a very young and rapidly growing company, AOL's fast paced culture was very different from that which CMIL members were accustomed. At times, the turnover among AOL employees made negotiations with CMIL discontinuous. Though active in marketing within the emerging online world, AOL's approaches to course marketing needed to adhere to the principles and standards of the University of California. Some members of the organization who were involved in negotiating saw these challenges as healthy. One of the key benefits that AOL provided was a means of rapidly crafting an online course presence. Message boards, chat rooms, email interaction and non-linear design of textual materials were incorporated into courses in two iterations. The first iteration consisted of merely converting traditional extension courses to an online medium. What designers found in the second iteration was that online courses could create more communication opportunities than traditional correspondence courses. Student to student interaction was possible while in the past the interaction was primarily between student and instructor. AOL's technologies were allowing course designers to create asynchronous learning experiences that were more collaborative than traditional correspondence courses, while offering students access to media-rich learning materials primarily online.

A second proposal to the Sloan Foundation submitted in June 1996 expressed the major lessons learned in what came to be known as Sloan 1. The findings, particularly the dealings with AOL, are illustrative. Marketing and support for students and faculty were also significant issues. The lessons learned from the first Sloan grant were considered valuable information and demonstrated enough progress to justify a decision to seek a second round of funding from the Sloan Foundation. The pilot program of 25 online courses was followed by a June 1996 proposal that was far more ambitious.

Sloan 2 proposed that the Sloan Foundation fund the development of an additional 100 courses so that by the end of the grant period (August 31, 1998) Extension would have 125 courses available online. The proposal requested approximately $2.1 million to support the development of these courses. The proposal also commits CMIL to develop an additional 50 courses at the end of the grant period. The proposal signaled an important shift in Extension's strategy of course development, that of making asynchronous learning and the new instructional possibilities that technology allows as mainstream as classroom based courses. The grant was also sought to expand the marketing efforts, which are seen as pivotal to the success of Extension's online offerings.

About the same time as the proposal to Sloan was being crafted, a strategic plan for the UC—Berkeley Extension program was being crafted as well. The plan, with its clear implications for and input from CMIL leaders, laid out a course that appears to complement many of the points expressed in the Sloan proposal. The plan contained two guiding principles. The first focused on creating a "learner-centered" approach, in which the needs and expectations of the learner are understood; customer service is consistent; and financial strength is sufficient to sustain learner-centeredness. The notion of "learner-centered" in the strategic plan is not defined, but a stronger definition is called for in the document. The second guiding principle is that of strategic readiness. Here the sense of adaptability and market responsiveness, which is evident in the Sloan proposal, is expressed. It states: "we will have to look objectively at our operations and be willing to reconsider and change many internal and external relationships, roles, policies, processes, systems, and attitudes" (Extension's Strategic Priorities, 1996). It may be intuited from the guiding principles that an organization that places the needs (and wants) of the student first, must continually rethink its organizational form and patterns to respond quickly to an evolving understanding of what it means to be a life-long learner.

As CMIL's past blends into the present day, organizational milestones are often measured by enrollment levels and number of courses available for online delivery. The pace at which members of the organization must work to achieve the grant established deadlines is typically stressful. The grant period that was expected to end in August 1998 was likely to be granted a no-cost extension by the Sloan Foundation according to leaders of CMIL. The atmosphere within the organization was summed up by one staff member in this way as she reflected on key milestones in the organization's history: "Oh god, I wouldn't even know what to call a milestone. That's a hard one. Everyday is a milestone. . .it's just like raising a kid, you know? You learn something everyday and you change the way you do it after you figure out something doesn't work."

In the next section, I examine CMIL based on the dimensions of the operational framework discussed in chapter 2.

ANALYSIS OF THE CENTER FOR MEDIA AND INDEPENDENT LEARNING

Extraorganizational Conditions Influencing the Organizational Form and Administrative Patterns of the Center for Media and Independent Learning

The analysis of extraorganizational conditions encountered by CMIL focused on the variable groups (uncertainty, dependence, normative and cognitive factors) explained in the conceptual framework. Imprinting (normative group), which concerns the degree to which the organization has acquired characteristics from its founding that are retained in the current form or patterns of the organization, was the only theme that did not emerge within this portion of the analysis.

Uncertainty

Complexity: The degree of organizational complexity experienced by CMIL has been defined largely by its relationship with UC—Berkeley Extension. As a statewide office, one might expect the potential for relationships with dissimilar organizations to be more likely. However, aside from interactions with textbook publishers and its online partner, AOL (which one could argue was a result of UC—Berkeley's influence anyway), the entities to which CMIL relates are somewhat limited. The operating structure of CMIL restricts unilateral alliances or partnerships with non-academic organizations, for example. Additionally, the decentralized nature of the University of California Extension system tends to undermine alliances across extension units on UC campuses.

Stability—Variability: Nearly every member of the organization that I spoke with seemed to have an example of how the changes in the environment of higher education were affecting his or her aspect of the operation. The notion of the shifting nature of markets for extension offerings, particularly online courses, was believed to be breaking down traditional boundaries in extension. In the past, campus extension units in the state would have informal agreements to market courses only within their locales. With online courses, boundaries such as this are obsolete and can create a new form of competition among units. The segmentation of markets was also viewed as a trend challenging the stability of the organization. One informant described market segmentation as consisting of two types, the residential market and the market of convenience. The convenience of time and place as well as easy access through technology is creating new demands on the organization. These demands have quickened the pace of the organization causing it to examine the processes and assumptions about delivery and support of educational content. Finally, turbulence in the publishing industry is another factor affecting the organization. Recent mergers and the revision of textbooks on a shorter cycle (at times each year or every two years) forces revisions in courses and course packages. As one senior administrator explained:

> It's a very, very dynamic and undefined time in the sense that I think the impetus for all of this is coming from so many directions that it's very hard . . . there's no way to manage it efficiently right now.

Threat—Security: The relative degree of vulnerability that CMIL faces within its environment is tied to its status as a self-supporting unit (although UC—Berkeley Extension is responsible for covering any deficit in CMIL's budget). In addition, it must rely upon the Berkeley faculty senate to approve courses and instructors, which limits the organization's ability to move quickly to seize market opportunities. Conversely, the procedure does grant CMIL's courses and instructors a solid measure of quality. In the online area, CMIL is faced with the task of attracting instructors with sufficient skills and ability in learning and applying instructional technology, and interest from instructors appears to be rather keen at this stage. A downturn in CMIL's partnership with AOL could pose a threat to the current manner of operating, but the continued development of UC Extension Online should help to minimize such a threat.

Dependence

Munificence—Scarcity: CMIL appears to face no accute scarcity issues concerning most of the key resources it requires for its operation. The development of the Sloan grant courses may be an exception in that the grant amount limits the director's ability to hire additional staff, despite the fact that the talent required to advance the project at a faster rate may be found in the Berkeley area. Another exception is the availability of technical personnel since CMIL must compete with Silicon Valley and other private sector firms in the area that pay much higher salaries.

Normative

Authorization of Structural Features: The organizational form and administrative patterns of CMIL are highly influenced by UC—Berkeley Extension due to the administrative relationship between the two organizations. This is most evident in the control that Berkeley exercised over the course and instructor approval process, which several members of CMIL viewed as overly bureaucratic. Course and instructors are first reviewed by UC—Berkeley Extension, then the academic department, then a discipline-specific sub-committee of the Berkeley faculty senate. The growth of online courses has tended to slow the process since reviewers have tended to examine online courses more closely than they had independent study courses. A notable outcome of the organizational reporting structure is the degree to which the offerings of an organization like Extension are integrated into the fabric of the campus. For instance, could an extension course be used to complete the degree requirements for a Berkeley undergraduate, residential student? As with all extension units in the University of California System, CMIL's relationship with UC—Berkeley does not permit the use of extension courses for completion of Berkeley degree programs. Those policies influence the strategic direction and administrative patterns of CMIL, particularly as they pertain to marketing and selection of courses for online development.

Acquisition: While members of CMIL were not specific about practices or structures that they incorporated within their operation, many were cognizant of what other institutions in the field were doing in regard to marketing, catalog development and program offerings. The University of Phoenix was mentioned on more than one occasion as an organization whose ideas and approaches were worth watching. However, most informants stopped short of advocating for the adoption of the University of Phoenix's practices.

Clearly, CMIL's contract with AOL (which was sought by the Sloan Foundation) is a visible outcome of actions undertaken by the organization to incorporate more modern practices. But as one administrator explained, alliances with an organization like AOL can demand persistence in negotiating contracts:

> When I returned the draft contract I sent it to him [AOL representative] not knowing that he had been reorganized to another area and there's someone new now who's reviewing that and I'm sure there's going be some discussion that's going need to go forward about what this is precisely. . . . AOL also because they're so fast moving tends not to want to necessarily nail everything down in black and white thoroughly, it's sort of like well . . . however the policies are today, and we're like no, no (laugh) we have to write these down. And this is precisely the reason, because we may have an understanding with one contact, but if that person leaves, which they do with regularity, how do we have any assurance that the next person is going to live up to the spirit of what our agreement was if it's not actually articulated in writing?

Incorporation: The degree to which CMIL has come to reflect structural features found within its environment is found mainly in the staff hired to perform certain functions for online course development. These staff members who are associated with the Sloan grant possess talent and skills that the organization had not needed in the past when independent study courses were the only type of course offered. However aside from specialized staff roles, the comments by one senior administrator tend to support the belief that the organization is influenced more by internal, rather than external perspectives. He explained:

> Our university's organizing itself to do online instruction and I think we're beginning to see some patterns, but very few organizations are like ours, devoted from the get go to non-matriculated students. . . . We're probably unique in the breadth of our seeking to go out and pull people in. And the fact that we don't offer degrees makes us different. We're quite uncharacteristically different from most other organizations, so I'm not sure that there are some real analogues that we could look at.

Cognitive

Legitimation: The Sloan Foundation grant provides the major source of external legitimation for CMIL's online courses. The exposure that the grant has provided has made CMIL the focus of news features, inquires, phone calls and awards. However, the principal legitimation sources are internal—structured by traditional academic review processes which, though bureaucratic, guarantee some check on course and instructor quality. Legitimacy is judged according to academic standards, rather than the ability to meet market expectations. Internal legitimacy is a constant struggle, as the comments of one administrator suggest:

> You lose that the minute you don't have the faculty support . . . the danger you have is being viewed more peripherally, and being even less important to the campus . . . at what point do they say you can't use our name anymore? A lot of the questions we get are . . . why should the University of California and Berkeley be doing this? Why should we be serving international students? Why should we be doing X, Y, Z, and there's faculty who don't really see any benefit to some of these activities. On the other hand what we have is all these campuses are finding it more and more difficult to find the funds they need, so they look to the self-supporting units as ways to bring funds back into other kinds of activities. . . . Something has to come back to them for their time and effort.

Because extension units like CMIL are intended to be self-supporting, return of revenue to the campuses may be a long term source of legitimacy. This realization by the leadership team makes the financial success of online courses all the more important.

Institutionally Shared Beliefs: Beliefs, rules and roles that shape the organizational form and administrative patterns of CMIL are primarily of an internal nature. The faculty senate, dean of UC—Berkeley Extension and other institutional actors are influential in shaping CMIL as an organization. There are, however, subtle but discernible patterns that suggest that the beliefs and roles of members of the organization are being changed by external influences. One obvious example that several informants spoke of was student expectations, particularly those of online students. In the customer service area, for example, student expectations about how long it should take to receive a response from a CMIL staff member was becoming shorter and shorter (especially when email was the communication method). Sensitivity to customer expectations was also in the process of being formalized. Course and certificate program development in the online area has been guided more recently by working closely with external advisors, such as the advisory board for the Hazardous Materials Certificate Program, to meet learner needs.

Interorganizational Conditions Influencing the Organizational Form and Administrative Patterns of the Center for Media and Independent Learning

This section evaluates significant collaborative influences that may shape CMIL's organizational form and administrative patterns. In keeping with the conceptual framework, the analysis focused on three broad variable categories—uncertainty, dependence and normative factors. Imposition of organizational form, the coercive influences exercised by external agents to legitimately change the organizational form and administrative patterns of the organization, did not emerge as a major theme group in this section of the analysis.

Uncertainty

Interconnectedness—Isolation: CMIL is not highly interconnected to external organizations that may affect its operations as would be the case with an actual virtual organization. Its alliances with external entities such as publishers, instructors and connectivity provider AOL are significant, but reflect activities that, with the exception of instruction, could be undertaken in-house. The strategic advantage they gain in marketing and infrastructure through AOL, for example, is but an alternative that the organization will pursue until it becomes disadvantageous to do so. CMIL's goal in uniting with AOL revealed the importance of an alliance with the organization as the comments of a mid-level administrator indicate:

Our initial goal there was the idea that we would be able to bring our expertise in designing online course materials, and they would bring in many ways, two things: the technical expertise so we wouldn't be worrying about the servers, and a large audience that they had already developed . . . it's a central hub. At the time we approached them, I think they had about 1 million members, but the idea was that there were a set of 1 million people out there already online whom it would be relatively easy for us to market to.

The strategic plan for Extension suggests that interconnections with external organizations like AOL are likely to rise in the future since the leadership team believes that resources within the organization may not be sufficient to meet student expectations.

Dependence

Coordination—Non-coordination: The degree to which CMIL faces a group of external entities whose actions are coordinated is illustrated in two coordinating mechanisms that informants saw as emerging within their environment. The first is the Instructional Management System (IMS) being created through the National Learning Infrastructure Project in conjunction with EDUCAUSE. The project was attempting to create a code that would allow an automatic cataloging of all online courses according to specified parameters or categories describing the course. The IMS system would allow comparisons across courses to be made, thus giving students or others the ability to compare courses fairly and accurately. As one senior administrator noted, it was difficult for a student (consumer) to know exactly what he or she was getting from an online course.

That's why this IMS thing is so important, because you know, theoretically if they were IMS compliant, you could go and find out whether they [the courses] were really even offered right now. How many of those courses are actually open right now I can enroll in? You as a consumer can't find that out very easily.

The second coordinating mechanism is the creation of the California Virtual University (CVU). CVU, as one administrator described it, "we're very happy to be involved in it, but it's right now not much more than a catalog that provides us with another marketing mark." The project was intended to provide a gateway to distance learning courses offered by California public institutions and provide an opportunity for marketing courses (soon after this interview, several key players in the CVU backed out of the arrangement).

Concentration—Dispersion: CMIL benefits from the physical location in the San Francisco Bay area with its high concentration of available talent for instruction and administrative support.

Interorganizational Power: CMIL's organizational reporting structure restricts the degree of control it may have over resources critical to its operation. As a central unit, CMIL has very little direct control over other extension offices in the California system. Internal relationships (its association with Berkeley Extension staff, faculty senate committees or departments, for example) tend to be marked by negotiation and give and take among members of those organizations. The interaction between CMIL staff and instructors provides an illustration of the negotiated atmosphere in which CMIL staff members work, as the comments of one mid-level administrator portray:

> Sometimes there are clashes, but usually I think a lot more often the case is that the instructor is also some kind of neophyte when it comes to online instruction, so they're usually very willing to accept the way that we develop it once it's demonstrated to them how the delivery works. But, we have had instructors who just have insisted that we've missed their intent, and sort of held out for something else, but again, I think it's a lot more often it's the other way around. These instructors are really looking for us to help them go through this process.

Deadlines determined by the Sloan grant parameters may also cause conflicts when instructor timetables do not correspond with the development team's expectations about course completion dates. The CMIL development team can exercise limited control over hastening the process. Contractual agreements with AOL do provide some degree of discretion over utilization of resources. This has occurred as a result of ongoing learning and revisions in the stance CMIL staff have taken in dealing with AOL officials, in which they pushed for more explicit contracts.

Normative

Inducement Strategies: The principal incentive that is causing CMIL to change its organizational form and administrative patterns are the Sloan grants that began in 1994. The infusion of Sloan grant money and subsequent online development has caused ripples throughout the organization. As one senior administrator noted, " grant funding has really allowed us to ratchet up our development in a way that we could never have done if we had not had that kind of money." The statement suggests that incentive strategies by Sloan were in no way coercive, but rather welcomed by CMIL. Groups such as the University Continuing Education Association, a group that recognizes annually the achievements of innovative continuing education and independent study programs, offer more subtle incentives. The selection of UC Extension Online for special recognition in 1998 reinforces the belief that online education is a valuable and innovative approach among its membership.

Intraorganizational Conditions Influencing the Organizational Form and Administrative Patterns of the Center for Media and Independent Learning

The organizational form and administrative patterns of CMIL appear to have been influenced by several internal conditions. Thematic analysis suggests that CMIL has been influenced by the nature of the organizational system of which it is embedded—UC—Berkeley Extension and the UC system. The themes also reflect strong linkages to goals set by the organization's leader and their selection of and investment in specific instructional technologies.

Brand Name Affiliation: CMIL's close association with UC—Berkeley Extension, the UC—Berkeley campus and the University of California system provide name recognition and a perception of quality to the courses and programs that CMIL develops. As CMIL develops courses for UC—Berkeley Online and UC—Extension Online, it is clear that brand recognition is linked to the quality and prestige of the residential institution. The affiliation influences the marketing approach that CMIL has taken as well as the academic standards that one would expect from a University of California course. As one senior administrator explained:

> Our brand is based upon the traditional classroom degree model . . . we're arguably the most selective undergraduate school in the country, and we have probably the best graduate school over all the country. Berkeley's name is out there. It's all in degree based . . . it's mostly in degree based research and all this kind of stuff. Extension has always been on the convenient side of the market, so how can we translate that brand/quality into the convenient side and keep our faculty happy and aware of what we're doing? And it's a tough one. We believe we can reach Berkeley quality standards in the convenience market.

Perceived Bureaucratic Atmosphere and Decision Making Processes: Informants at various levels of the organization were quick to point out a story or experience that revealed bureaucratic inefficiency and frustration. At times, the innovative educational products developed by CMIL seem to have been created in spite of the bureaucratic processes of the university system. One humorous story involved five different colors of "white-out" to correct typing errors on each sheet of an often used UC—Extension form. For example, some found the faculty senate course approval process as unjustifiably slow for responding to the pace that is being set in the market for online products and services. For other members of the organization there was a realization, however, that quality courses must carry the imprimatur of the University of California and therefore the seemingly bureaucratic processes that accompany course approval are simply part of the equation. The decision making atmosphere, one that is deliberate in an optimistic rendering, seem to have shaped the processes of the organization more than any other environmental factor(s).

Perceived Intraorganizational Competition: The emergence of online courses as a portion of CMIL's offerings has raised issues of competition among continuing education units in the UC—Extension system. CMIL's close association with UC—Berkeley Extension is perceived by some members of CMIL as a long standing issue of contention for other continuing education offices, who feel that as a system wide office CMIL is too closely allied with UC—Berkeley Extension. CMIL's role in developing online courses for Berkeley Extension has added to that perception. Programming CMIL online courses is perceived to have had the opposite effect, making some at Berkeley concerned because the courses included in the catalog may be competing with their program.

The nature of an asynchronous, online product is itself a source of unintended competition among continuing education units in the California Extension system. Structures such as the California Virtual University tend to add to the spirit of competition by juxtaposing institutional offerings in a public manner. Where geographic boundaries had created informal marketing boundaries, online offerings negate any semblance or need for such boundaries. Any extension organization in California may compete with any other California institution (or national or international institution) for students.

Presence of Organizational Champion: Many members of CMIL viewed the role of the Dean of UC—Berkeley Extension as a critical force in shaping the organization and particularly in growing the online component of the organization. Working with the Director of CMIL and members of the Berkeley Extension leadership, the dean was influential in securing two Sloan Foundation grants, which launched the online effort for CMIL. One staff member described the dean in this way:

She's very enthusiastic. She's really turned both extension and our program around. . . . She's kind of come onboard and given a push with letting us collaborate with UC Extension, so our program has grown in that way and our enrollments have gone up.

Selection of Educational Technology: CMIL's emphasis on asynchronous learning (influenced by existing structures) has led it to select specific educational technology. The decision to implement Web-based applications had a very direct influence on the structure of the organization, its strategies for course development and marketing and the processes by which courses were developed. The partnership with AOL has prodded CMIL to accept technology standards and templates for educational products, while also giving course developers a point of comparison for creating the UC—Extension Online Internet site, which is not associated with AOL. As one mid-level administrator explained, the decision over technology was intended to create as much flexibility as possible:

> There were a variety of technologies out there that we could develop, that would give us some flexibility and experimentation. We didn't necessarily know how the market was going to evolve in terms of whether people would be moving away from AOL or to the Internet or the market would sort of split as it is now.

Indirectly, selection of Web-based technologies redefines the processes and pace of affiliate areas such as customer services and technology support.

The Nature of the Organization

In the next section, CMIL's organizational form and administrative patterns are explained according to the conceptual framework presented previously in Chapter 2.

The Organizational Form of the Center for Media and Independent Learning

Strategy

Intraorganizational Strategy: Activities and policies designed to shield CMIL from potentially detrimental environmental events tended to be expressed through the partnerships that CMIL has formed with AOL, Berkeley Extension, as well as potential partnerships that were possible with other extension units in the state. As the strategic plan outlines, strategic readiness by way of partnerships will be necessary to ensure that Berkeley Extension and CMIL have the resources needed to create learner-centered programs. For example, with partner AOL, CMIL has the ability to take advantage of innovative online marketing techniques that in their absence might undermine enrollment in online courses. Fulfilling the strategic objectives and buffering the organization may include future partnerships and grant funding for projects such as the one described by one senior administrator:

> I'm onto what I'm calling Sloan 3, which is looking at the possibility of making a grant proposal to the Sloan Foundation a third time for a statewide project that would involve many, if not all of the extension campuses in the system.

Interorganizational Strategy: CMIL's principal strategic approach is one designed to change the nature of the environment for its educational services and products. As a statewide office, a key aspect of CMIL's strategy is educating other extension offices throughout the state by exhibiting political adroitness in managing expectations about online courses. This focus is described by one mid-level administrator:

> It's kind of a combination of marketing and PR [public relations] really for us. . .It's important to educate the other campuses and that's reall . . . .the mandate of CMIL is that we're a statewide organization, we only, are sort of able to push beyond any kind of geographical boundaries.

Clearly, the redefinition of geographic boundaries built around the unit's online offerings is a desired outcome for CMIL and is likely to be the growing focus of their business.

The pressure to internationalize offerings by both Berkeley Extension and CMIL is an area in which the organization's environment may be influenced quite dramatically. By partnering with AOL and developing their own website, CMIL has attempted to offer choices that are suitable for the technologically sophisticated and less technologically sophisticated (Berkeley Extension is sponsoring projects that mix media such as CD-ROM, Internet, print, video). Similarly, by diversifying the types of programs being offered (certificate programs, for instance) CMIL intended to attract new groups of learners.

Resource Strategy: As a self-supporting unit, CMIL has for years faced the challenges of having to generate a sufficient revenue stream. The revenue stream has been drawn largely from independent study courses and media sales and rentals. The Sloan grant funds that were transferred to CMIL from Berkeley Extension have been the major impetus for the development of online courses. Early indications were that online course offerings were not yet profitable, as the comments of one senior administrator make very clear:

> At least to the point that we have collaborated with Berkeley . . . their online courses are not generating enough income to sustain this infrastructure. What

is sustaining this infrastructure is the 3,000 independent learning students who are still taking traditional based [independent study] courses.

There are several reasons why profitability may be difficult to obtain, as this passage from the Sloan II grant application explains:

> We currently are budgeting $20,000 per course. However, the per-course development cost is extremely variable depending upon the scope of the course; the amount of instructional design, writing, and editing required; the technological features incorporated; the abilities of the instructor in writing appropriate course notes, identifying Web resources, and developing other course features such as message board threads; and the extent of coordination of team members.

Because of CMIL's diversified product lines and grant funding, online courses are buffered from an immediate need to be profitable. However, as the focus upon online courses becomes a larger aspect of CMIL's educational offerings, it is apparent that new approaches will be necessary. Indeed, this is evident in CMIL's approach to course development, which is the subject of the next section.

Course Development Strategy: CMIL's course development strategy is an aspect of the organization that is unique to this case and worthy of inclusion for understanding this organization. The course development strategy involved critical choices that leaders of CMIL needed to make, which could have implications for profitability, course quality and general levels of job satisfaction on the part of the course development team. Aspects of the course development strategy are expressed in the second Sloan Foundation grant proposal:

> In our strategy to diversify our course offerings and build critical mass in the program, we are selecting programs that have already been successful in the classroom. . . . Also key to a program's selection is the identification of experienced instructors who are interested in using technology in their courses.

The choice of which courses, programs and instructors to begin with is not a trivial point. Success in traditional formats was used as a guide to online course development. Once the course development process is underway (and the grant from Sloan received), the strategy appeared to be one of crafting the largest amount of courses as quickly and economically as possible. The approach had raised questions among some on the staff as compromising quality for quantity in order to meet deadlines established by the grant.

Organizational Learning Strategy: Another strategy that leaders of CMIL have undertaken is to document the processes of the organization and create performance standards for development of online courses. The sense of experimentation is pervasive in the office, as one mid-level administrator explained: "We were one of the first and we did a lot of things just. . .we just went about doing it. We didn't really know what we were doing, we were inventing the wheel." That initial impulse to jump in has given way to a strong emphasis on organizational learning—tracking processes, noting inefficiencies and implementing new techniques. Outsourcing aspects of the operation is continually evaluated—more informally, than formally. Several members of the organization believe that an essential outcome of the learning strategy should be the standardization of processes, which will allow online development and delivery processes to be more time-efficient and cost-effective.

Structure

Centralization: CMIL is an organization that relies heavily on its senior leaders to guide the direction of the organization. Because of the reporting structure, the Director of CMIL is both a project manager for the Sloan project and the director of the independent study and media areas. Decision making by virtue of this arrangement is centralized, with the director making most of the key decisions in the organization.

Formalization: Expectations about the means and ends of work at CMIL are becoming increasingly more formalized. The introduction of online courses has caused ripple effects in the organization that have prompted the management team to look closely at the processes across several areas. The influence of online delivery seems to have hastened the pace of many parts of the organization. This is caused primarily by the terms of the Sloan grant, which specify an aggressive timetable for the creation of new online courses. The more rapid pace is forcing CMIL's managers to make the means and ends of work more explicit in order to reduce the time it takes to develop online courses.

Complexity: The organization has in recent years become more highly differentiated by adding media services and the Sloan project to its independent study operation. Plans for future partnerships with other extension organizations may create opportunities for increased differentiation. As this statewide unit develops expertise in the development of online courses and new media, additional grant opportunities and alliances may be cause for the addition of new components to the organization as well.

Configuration: CMIL's structure is traditional as formal roles are located within the confines of a single organization. Alliances with AOL, instructors, textbook publishers and printers make the network of relationships in the organization extend beyond conventional boundaries. What is obvious from both interviews and review of the organization chart was the lack of a project manager for the Sloan project. Due to financial constraints, hiring someone for this role was not possible. The decision to have the director of CMIL fill this role suggests how important the project is to the organization, but also a tendency toward centralization in managing the online project.

Process

Design and Management of Technology and Tasks: CMIL is currently undergoing transition in how it thinks about the design, management and integration of materials, operations and knowledge. As one supervisor explained, "everything that one of us does impacts another person, so for instance if I enter an enrollment, and make a mistake, that's going to impact one or two other people at least." The tight integration of functions within this office makes change in one area immediately felt in another. The online operation is viewed by most as the principal factor driving change in the organization. It is because of this that managers in the organization are very concerned about process, having completed extensive process maps of the online operation and its connection to other parts of the organization.

The organization appears to be reconsidering some of its original assumptions concerning how well independent study processes will transfer to online course development, online student services, online marketing and other related aspects of asynchronous course delivery. One mid-level administrator described (in a manner typical of a start-up organization) the initial phases of the Sloan project—reporting lines were initially unclear and were reconceived once the new operation was underway. Initial assumptions about the applicability of independent study data management systems for online courses were quickly found to be inappropriate and required changes. One response has been to have the director of CMIL assume the role of both project manager for online course development activities and director of the independent study and media services operations. The move has had a centralizing influence on the decision making of the organization since all major decisions (and potentially minor decisions as well) must then flow through the director.

The pace within the organization is also of concern. The pressure of keeping up with work demands was voiced by most every member of the organization. The response by leaders to the quickening pace of the organization has been to track organizational processes and by forming process maps to seek standardization of processes where appropriate, beginning with the online project. The approach exposed the course design procedure since finding a balance between standardizing aspects of a course and uniquely crafting each course can come into conflict under time constraints established by the Sloan grant. The team approach to online course design also tends to make the process quite linear and integrated. Supervision of course development tends to be deadline driven. Periodic meetings are held to evaluate progress and determine why development deadlines were not achieved.

Political Process: Sources of conflict within the organization have much to do with the time constraints and rising work demands placed on the staff. The ambiguity of developing online courses without established patterns of operation (or patterns that differ from the independent study operation) is also seen as a source of conflict among members of CMIL. The effects of online courses and the speed at which they must be developed have left gaps in the system of communicating and resolving conflict as the comments of one staff member indicate:

> I think that because we really don't have many systems for making sure that opinions are heard and then dealt with in some way, not that every opinion has to be followed, but just that you're being heard. I think people have developed sort of back door ways of being heard.

Conflict resolution has followed several paths. Regular meetings among staff tended to be a forum for airing superficial issues or heading off problems between departments or individual staff members. For example, coordination meetings on online course progress are intended to surface potential problem areas before they become real concerns. Members of the Sloan project staff participated in a seminar intended to facilitate more effective communication among members of the team. One implicit message in documenting organizational processes within CMIL is that more efficient processes may reduce levels of conflict by eliminating redundancy and easing time constraints.

The Administrative Patterns of the Center for Media and Independent Learning

Normative Structure

Values: One overarching value expressed by the senior leaders in the organization has been an emphasis on standardizing aspects of the online course development process. The concern over process and focus on process mapping is an overt sign of this value. Personal values do, at times, conflict with general organizational values such as standardization, as this comment by a staff member suggests:

> The main thing that I see in terms of values is people are very concerned about the details or the quality of the classes. . . . I think that's a combination of concern for the student, and pride in their work. I just think you have a very high level of performers who want to make perfect, perfect software almost to a fault . . . in a private industry, you see that there's a lot of give and take as far as . . . quality versus meeting deadlines. . . . I'd say that more so here than in other places I've been, people are . . . almost anal about making sure that every single detail is absolutely perfect.

The dichotomy of quality versus standardization is a value that seems to be in conflict within the organization.

Responsiveness to student needs is another major value expressed by informants in the study. Whether this was conveyed in terms of strategic goals of learner-centeredness, timely responses to student questions or new program delivery methods, the student is foremost in minds of the staff. This value was explained plainly by one senior administrator:

> I think we're trying to be responsive to their [students] needs, both by developing the program in the first place and then also by providing strong student service, which I see as a real key to having a good program.

Norms: The rules governing behavior in the organization are, in general, subject to the terms of the policies set by the University of California. For example, the University's hiring policies tend to complicate the nature of temporary work. A senior administrator described the norms of hiring in this way:

> Because of the university setting . . . it's not like a private business where I could say you're hired for three years, see the curious thing is I did hire all of the people in the online project. I told them their jobs would end on X date, but in reality the way the University works, once you have worked here twelve months non-stop, you are a permanent employee, and I have to go through a layoff procedure even though I've told them . . . that their job ends because there's no money after X date, I have to go through a layoff procedure, so I just wanted to make it clear from the outset.

At the micro organizational level, the Director of CMIL and others in supervisory roles set the organizational norms. Most staff members describe the rules of the organization as "casual" or "relaxed," which suggests that professional standards are the responsibility of the individual. This seemed paradoxical given the pressure that many members of the organization are under to meet the deadlines of the Sloan grant. One might expect the rules governing behavior to be much more explicit in order to ensure that goals are being achieved.

Role Expectations: Role expectations for the staff of CMIL are, like the norms of the organization, influenced to a large extent by the policies of the University of California. Performance standards and performance reviews are used to assess the performance of employees. However, sub-group role expectations can develop separate from the larger patterns of the organization since the outcomes of the sub-groups can differ. As one member of Sloan project team noted, "the only expectations that really matter for me, are the team's expectations." The strong group identity of the Sloan project team tended to guide behavior and set the performance standards for that group. It is clear that the influences of the Sloan project group on the performance standards of the other areas of the organization are indirect, but significant. The pace of work and expectations about customer satisfaction appeared to be changing as a result of the online course development process.

Behavioral Structure

Activities: The types of activities that the CMIL staff performs are diverse, but are not atypical for organizations that perform extension or continuing education functions. Major areas that CMIL staff are responsible for include marketing, catalog preparation, course development, instructor recruitment and payment, student services, bookstore and course material services and media sales and rentals. They work closely with programmers at UC—Berkeley Extension to create and offer online courses and coordinate the course approval process with academic departments, the Berkeley faculty senate and Berkeley Extension. Some members of the staff have relationships with external organizations and negotiate the terms of outsourced activities such as textbooks and catalog printing.

With the addition of the Sloan project, new activities have been created and older activities have been redefined. The online course development process has given rise to a team approach to development in which instructors are part of a team of instructional designers, online editors and technical support staff. The team, working with members of Berkeley Extension and other CMIL staff, is responsible for the entire online course development process: from conception through testing to student enrollment. The online course development process has influenced the activities of other members of CMIL by adding additional work, most assuredly, but also by changing expectations about work deadlines and timeliness of completing routine activities such as responding to student requests.

Interactions: The interactions among members of the CMIL staff and between CMIL staff and external entities are determined largely by patterns established through the organization's historical approach to independent study. The reporting structure of the organization and the patterns of interaction with Berkeley Extension and UC—Berkeley prescribe the nature of contact for many CMIL staff members. The introduction of online courses has expanded the scope of interaction for several members of CMIL, as has the organization's continuing assessment of outsourcing opportunities (e.g., delivery infrastructure, textbooks and print material).

Among members of CMIL, email is a convenient method of communication. The growth of technology-mediated communication allows members of the organization to determine the time and nature of a response. This pattern of interaction appears to coincide with the increasing workload and time constraints faced by members of the organization. Email, even among this rather small organization, appears to return some control over work patterns to the individual.

Sentiment: The feelings or attitudes that members of the organization exhibited toward their work were quite expectedly diverse, particularly since the organization is undergoing significant change as a result of the development of online courses. Many felt they had little control over changes taking place in their individual position, but most were optimistic about the changes overall. The essence of statements such as this one were common, although most I spoke with felt no embarrassment about their work:

> This sounds like the party-line, but I really am proud of the courses that we produce. . . . I used to feel embarrassed about telling my friends that I go work for the place [CMIL], . . . but now you know, we offer on-line courses, and it's like whoa, you guys are on the cutting edge.

But frustration with the rapid pace of the organization was troubling to many as well. Many of the comments expressed by members of the staff are captured in the comments of one staff member, who explained:

> I guess my greatest frustration is that I feel like I come into work and just speed around doing all of these things that I'm not sure why I'm doing a lot of time. I get very caught up in it and by the end of the day, when I'm walking home, I start to consider what's the bigger picture and it doesn't make a lot of sense to me.

The sense of experimentation and leadership in creating online courses is attractive and challenging for the staff at CMIL. However, deadlines and the press of the work at hand give them very little time to reflect upon the progress they have achieved or challenges that remain.

CONCLUSION

The University of California Extension Center for Media and Independent Learning is an example of a publicly sponsored, statewide continuing education organization that offers independent study and innovative online certificate programs and courses. CMIL was established in 1913 to extend the University of California's learning services to a community that now includes local, national and international students. The organization has strong administrative ties to the UC—Berkeley Extension Center, which guides many of the administrative procedures that CMIL follows. As a recipient of two Sloan Foundation grants, it is considered by many to be a pioneer in asynchronous course delivery. While the grant project has increased the capacity of the organization and expertise with new delivery mechanisms and partnership arrangements, it has also created new expectations and changes in other parts of the organization. These changes offer valuable lessons for any organization considering the development of online programs or courses.

CMIL's structure and approach to online learning raises several important issues, particularly for institutions that possess a well-established history. One issue concerns CMIL's reputation and association with the University of California – Berkeley. Such characteristics enhance its ability to establish a unique presence in a volatile educational marketplace. The imprimatur of the University of California offers CMIL a tremendous advantage for staking out an identity, which many institutions of lesser name recognition and reputation may not be able to establish. Their ability to draft off of the reputation of UC—Berkeley, for example, also presents some disadvantages. A major disadvantage is the measured program and course approval process. While it is clear that the quality of CMIL courses is not likely to be hindered by rigorous academic reviews, the policies of the university may undermine CMIL's ability to move courses to market in an expeditious manner.

Next, CMIL has been effective in learning from its educational partners, namely AOL, to improve the design and marketing of its courses. By observing AOL, the organization has been able to bring key aspects of course design in-house and modify templates supplied by AOL for their own purposes. This has given them an advantage in streamlining the course design and production process. The case study of this organization also illustrates how internal positioning and organizational structure influence the organization's ability to innovate. Grant funding from the Sloan Foundation offers an external form of recognition concerning innovation. However, it is unclear as to what this will mean for an organization that is embedded within a university system structure and must answer to various bodies whose interests are not necessarily tied to success in a marketplace that is driven by design and delivery innovations. New course design and delivery approaches may in the short run limit CMIL's ability to reach out to learners in a timely manner, since they must spend more time internally providing evidence for the efficacy of new programs and courses. It is evident also that CMIL is looking for ways to reuse its learning architectures and learning design approaches, while customizing its course content. Their concern with documenting process and success in discovering the consistencies that exist in the course development process may provide evidence for how organizations can realize efficiencies and reduce development costs.

CHAPTER 6

The Colorado Electronic Community College: Innovator, Consortial College and Degree Broker

We are exporting curriculum, and bringing dollars into the state
that we would have never have had before, because of a Colorado
grown product. It has an international trade aspect to it.
- A senior CECC administrator

ORGANIZATIONAL OVERVIEW

THE COLORADO ELECTRONIC COMMUNITY COLLEGE (CECC), ESTABlished in 1995, was the thirteenth college created within the Colorado Community College and Occupational and Education System (CCCOES). It is conceived as a virtual campus within Colorado's community college and occupational education system. CECC offers a distance education, Associate of Arts degree that is awarded through Arapahoe Community College. CECC is also a broker of degrees and certificate programs. Through Colorado Community College Online (CCC Online), a consortium of thirteen of the system's community colleges, students may earn an Internet-based Associate of Applied Science degree in Business that is recognized by all thirteen colleges of the system, with courses completely transferable between the colleges. Degrees are not awarded directly from CECC. The North Central Association of Colleges accredits the degrees and Schools because each one of the CCCOES colleges holds accredited status with that association. Internet-based certificate programs are offered through several of the system's community colleges, with CECC in the role of broker for those programs.

Since its inception, CECC has served over 1800 students. It is an open admission institution. It has extensive course transfer agreements with four-year institutions within the state, as well as several out-of-state baccalaureate institutions. Each student pays the same tuition rate, regardless of in-state or out-of-state status. Although most students are from Colorado, enrollees have also included persons from 48 different states, Canada, the Caribbean, Brazil, Sweden, Asia, Africa and some northern European countries. All instruction is available at a distance, as are the administrative and student support services. For many students the experience is completely at a distance. Students may enroll by phone and take classes via instructional television at home through the Jones Cable System or participate in a Web-based class from home or at work. Instructors are drawn from the system's community colleges and are overwhelmingly full-time faculty members (80% of instructors). The Colorado Research Libraries Association provides library access to students for services, including interlibrary loan and various Internet-based library resources.

CECC is perhaps the most virtual (in an organizational sense) of all of the institutions in this study. The core operation group is comprised of just 3.5 full-time equivalent staff. CECC's funding is achieved primarily on cost recovery basis (approximately two-thirds of revenue) while the remaining one-third is acquired from the general fund. Extensive outsource contracts are used to provide the basic services of the organization. The content is outsourced from the faculty teaching within CCCOES institutions. Maintenance of student records and other administrative services are the responsibility of the individual college within which the student registers. An alliance with Colorado-based Jones Education Company is in place to provide a majority of the initial student service functions and the broadcast course production functions for the Associate of Arts degree. Another Colorado company, Real Education (later renamed e-College), provides the entire course development and delivery infrastructure for the online courses developed at CECC's partner campuses. CECC staff are engaged in managing these key relationships and ensuring that services handled in-house are of high quality, such as: providing students with informational and course materials; student advising; and course content review.

The CECC is embedded within Colorado's largest system of postsecondary education (217,000 students). It is a system devoted to community college-level and occupational education. The CCCOES is governed by a nine member state board (there are two additional non-voting members), which is appointed by Colorado's Governor and confirmed by the state Senate. The President, who has a system staff under her control, reports to the State Board for Community Colleges and Occupational Education. The Presidents of the community colleges within the system report to the system President. CECC is best viewed as a college that was created from the existing system staff, as opposed to persons not previously affiliated with the system. The President of CECC reports to the system President, as would any other campus president.

The purpose of CECC is to be both a symbol and source of innovation for the system. The leadership believes that CECC is a powerful mechanism for collaboration among the System's 12 residential campus institutions. As one senior leader commented:

> It really is set up to build capacity within all of the institutions. As a result of that, it takes a heck of a lot of coordination and outreach and bringing people along, but as a result of structuring it that way, I think we have in fact brought the mindset and helped that paradigm shift occur much more uniformly across the system, than what we would have ever accomplished before.

CECC's central purpose is to offer Associate degree and certificate programs that are intended to be low-cost, high-quality, accredited, flexible, learner-centered and of suitable curricular variety to meet the needs of students and potential employers. CECC's educational products and services are, as some administrators within the organization readily admit, a blend of training, recreation and general education offerings. These offerings appear to be in line with the broad educational mission of the system, which emphasizes vocational, career, technical and general education programs.

ORIGINS AND HISTORY OF COLORADO ELECTRONIC COMMUNITY COLLEGE

The origins and history of CECC reveal a confluence of events and decisions that are at once unique to Colorado postsecondary education and the region, but are also a response to fundamental concerns about access, affordability and convenience for students. The influences that provide the backdrop to the CECC context are not uncommon issues for postsecondary education leaders. The creation and nature of CECC however, which are influenced by this context, are indeed unique.

The history of CECC is chronologically a very short one. Its origins may be traced to the formation of the community college system, which occurred in 1967. In 1986 the legislature consolidated the vocational education and the community college divisions and formed the Colorado Community College and Occupational Education System. The structure is distinctive and has created closer ties between vocational and academic education. One informant characterized CCCOES as a "loose federation of community colleges." One key leadership challenge since the reorganization of the system was to bring all of the community colleges in Colorado into a common system capable of working toward a unified goal of collaboration rather than competition. The successes of the system are evident in its growth. Three new campuses have been added since 1986 and enrolled students have risen over 71% in the period 1986-1996. The system has forged strong alliances with business and industry in Colorado. It has expanded its once regional training and general education programs to national and international audiences. By the late 1980s, there was a sense among some system administrators that alternatives to the traditional college education model were needed for Colorado students, as well as for people from all over the country.

The nature of decision making and goals for the system during this period were also viewed by some members of the management team as critical to the future direction that CECC would take, as the comments of this system-level administrator illustrate:

> My perception is that this was a top-down initiative, and that the . . . then President of the community college system saw an opportunity to jump out ahead, and took this opportunity . . . my sense is that it was a real positive step, one we needed to make, which put us as a system out on the forefront.

Clearly, national leadership was on the minds of many people at the system level who saw CECC as a way to showcase innovation within the system, while at the same time provide an excellent vehicle for collaboration among the System's colleges. It was unlikely that such collaboration would occur naturally, according to one former top administrator. The top-down approach from the System-level seemed to have the best chance of fostering collaboration since the board structure places the System president in a position to guide the decision making process. A coordinating board structure, it is believed by some administrators close to the process, would not have given the president sufficient control over the decision making environment.

As the System matured, the leadership, drawing on advice from business and industry, began to consider truly new models for postsecondary education that involved the use of emerging information technologies. One might find few places in the country better equipped to initiate a conversation on new organizational models. Colorado was and is a fertile place for technology innovation—home to prominent telecommunications firms such as Jones International, TCI and U.S. West. Colorado's community college leaders found CEOs at these firms enthusiastic about working together to re-envision the future of education. The conversations turned into an alliance with Mind Extension University (now Knowledge Television Network) and its founder, Glenn Jones. A former administrator described the alliance with Jones in this way:

> His cable company was reaching 26 million homes all over the world, and while Mind Extension University was going along, in my mind and in even Glenn's was the distinct lack of pizzazz . . . the talking head, a video camera

and a lecture. I think we both saw the potential. We got together and formed a partnership . . . where we would deliver some programs through what was then Mind Extension University. . .through that partnership we were able to raise money and went to the legislature and got some grants.

The alliance with Jones provided the System with immediate capacity to deliver courses in a new way and to new audiences. The alliance also brought the System and its colleges to the attention of others in the state, namely the legislature and the Governor.

In the early 1990s, leaders of CCCOES discovered that there was a possibility that Lowry Air Force Base, a major Department of Defense finance operation and vocational training post located in Denver, would be closed. In a fortunate move for CCCOES, the Department of Defense eventually decided to close Lowry. CCCOES leaders, with prompting from the Governor, worked behind the scenes to have the Air Force base become part of the System. The base—158 acres of land, 1 million square feet of space, replete with furnishing and equipment—was transferred free of charge to CCCOES in 1993. Legislative funding ($12 million) and funding from business and industry ($12 million) followed. With a physical location secured and alliances in place, the next step was to create a new college with a very different organizational concept.

Support for a new college was secure among many key players. Partnerships with business and industry that grew out of the training services the colleges offered helped to demonstrate the need for new ways of delivering educational services. The support from industry also helped to show that CECC as an educational experiment would not have to be underwritten by Colorado taxpayers, which was undoubtedly important to the legislature. By the end of the 1994 legislative session, changes were also taking place within the entire system of postsecondary education in Colorado as the legislature was revising the state's institutions into tiers, which placed the community colleges into an "open admission" tier. As one administrator explained, "we just added a college, and called it the Colorado Community College and Occupational Education System College, which was the birth of the virtual college." The establishment of CECC in 1995 as the System's thirteen college proceeded without conflict, as one administrator explained:

> The approval of Colorado Electronic Community College was done with very little controversy, very quickly, kind of to the surprise of the entire higher education committee. I've got to tell you that if the universities had, if this had been a dragged out affair, I'm sure they would have killed them [CECC]. But this came through very quickly and once that happened, we had a device in the model that was wide open. . . . Here's a new community college . . . and you can do whatever you want with it, so we could hire faculty in new

ways, and that was a key part of it. I think that the key part of it was the Western Governor's University [WGU] coming on and getting all this publicity . . . making people wonder. They actually had to think about, my god, with all this political support, these guys could get a lot of money, they could get our money, they could get our students, and we better react or respond and the response was let us do it, they're [WGU] unnecessary.

The emergence of the highly publicized Western Governors University (WGU) seems to have played a pivotal role in shaping CECC. The vision of Colorado Governor Roy Romer and Utah Governor Michael Leavitt, WGU is intended to be a university in which students are free from the constraints of time and place in taking courses and would have the flexibility to construct degree programs by taking courses at multiple institutions or even from non-traditional education providers. WGU would then certify the body of courses and award degrees or certificates. The hype surrounding WGU created urgency and responsiveness on the part of CECC leaders to move ahead quickly and establish themselves within this politically charged environment.

Another key decision pending in 1995 was how the new institution would award degrees. The leadership decided to have a single institution award an Associate's degree via the Jones Education Company infrastructure. Arapahoe Community College was selected because it was very strong in transfer degrees and had an established record of awarding Associate of Arts and Associate of Science. As one administrator explained, the strategy "was that [Arapahoe's] reputation and history would be a good one for establishing credibility for a distance delivered degree." For a while, according to one administrator, the other colleges in the System seemed to avoid CECC because it was "doing this weird stuff." The turning point came when the revenue model became clearer. With faculty drawn from each community college and the curriculum drawn from courses at individual institutions (coherence is given to the curriculum because it is standardized at the System level), it became evident that every college added would reduce the cost of the entire venture. As a result, tuition costs might very well decrease. As one administrator described, "it's a shopping mall approach. The more colleges you have, you increase the consumer demand for it."

By 1996, it was becoming obvious to leaders within the System and at CECC that one-way transmission of educational content would not be a long-term solution. As had been the case with Jones Education Company and other partners in the Denver area, CECC again used its geographic advantage to move in new directions. A young, Colorado-based company named Real Education approached CECC with new instructional management software and web infrastructure tools designed to convert courses quickly to a Web-based medium – the preferred delivery mechanism because it provided greater interaction among students and between student and instructor. Although its client list was small, CCCOES decided to contract with Real Education because it saw value in the start-up and decided to gamble on what the company was offering. On August 1 of 1997, the System President announced that a full Associate's degree program would be online by January 1 of the following year. The venture turned into what is now Colorado Community College Online (CCC Online)—a partnership of thirteen colleges within the System. A former administrator admitted that competition was a significant factor in what, at the time, must have seemed like an impossible task. The reflections of a former senior administrator attest to the demands of this period:

> Everybody thought that was nuts, I mean, it was impossible, it was a joke, and I went and talked with [name of Real Education representative] and said look, 'I'm going to roll the dice here and give you guys a shot and if you can do this, we're all going to be happy' and they did. We got it up by January 15th. The reason I did it was I knew that the Western Governor's University was scheduled to come out with their whole program and course catalog on January 15th, and I wanted to be there ahead of them. So we just pulled out all stops and turned the whole System loose at it. . .It was a political decision and I wanted us to be Western Governor's University here [in Colorado] and when they came up I wanted us to dominate the course offerings.

With the development of CCC Online, CECC had a strong online presence and perhaps more important, a partner that was able to meet its needs rapidly and in whom it could trust.

The future of the organization remains one of continuous redefinition and reassessment of policies and practices. This is in part intentional since the concept of distance education and virtual organization were conceived of first and foremost and the policies and practices followed. Agility and speed were paramount, as one administrator explained:

> The idea is that if the institution was made to be virtual, that all the policies, practices and philosophy could wrap around that . . . with other colleges, they have their traditional organization and then they have to hang distance education practices off of it. Ours is going to be the opposite. The distance education 'virtualness' came first, so policies have to follow it, and that was the idea behind the organization that by centering that idea, that practices, policies, and philosophy would come much more easily and . . . much faster than at the other community colleges.

Another area that is critical for CECC's future growth will be its relationship with faculty. The organization's approach was to focus first on the

top 20% of faculty who were comfortable with technology—the innova-
tors. Then they would bring along the next 60% who may have doubts, but
would eventually embrace technology-mediated education. As one administrator expressed, "there's going to be 20% of those faculty who will never
ever move or accept even talking about this. . .we made a decision to ignore
that 20%." CECC's desire to innovate will push them toward new partnerships in the coming years. Whatever the conditions, the leadership of
CECC and CCCOES are convinced that the organizational form must continue to evolve and emphasize collaboration among the System's community colleges, particularly if projections for job growth in areas requiring
community college or technical training are accurate.

In the next section, I examine CECC based on the dimensions of the
operational framework discussed in chapter 2.

ANALYSIS OF COLORADO ELECTRONIC COMMUNITY COLLEGE

Extraorganizational Conditions Influencing the Organizational Form and Administrative Patterns of Colorado Electronic Community College

Extraorganizational conditions faced by CECC focused on the variable
groups (uncertainty, dependence, normative and cognitive factors) developed previously in the conceptual framework. Numerous sub-variables
within these categories were evident as influences upon the organizational
form and administrative patterns of the organization. However, incorporation (which includes salient structural features within its environment that
are observable within the organization) and inducement strategies (which
relates to externally generated incentives for change) were not found to be
themes within this analysis.

Uncertainty

Complexity: The organizations with which CECC associates are diverse,
bridging higher education and the for-profit sector. CECC's operating
structure reflects a rich mixture of System's community colleges, content
packagers and infrastructure providers, and educational publishers. Large
publishing houses, for instance, have viewed CECC as a partner to experiment with new multimedia educational products and content delivery services. CECC has also drawn the attention of institutions in other states and
countries that are seeking partnership arrangements in which CECC would
offer the first two years of a baccalaureate degree. The institution's tendency to outsource critical functions is likely to place it into contact with
increasingly more diverse partners, thus creating the probability for higher
levels of complexity in its organizational dealings.

Stability-Variability: Leaders at the System level and within CECC are keenly aware of the environmental changes taking place in the organizational environment. As a result, the management team is focused on understanding and responding to the needs of students and building strong external relationships and an atmosphere of internal collaboration among community colleges in the System. A senior leader expressed the changing nature of the environment in this way:

> I think that's what's happened within our consumer society. . .people are well aware of choices, and they want choices . . . we in higher education have got to adapt and I think it's characteristic of community colleges to be much more flexible and adaptable and responsive . . . when you look at it from an entrepreneurial perspective . . . with all of these shifts that have occurred in every aspect, every dimension of our society, is that geographic boundaries mean nothing . . . we know that the competition is such that it isn't a monopoly any longer. There are a lot of businesses that are in the learning business, and in order for us to be competitive we've got to continue to create new ways to deliver our products and services.

The community college mission is closely tied to the needs of the local community, however geographic boundaries associated with technology-mediated course delivery no longer make such boundaries realistic. Strongly influenced by customer needs, CECC as an organization adjusts to the perceived needs of students by creating new alliances, new educational programs and new delivery methods. Instability within the organization, because of the response strategy, is likely to be a permanent organizational condition.

Threat—Security: The degree to which CECC is vulnerable to the environment is affected by numerous factors that are both broader trends in postsecondary education and also issues that are particular to the college's current manner of operating. A key issue influencing CECC is the threat of substitute products and services from other higher education and non-higher education institutions. As a community college, it has both vocational and general education offerings (which suggests it must be closely tied to the needs of business and industry) in addition to courses for students seeking more academic and professional education. One former administrator described environmental threats in this manner:

> There was a time when public higher education had a monopoly on all of this and we don't any longer. . . . We certainly have no monopoly on content. Content is coming from the General Motors Institute, from all of these businesses, Novell, McDonald's University . . . hundreds of them, not only the content, but the context. All higher education has left now is the ability to certify.

Because CECC is a virtual organization, its degree of security is highly associated with the strength of the alliances and partnerships it is able to maintain between external organizations and the System's community colleges. Also, because the organization has only a small core management team, it is vulnerable if a partner or vendor ceases to offer a function or service it currently outsources. As one administrator acknowledged:

> I think about strategic partnerships. I'm getting chased. What if my out-sourcers go out of business, how do I spread it out so I keep alive with 3.5 people? And then of course, how do I bring in revenue so that I can get better and make the product better and do all those things?

Dependence

Munificence—Scarcity: The availability of financial resources within CECC's environment is declining, even as the sources of expertise and talent that are vital to the organization are expanding. The financial resources that CECC requires from the System are likely to be constrained in light of the expectations that are occurring at the state-level. Funding and expectations about how the funds might be used create an atmosphere within the state that is likely to reduce new spending on higher education. As one senior administrator explained:

> We have a situation with what we call the [Name] taxpayer bill of rights that was kind of Colorado's version of Proposition 13. And that is going to begin to have a more and more profound effect on ratcheting down what is available as far as new resources. At the same time you have a climate that I think is expecting more and more accountability, and is recognized or is asking tough questions about what are you getting for the money that we're investing.

However scarce the financial resources may be in the future for CECC, the organization is operating in an environment in which those functions that it may choose to outsource are gaining in sophistication and potentially in efficiency. For example, its partnership with RealEducation has benefited from the increasing expertise that the company has gained as it has grown its business and taken on more clients. Surely competitors with innovative (and potentially better) products will follow. This may allow CECC to reduce costs, while simultaneously increasing efficiency and effectiveness.

Normative

Authorization of Structural Features: The organizational form and administrative patterns of CECC have been linked closely to policies at the

System level. CECC operates as the System's college and therefore it is not surprising that the internal operations of CECC are influenced by System officials. In fact, as this comment from a former administrator suggests, CECC was used initially as a lever for change within the System, revealing the control System officials had over the college.

> We really worked behind the scenes. . . . Because if a college was reluctant to put a major emphasis on the use of technology and teaching/learning and delivery process, I could simply say okay, fine, then we'll do it with Colorado Electronic Community College. Because of turf, and egos, fear of losing their student enrollments, I think our colleges moved probably in one year, what otherwise would have taken ten years.

Acquisition: CECC and CCC Online are replete with examples of ways in which the leadership has adopted practices and models that are believed to be more modern, appropriate or rational. In the instructional process, for example, the faculty is using innovative technology tools to reach students both synchronously and asynchronously. Indeed, the college's very structure of outsourcing key functions is itself an approach deemed more appropriate for success within the emerging Knowledge Industry. For CECC, as one administrator explained, technology, while critical, is not always the basis of comparison for more modern practices, as this comment implies:

> University of Phoenix . . . that's a model, just not necessarily for virtual education, but just the standardization of your product, the customer orientation that would be one that I looked at and thought now, this is something we want to think about and do.

Standardization and the ability to meet customer needs quickly and effectively are practices that CECC administrators hold in high regard.

Challenges remain, however, particularly in areas in which the organization must think about how to continuously improve services to the student (customer) at a distance. A key challenge is the effective and stable delivery of what one leader described as "electronic student services." The importance of seeing students as customers, which is a practice believed to be essential for CECC's success, is often demonstrated in how quickly questions are answered for students. This was explained by one administrator as the imperative of "getting everybody to understand that a student needs a response within 24 hours." But also the desire to, "keep that down to 4 or 5 hours." One administrator found that after participating in a benchmarking study of student services that customer service models from other industries should be considered to make CECC more effective.

Imprinting: As a very young organization, CECC's founding characteristics are infused throughout the organization. This is seen most forcefully in the intent of creating collaboration among the institutions within the System. Competition among the System's community colleges is present, but CECC is a mechanism for directing the institutions toward common goals that they would not likely pursue unilaterally.

Cognitive

Legitimation: Because of CECC's and the System's close ties with professional and business communities, the degree of legitimacy that the college may receive is in large part determined by their service to students within these sectors. As a senior leader pointed out:

> We never build occupational education curriculum without a board of employers defining for us what the competencies are of our graduates. That's how we build an occupational program. We invite employers in that industry to the table and we have curriculum writers talking with them. . . . What does this graduate do? What is the level? . . . We write down the skills that they need, and that's how we build curriculum, based on what employers want.

While employers are a key constituency and source of legitimation, constraints placed on distance learning organizations by the Federal government create a second entity whose approval must be obtained. Just as those policies tend to be reflected in CECC's operating structure, so too do federal policies create structures for receiving legitimacy. As one administrator remarked sarcastically:

> We've been working very hard with the Department of Ed., and others to get that bill changed [Higher Education Reauthorization Act], but U.S. Legislators don't know how to spell distance education. . .They're all probably living in the 40s and 50s . . . 'this is a bunch of diploma mills who dah, dah, dah, dah, dah, dah.' They've got to have another whole mindset, and they are the ones who the U.S. Congress has to change.

Institutionally Shared Beliefs: The overarching structural constraint found within CECC's external environment that greatly determines the beliefs, rules and roles of the organization are the current Federal financial aid policies, which were affirmed in the 1998 Higher Education Reauthorization Act. The policies state that in order for students attending a postsecondary education institution to receive financial aid, the institution that he or she attends must have no more than 50% of its offerings delivered at a distance. As one System administrator explained:

A developing institution like CECC is unable to become actually its own stand alone college . . . if it wants to provide financial to students, which of course in the community colleges is absolutely critical. . . . The organization that emerged was to a great extent driven by this particular fact. . . . [The Act] specifically prohibits an institution from providing federal financial aid in an institution in which more than half of their offerings are either correspondence or distance, or any combination of the two.

Another constraint tied to the policies of the federal government has to do with proctoring of exams for financial aid students, which does not allow CECC to offer a completely asynchronous degree for the financial students. If a student qualifies for financial aid, he or she has to go to a testing center and be proctored.

Interorganizational Conditions Influencing the Organizational Form and Administrative Patterns of Colorado Electronic Community College

Variables discussed in this section examine CECC's relationship with organizations within the external environment that may shape its organizational form and administrative patterns. In keeping with the conceptual framework, the analysis examined aspects of the competitive and institutional environments reflected in three broad categories—uncertainty, dependence and normative factors. Imposition of organizational form, the coercive influence exercised by external agents in order to legitimately change the organizational form or administrative patterns of the organization, was not observed in this analysis.

Uncertainty

Interconnectedness—Isolation: CECC is highly interconnected to entities both internal (within the System) and external (outside of the System). This is so by virtue of the significance of their relationships to the operation and in terms of the number of relationships it has with these partners as a function of activity within the organization. First, CECC relies heavily on its partners to form the network that is the organization—content, content development, bookstore operations, various student service functions, infrastructure, etc. – all are critical and all are outsourced. Without any one of these functions, the organization would be less effective, if not unattractive to students. Second, the sheer number of the relationships the organization maintains with community college faculty and its vendors in relation to the number of services it provides is quite large. For example, only student advising, informational mail-outs and various coordination tasks (which are voluminous) are conducted in-house. Of these, managing and coordinating relationships is the principal activity for CECC's administrators.

Dependence

Coordination—Non-coordination: CECC does not face a group of external entities whose coordination affects their operation in a significant way. As a member of various lobbying groups such as the American Council on Education, for example, it operates within an external environment in which there is loose coordination among organizations, but this coordination has no discernible outcomes within CECC. However, CECC does operate within an internal System (CCCOES) in which coordination among the community colleges is emerging. Lack of a common grading system among the colleges and an inability to share data about students complicates the coordination that could lead to more effective student services.

Concentration—Dispersion: The resources that are needed to operate CECC and CCC Online are competencies that the organization has found within its environment or within the CCCOES colleges. The organization benefits from the geographic concentration of businesses with which it could form relationships early in its history and from which could be obtained the critical expertise and services it needs to function. Similarly, the arrangement draws on a large group of faculty who may have an interest in developing courses for this new medium, as the comments of one administrator reveal:

> It's a small business plan model. . . . You don't need to own everything. You can just use the services up. I have no faculty. Why should I? I have 800 full-time faculty to choose from and 3,000 part-time faculty in our System. We've got a huge pool, and it's wonderful for faculty because I say do you want to do this, and if they say 'no,' I say okay, well, thank you very much, and then there's somebody else who can, so they're not forced into it or pressured into it, so I have a group of faculty who love doing it. What a better way to do it than that?

As the organization considers partnerships with four-year institutions from outside of the state, it is likely that CECC will be able to draw upon a larger and more dispersed pool of faculty to create new educational offerings.

Interorganizational Power: The control that CECC is able to exercise over the resources that are important to its operation differ in accordance with the type of relationship it has with a specific partner and established customs and procedures for dealing with that partner. For example, as one administrator explained, relationships with faculty who provide the course content are influenced strongly by how the curriculum is constructed. She pointed out:

We have very structured ways to build curriculum, we have a content guide that is formulaic based on Bloom's Taxonomy. . . . We train the faculty in our way of doing things. . . . In fact, when I was telling Real Ed., that we were going to do it this way. . . . I said trust me they'll [faculty] know exactly what I'm talking about because they've been building curriculum this way forever, and all we did was make a standardized way of doing it, almost so that we could shrink wrap curriculum and maintain standards in quality in that regard.

Vendor relationships have proven to be the linchpins of CECC's success. As is often the case in virtual organizations, contractual agreements hold the parties to agreed upon terms. Performance is stipulated in contractual ways and, particularly among distributed partners who do not often meet face-to-face, becomes the essential quality of the business relationship. In CECC's case, its contract with Jones Education Company is surprisingly a handshake agreement, which is re-negotiated on a year-to-year basis. An administrator explained, "really, it has a very strong contract. . .we make them one year at a time. . .there are specific performance contracts, I just haven't had a problem. Their customer service is phenomenal." The means of maintaining the relationship between Jones and CECC is clearly forged on trust and a track record of meeting the performance objectives sought by CECC.

Normative

Imposition of Organizational Form: CECC seemingly receives very little pressure from external agents to change the organizational form and administrative patterns of the organization. In fact, in areas such as accreditation review, CECC has invited accreditation officials to its offices to discuss how CECC might be influential in revising accreditation policies. It appears that CECC is attempting to change the environment as opposed to being changed by it in this circumstance. Subtle changes such as grants to faculty for developing new courses may alter minute aspects of administrative processes, but not in any significant way. Relationships with publishers and business and industry representatives are typically reflected in curricular changes (e.g., publishers promote a new CD-ROM to accompany a course or industry representatives suggest a new course or program). To date, the strong reputation that the college enjoys with the legislature and governor have sheltered it from government directives for change.

Intraorganizational Conditions Influencing the Organizational Form and Administrative Patterns of Colorado Electronic Community College

The organizational form and administrative patterns of CECC are emerging, which is consistent with its youthfulness as an organization. However, despite its relatively short history, distinct themes are evident that reveal much about how the decision making approach, technology choices, organizational purpose and role within the System, and other historical and management related themes shape the organization. These are addressed in this section.

Agent of Change: One of the pivotal roles that CECC plays within Colorado's Community College and Occupational Education System is that of a change agent and vehicle for experimentation. Leaders within the System have noted its impact on the other community colleges. One senior leader explained the influence of the virtual college in this way: "The effect that its presence had was phenomenal because in that one year [CECC's first year], the rest of our colleges increased their use of technology for instruction both in the classroom and at a distance, 350 percent in one year." The tendency toward experimentation and innovation in CECC's educational services and products is likely to continue. One administrator explained her uneasiness about becoming too comfortable with what the organization has achieved. She noted: "Every year we're doing something that takes me on the road. . .it's not the fact of a delivery of a degree online, which is so amazing, you know? Now that's old stuff." The irony here is that for many, the "old stuff" is indeed the new stuff.

Redefinition of the Educational Product/Service for Broader Markets: Several leaders within CECC opined that long held distinctions between educational services and products and training (occupational) services and products were becoming more difficult to differentiate. This breakdown in distinctions between education and training signals that CECC's leaders perceive that students want and need skills that will serve them well in a particular job and more generally in life. The opinion is based in part on a belief that the products and services offered by CECC should lead to enhanced economic return for students and taxpayers within the State of Colorado.

Leaders within the System also admit that the nature of distance delivery gives the System other ways to demonstrate their value to the state and presumably to lobby the legislature for increased funding. Leaders explained that the technology-mediated products and services they offer may be viewed as export products since technology gives them the ability to cross state and country boundaries. No longer are regional notions of markets applicable to CECC's conception of the audience that they serve. This has led to a tacit expansion in mission – no longer is "community" college a local endeavor, but rather a national or international knowledge enterprise that attempts to benefit the local community and the state by generating revenue brought in from outside of the state.

Outsourcing Evaluation-Re-evaluation: The partnerships that CECC maintains with its vendors and faculty members are subject to informal, but continuous re-evaluation. As one administrator explained, "if you want to get an organization to outsource, you make them real poor" and according to this administrator such is the case with CECC. The organization's inability to undertake critical functions internally due to a lack of financial resources places it in the position of constantly evaluating and assessing its relationships with its partners and considering potential new partners whose services might be more cost-effective and provide greater value to students.

Presence of an Organizational Champion: Another key theme that is critical to understanding the managerial influences on the organization is found in the persistence and decision making strategy of the former System president. It is clear from discussions regarding the organization's inception that the former president of the System used CECC as a lever for the System's colleges to adapt to technological opportunities. One administrator described the former System president's role in creating CECC in this way:

> We had a President who was very keen on being able to leapfrog in innovation. . .and he was very good at being able to not just see the next step, but see the steps beyond the next step, and would take that next step leap, and he saw that the technology in education was coming and was going to make major shifts and changes in the way we do things. . . . The rationale of course was that we had to . . . prepare colleges for the 21st century, that there was going to be what I call an orbital shift—not just a paradigm shift.

Concerning the creation of CECC, most informants with whom I spoke seemed to believe that the decision was one made from the top down. The System president championed the creation of the organization and demonstrated that he understood well the control he possessed in working with presidents at individual colleges within the System.

Perceived Intraorganizational Competition: One of the main challenges that CECC faces is managing how the other colleges within the System perceive it. As an agent of change, it is particularly vulnerable to charges of generating competition by introducing new programs and delivery methods. As one administrator explained:

> The colleges still aren't sure that CECC is so consortial because it was set up to be a separate competitive institution with the rest of the schools by the previous director, for interesting management reasons, but we have moved to a consortial thing. . . . We haven't proved ourselves yet, so we're very keen on

having the colleges use this and see it as a resource and putting it under CECC.

CECC leaders are keenly aware that they must demonstrate the financial attractiveness of revenue sharing within the consortium. They must also prove that a college's participation is likely to provide access to innovative technologies that an individual college acting unilaterally would not be able to afford.

The Nature of the Organization

The organizational form and administrative patterns of CECC are examined in the following sections, corresponding to the outline presented within in the conceptual framework.

The Organizational Form of Colorado Electronic Community College

Strategy

Intraorganizational Strategy: CECC's strategy for shielding itself from detrimental events is one based on speed. The approach is to keep a step ahead of the competition, which one administrator described as for-profit educational organizations such as the University of Phoenix or any organization that can prove the value of its educational offerings in areas for which CECC and CCC Online are known. CECC also constantly reassesses its relationships with vendors to ensure that their operation is as efficient and cost-effective as possible. The thoughts of one administrator illustrate how this strategic approach plays out in everyday affairs:

> I have a general day-in and day-out feeling that they're nipping at my heels, and I'm about to be put out of business—that I can't compete with the big guys who are coming to town. . . . The only way I can compete is to do it faster, sooner. I don't think I can do it better, I can only do it faster, sooner, because once they get their ducks in a row, they're going to be able to do it better, and more capitalized. . . . I think strategically by thinking what have I got to do, and I've got to do it tomorrow. It's got to be there for good or bad. I go to market 65 percent ready, so that by the time they catch up. . . . I'm in a second stage development.

At the System-level, activities and policies that are intended to shield the System campuses from harmful events are aided by the design of the governance structure. A member of the System management team explained: "All the Presidents [of the System campuses] report directly to [CCCOES President]. They don't report to the board." This governance structure provides the System leadership with the ability to respond more quickly to environmental events of strategic importance than would be the case if the presidents reported to the board.

Interorganizational Strategy: CECC's approach to shaping its external environment is linked to the partnerships it is creating with vendors and others that will allow it to offer new educational services. One striking example, which was in negotiation during my site visit, was a plan to create a partnership with a Missouri university in which students from that institution could enroll in CECC or CCC Online courses for the first two years of their business degree, then complete the final two years of the degree, online, under the auspices of the Missouri institution. In theory, faculty members from a particular institution may affiliate themselves with the other institution. This strategy of forging new partnerships to change the nature of the environment is, according to one leader, taking the institution into areas with plenty of unanswered questions:

> The enormity of the thing . . . we just make up rules as we go along. I mean, not make up the rules, we're just making it up as we go along on what it is that we want to do, for example. . . . The NCA [accrediting association] question is faculty have to belong to the college that is the accredited college, and so these are community college faculty, how do they belong to the Missouri college?

CECC's strategy for changing the nature of its external environment is also shaped from the System-level. Leaders there, bolstered by the thinking of contemporary business scholars and strategists, consider market leadership and CECC's role in this leadership as essential for future success. This comment from one senior leader captures the strategic application of market control and leadership:

> There are the drivers and they're the ones that get there first and they really have control of the market because they are creating the new advantages and they will be very richly rewarded for that leadership role. There are the passengers, they will survive, but they are not in control. . . . Then there's the roadkill that will not survive because they can't respond rapidly enough and adapt . . . it really goes back to . . . that understanding that the real capacity that a learning organization has is the ability to add new advantages, all the time, to the people and the products that they're serving . . . how are we going to anticipate what your needs are even before you know that you have them?

Resource Strategy: CECC's resource strategy is a mixture of self-funding (two-thirds) and central System support (one-third). However, it is CECC's ability to enhance the resources of other System colleges that is one of its inherent strengths. As one administrator explained that the "cost savings for curriculum construction of one course divided by 12 colleges and one set of faculty divided by 12 colleges—the cost efficiency is amazing." The course development model employed by CECC and CCC Online are based on shared costs, that is, the twelve residential colleges divide all course development charges, faculty instruction costs, etc. Conversely, any revenue that the courses earn (less CECC's small administrative overhead) is divided equally among the colleges. Another administrator explained the arrangement in this way:

> If you have no students in the class, you still end up paying. You still end up paying 1/12th of the cost of the faculty person, and that has been a bit of a problem for some schools because . . . they might not have a student and they're kind of resentful, and yet on the other side, they could have students in another class that nobody else has students. . . . Maybe Lamar doesn't have students in accounting, but they have them in math, so they end up paying 1/12th of the accounting teacher, but they're also only paying 1/12 of the math teacher even though they might have six or seven students in the math class.

Structure

Centralization: There is an understanding among several leaders that, at times, a top-down approach to management is critical for creating an organization—both at the System-level and at CECC—that is responsive to the environment. However, these same leaders agree that collaboration is clearly the goal in terms of decision making with the CCCOES organization. As one senior administrator explained:

> What you really need is a sort of top-down, you need to make it happen now, sort of approach to decision making if you're going to move very quickly. That's absolutely the idea, there are times that you know, you have to be much more autocratic, but ideally you'll be much more collaborative. . . . I think it has to come from the consistency of message with an articulated vision of what it is that we're trying to do and you have to get that out there over and over again, so that people can begin to embody that in their thinking, meanwhile, there has to be a concurrent effort focused on helping them understand the larger context.

Several administrators explained that the press to compete more effectively in this highly charged environment often truncated debate or shortened the decision making process, thus creating fewer opportunities for input. Most, however, understood that participation in decision-making by lower level staff was important despite an atmosphere that tends to obviate such participation.

Formalization: CECC is not a highly formalized organization. As a new entity, its procedures and processes are emerging, seemingly as issues arise with the faculty or its vendors. New programs and expansion projects, such as the partnership with a Missouri institution, tend to reduce the explicit connections that members of the staff make about the means and ends of their work.

Complexity: CECC is the core of a network of differentiated units that are geographically distributed. The inclination of CECC's leaders to outsource functions and activities as a principal mechanism for structuring the organization creates complexity by differentiating the organization's partners. A good example is a new multi-media project that is a partnership between CECC, Bellevue Community College's Northwest Center for Emerging Technologies and a very large publisher who is going to pay the faculty time for course development. Most partnerships with external entities and System partners are stable, as in the case of CECC's relationships with Jones Education Company or the System faculty. However, some, like the partnership with the large publisher are more temporary.

Configuration: With just 3.5 full-time equivalent staff members, CECC is a rather archetypal virtual organization. Its extensive network of partners allows it to reconceive the functions and activities of the organization by establishing or ending alliances. It is somewhat constrained by its affiliation with the CCCOES faculty however, as its recent negotiations with institutions beyond the State of Colorado suggest, it is considering ways of incorporating new faculty within its operation. Publishers and technology companies, in alliance with other CECC partners, seek to provide educational services that are seamlessly integrated for the student, that is, the "college" is configured to be functionally transparent in the manner in which students interact with it.

Process

Design and Management of Technology and Tasks: One of the pivotal issues that emerged concerning how materials, operations and knowledge are combined within CECC is the degree to which the leadership is attempting to integrate the organization's processes. Supervision of the processes that create the learning experience are largely out of the direct control of CECC administrators. Contractual obligations bind CECC's partners to achieve specified levels of performance. Therefore, the design and management of technology and tasks lies with supervisors of the functional areas or sub-processes, which are primarily beyond the immediate control of CECC managers.

This drive to respond very rapidly to the needs of external constituents is also essential for understanding how work in this organization is designed and supervised. One administrator described the expectations of industry, a key constituent, as "ask today, get it tomorrow sort of thinking." This approach urges CECC staff to constantly seek alternatives to their current outsourcing arrangements and understand emerging developments in information technology and instructional management systems. The desire to be innovative and efficient was viewed by one campus administrator as having a paradoxical influence on the organization. He explained:

> One of those little ironies that I have seen that's embedded deeply within the use of technology . . . in our case, the teaching and learning is distributed . . . the instructor can be anywhere, the student could be anywhere . . . but the irony here is that while the application is distributed, a lot of the administrative functions . . . have to inherently be centralized . . . so that's the catch.

Political Process: The organizational environment of CECC is changing very quickly, which is forcing members of the organization to think creatively and respond intelligently to these changes. Conflict and the process for its resolution can become muddled as solutions to new and pressing issues continually come to the fore. As one staff member explained: "I think part of the problem is that this place is changing so fast, and moving so fast, that things don't get resolved. . .We don't have time to deal with that, let's move on, and that's frustrating." One approach that has been expressed in terms of dealing with conflict within the organization has been to place management responsibility in the hands of the organization's managers and staff person. The approach, according to one administrator, is to delegate responsibility in an effort to solve problems without having to raise them with the entire staff:

> The President has, I think, selected people who are fairly experienced, so she has put a lot of trust in all of us to handle a lot of things on our own and after the fact. She's busy enough that when conflict has arisen, a solution was found or not found, and then reported later . . . the more time and money that particular conflict requires, the more we have to take it up to her—to a staff meeting in a public way.

The Administrative Patterns of Colorado Electronic Community College

Normative Structure

Values: While CECC's originators may have seen the organization as an agent of change, it is clear that collaboration among the System's colleges is today highly valued by administrators at the System and the organization level. The values expressed by members of CECC are focused in large measure on creating more effective and convenient learning experiences for students and engaging the community colleges in the processes of accomplishing this. For several administrators, the System of postsecondary education is moving from one of sponsorship and restrictions, described as a system for "people who have patrons, either the government or their parents, or some other sources," to one that must encourage continuous renewal and access. Toward that end, the leadership team encouraged an educational environment in which students have convenience in their interactions with college personnel and likewise, college personnel have the ability to handle a wider variety of organizational activities.

Norms: Rules governing behavior within this organization are not formally established. As one staff member explained:

> It's an atmosphere where I guess it's so innovative that if someone wants something and wants it now, you're expected to provide it. You're expected to find the solutions to be able to do it. . . . We don't have time to establish policies. We don't have time to say well, how should we do it? I mean, you just do it.

The comments of this staff member would tend to reinforce the belief that responding in a timely manner to requests is the overriding rule governing the behavior and expectations placed on staff of CECC. This was supported by another administrator who noted: "because we're so dynamic, we do shift gears, you know, in and out of the priorities, change faster than I've ever seen anywhere else." It appears that rules for behavior within the organization would be subject to the dynamism and shifts in the organization's priorities.

Role Expectations: Standards employed for assessing the behavior of employees within the social system of the organization are complicated by the seeming lack of formal rules that govern behavior. However, state requirements to have an employee evaluation do tend to place some expectations upon the management team for assessing employee performance, but perhaps not behavior. The comments of one administrator seemed to express the difficulty of goal setting and by correlation, assessment of employee behavior in meeting those goals:

> [The president] and I are working on my specific goals for this year. . .she asks us to write our own goals, and I think she's a little concerned . . . we're changing every day. I think she'd be a little concerned about setting out specific goals for me that said you have to you know, create X FTE in X amount

of time . . . she knows I don't have a lot of control over that anyway, because it's coming back from the schools.

Behavioral Structure

Activities: The actions that CECC staff members undertake in the course of their work, because of the nature of the organizational structure, involves a good deal of coordination. The staff is involved in nearly all aspects of developing and operating the degree programs and courses, although not directly, as the outsourcing arrangements provide the functional expertise of the institution. Members of the organization manage relationships with vendors that handle most aspects of student services, course material conversion, textbook and bookstore operations and infrastructure and course management applications. Staff members work with vendors and representatives on individual campuses to ensure students are registered properly and grades are submitted accurately. CECC staff work with faculty to modify curriculum and also to ensure that payments are made to faculty for developing and teaching courses.

Interactions: Because of the distributed nature of the organization, interactions among the staff and among CECC's many partners are often technology-mediated. Email, phone and fax provide linkages between partners. The nature of the interactions can, at times, be contentious. One administrator expressed frustration at the perception that some individuals at the campuses had about the motives of CECC. One administrator remarked sarcastically:

> You really do have to put your ego to the side, and thank goodness there's e-mail because you get an opportunity to think about your responses before you respond. Because some of this stuff . . . I spend all day on e-mail, and . . . some of the things you can just tell by the tone, it's like you did this to me, you know? Like I lay in bed at night and think of ways just to make people upset.

Sentiment: For many members of the organization, the larger context of the community college mission, a mission they had carried out for years, is a key element regarding satisfaction in their jobs. As one administrator explained, "I'm in education because I believe . . . I still believe in the power of shaping citizenry." For others, the excitement of experimentation and shift toward the student as the center of the educational enterprise was most important. As one campus administrator explained, "for the first time, a learner has options, and you don't have to go to get the real full experience, you don't have to go live some place on a campus and be a full-time student." For many members of the organization, this approach provides a great deal of satisfaction in their work. However, the challenge of managing an organization, which has very little historical precedent, can be burdensome, particularly when the eyes of other System administrators are on you. One member of the management team admitted:

> I don't know if I'm sure about what I'm doing, and that's a very unsettling feeling. The other one is the slings and arrows, when you're doing stuff like this, although I get lots of good support and that's what will keep me going.

Clearly, managing innovative (and potentially threatening) organizations can place one in a disconcerting position.

CONCLUSION

The Colorado Electronic Community College is an example of a publicly sponsored, System wide virtual organization that offers associate's degrees and general education courses via cable, the Internet and multi-media delivery. CECC was established in 1995 to act as a lever for change among the CCCOES campuses. CECC has an organizational structure that relies on a series of external and System wide alliances to provide the functional differentiation it needs to operate. A small staff of functional specialist/managers is responsible for coordination and management of alliances. As an innovative organization, it can be viewed critically as a source of competition by other community colleges within the System. CECC is keenly aware of its competition externally and has consistently, in its short history, sought to add new features to its educational services in order to compete more effectively. The organization sees itself as an exporter of knowledge that must constantly innovate or become a marketplace anachronism.

Educational leaders may find CECC's organizational model and series of alliances a marked contrast to the structure and organizational philosophy often encountered in many higher education institutions. The organizational design approach suggests that an alliance strategy is particularly important for this type of organization. CECC's decision to minimize head count presents some points for consideration. Because the organization received limited funding, by its own admission, it had to find innovative ways to achieve its mission. By retaining functional area specialists/managers, and outsourcing much of the day-to-day work, CECC is able to scale the organization as needed to meet learner and faculty needs without having to hire new staff. By doing so, it focuses upon the areas of the organization for which it has the greatest competency while outsourcing unstable areas like delivery, which are dependent on emerging technologies. This structure gives the organization the flexibility to reconfigure the players based on changing environmental conditions. Next, CECC shapes its alliances in two major ways. The first type, a long-standing relationship with Jones Education Company, for instance, is strategic in nature and offers unique forms of knowledge for the organization. However, the organizational structure also permits a second, less strategic, supplier-oriented approach that might be categorized as a vendor relationship. In this case, the organization has the ability to switch to vendors that provide price advantages, for example, since the relationship is neither critical to their overall success nor the services provided difficult to find. In either the strategic partner or vendor situations, CECC is positioned to manage the relationship to its benefit. A final point that must be raised about these organizations is a concern over how institutional knowledge and memory are grown and maintained within an organization of this type. Advantages accrue to organizations that can learn from their experiences and execute what they learn in a timely manner. In a stable network organization like CECC, much of the organization's knowledge resides within an external organization—its strategic partners and vendors. Leaders that are considering this type of organizational structure should be certain to define which functions within their organization might benefit from an outsourcing alliance and which might not. By viewing CECC from a knowledge ownership perspective, leaders may evaluate the relative advantages and disadvantages of this design approach for their organization.

CHAPTER 7

The Pennsylvania State University World Campus: Extending the Research University and Solving an Entrepreneurial Problem

The train has already left the station and some people still want to debate the color of the caboose.

-An Administrator

ORGANIZATIONAL OVERVIEW

IN THE FALL OF 1996, DURING HIS STATE OF THE UNIVERSITY ADDRESS, the President of Penn State announced that the University was considering a new venture that would address the educational needs of adult learners in the Information Age. Through the use of innovative educational technologies, Penn State intended to extend its finest undergraduate and graduate programs to adults around the United States and abroad. The initiative ultimately became Penn State World Campus, which was inaugurated in the fall of 1998 with the enrollment of students in its first, signature certificate program—Turfgrass Management. Penn State's commitment to educational outreach began in 1892 when it became a pioneer in distance education founding one of the nation's first correspondence study programs. The concept of outreach has evolved in sophistication, but remained true to the land-grant principle of extending the University's resources upon which Penn State was founded. World Campus is intended to place Penn State in the vanguard of land-grant universities in the 21st Century. Convenience and customization for each student are central notions of World Campus. In a report for discussion by the Penn State community (Ryan, 1997), World Campus was envisioned as an organization that could provide the educational resources that were lacking in many communities where learners live and work. In particular, the report empha-

139

sized the need for extending the University's resources in order to enhance the personal, cultural and economic success of students.

Penn State University in the context of its larger organizational structure was described by one informant as the "un-system" in that the University's President is responsible for the entire university—all 24 campuses—with World Campus being the 25th, but is not organized under a statewide board. Each campus has a Dean that reports to the Provost and a Provost that reports to the President. Penn State is perhaps best viewed as a single university that is geographically distributed. The University has one academic structure, one faculty, one faculty senate, one curriculum and one set of degree programs. The reporting structure of this "virtual campus" is not truly a separate campus entity in comparison to the residential campuses within the University. Nor is the campus virtual in an organizational sense because the outsourcing relationships one typically sees in a virtual organization are not present in World Campus. It is an internal network organization, as opposed to a stable or dynamic network form. Rather than a campus with its own provost, Penn State World Campus is a unit within Penn State University, which reports to the Vice President for Outreach and Cooperative Extension. An Associate Vice President— Executive Director heads the unit. World Campus is operationally a matrix organization as various committees and teams provide the functional expertise for the organization. Cross-functional teams comprised of staff from World Campus and non-World Campus units develop and administer the distance learning courses and services that the organization creates. Internal committees, such as the World Campus Strategic Management Group (directors of the major functional areas), provide the major policy and management direction for World Campus projects. An external advisory group made up of business and educational leaders contributes a community perspective for the direction of the program. The World Campus Steering committee provides University-wide perspectives on policies and programs by advising on areas of development for the World Campus and ensuring that the educational experiences are of high quality.

The organization was the recipient of a $1.3 million Sloan Foundation Asynchronous Learning Networks grant, which has provided much of the start-up capital to create its initial programs. It also has a long-standing relationship with AT&T, which has strengthened the organization's experience in structuring relationships with corporate clients and generating business for this client segment. The goal is that ultimately the World Campus is intended to be a self-sustaining unit. It has considered several revenue sharing models for generating faculty interest in its programs, attempting to blend both market influences with the desires of faculty to participate in World Campus programs.

ORIGINS AND HISTORY OF PENN STATE WORLD CAMPUS

The development of Penn State World Campus appears to be a logical extension of a century-long commitment to educational outreach and the University's land-grant mission, which dates back to the early 1890s. It is not surprising then that an institution that has cultivated close ties to constituents such as farmers and corporate employees, would take advantage of innovations in instructional technology to reach an ever widening array of learners. Drawing on its experiences in offering programs to adult learners through independent and correspondence study, workplace outreach, and institutes and conferences, the World Campus was constituted in part based on lessons from these educational endeavors as well as an adroit reading of the political climate. The political climate is one that continues to evolve and may determine the success or failure of this venture. As one senior administrator explained, historical precedents were catalysts: "One was the fact that we started doing distance education in 1892. If we did not have that history to build on, we probably wouldn't be talking about a World Campus today. We'd be talking about it, but we wouldn't be doing it."

As several informants explained, understanding the growth of Penn State as a university is critical to understanding the historical context from which the World Campus has taken shape. Penn State University initially existed only at University Park in State College, Pennsylvania. But, by the 1930s and through the 1960s, Penn State was extended to a variety of locations throughout Pennsylvania by creating extension continuing education centers or schools of forestry. Over time, several extension centers developed into campuses that provided a wide array of offerings beyond merely extension courses, such as associate's degrees, the first two years of a baccalaureate degree, or graduate offerings. The growth of these campuses coincided with the development of community colleges in the 1960s and 1970s. The campus structure, as one administrator noted, "was very much Pennsylvania's response to the development of community college systems," although it is important to point out that Pennsylvania does not operate under a community college system, then or now. As a land-grant institution, Penn State has "always been extending education, either via a physical location, through continuing education, or through cooperative extension, we've been in that business for 80 years with local cooperative extension offices in every county."

By the 1960s and continuing through the 1980s, the extension operation became more technologically sophisticated. It became a public broadcasting affiliate, developed a satellite network for all of its campuses and cooperative extension centers, and created high-speed connections to a number of campuses as well. It developed a capability to produce video and audio content. The first satellite downlink site was established in 1978. And by 1987, all 17 of Penn State's campuses possessed downlink capabilities, with satellite uplink capacity at the University Park campus. In 1988, the American Center for the Study of Distance Education was created, which made Penn State a focal point for the study of distance education and research dissemination through *The American Journal of Distance Education*. At the same time, the independent study division was producing a series of new instructional modules that became the foundation of the independent learning program.

1990 brought new leadership of the Outreach and Cooperative Extension unit. The leadership of the new Vice President would prove critical in redefining the nature of outreach at Penn State. One administrator recalled the consolidation process that followed over the next few years:

> He [the Vice President for Outreach and Cooperative Extension] only had the continuing education responsibility . . . when he came on board, we merged the distance education units that included Public Broadcasting and Independent Learning into continuing education and then later on we included Cooperative Extension, in 1996, and that accomplished [sic] all the outreach arms of Penn State.

Along with the organizational changes, University leaders were sensing changes in the climate of postsecondary education. In 1992, a task force was created to examine the role of distance education and its potential influences on the University. Distance education's migration from the periphery to the mainstream is evident in the words of one senior leader, who explained:

> The task force of the University made a report to the President that recommended that distance education be moved more into the mainstream of Penn State's academic life. That was a significant change in the tenor of distance education of Penn State, and it really paved the way for us to be doing the World Campus, because out of that report came a whole series of events.

The report spurred several key outcomes. First, a distance education advisory board was created. The formation of the board pointed to the necessity of incorporating multiple perspectives in what would become a university-wide distance education effort. The second event marking the seriousness of Penn State's involvement in distance education was the creation of a department of distance education under the auspices of the Vice President for Outreach and Cooperative Extension. The office, though seemingly on the periphery of the institution because of its association with the outreach and extension operation, was perhaps the most logical choice for its placement due to its expertise in repackaging educational programs that was developing in related areas of the organization (e.g., independent study). Third, a partnership was forged with AT&T to develop projects that would change the academic culture of the institution in order to "make it more welcoming," as one senior administrator described it. The confluence of these events prepared the campus for expansion of distance learning efforts that were to follow in the next two to three years. One senior administrator explained in speaking of this period: "It gave the university a sense of confidence that we could talk about this." The institution's recognition that distance education was both a larger external force influenced by the expectations of potential learners and an internal force by which the land-grant mission might expand became evident in the policy decisions that were to follow.

If 1992 was a milestone for legitimizing discussion about expanding distance education at Penn State, then 1994-95 became the years that preparations for distance education on a university wide basis began to take shape. In 1994-95, The Innovations in Distance Education project was initiated to aid faculty at Penn State and two historically black colleges in Pennsylvania to create a supportive environment for the cultivation of distance education. Supported by a $500,000 grant from the AT&T Foundation, the project remains a catalyst for developing guiding principles and practices for distance education, fostering new approaches to teaching and learning and supporting faculty in effective applications of distance education tools. Several administrators noted the groundwork set by the Innovations in Distance Education project was critical for examining policy issues and readying the faculty for the World Campus initiative.

The momentum driving the creation of a unique, technology-enabled campus was finally recognized as an opportunity for change when, in 1996, the new president of Penn State took an active interest in reshaping and extending the campus by building upon the University's technological strengths. As one senior administrator recalled, the circumstances surrounding the exploration of a World Campus appeared to be tied to a broader set of initiatives that the president and his leadership team were considering:

> In 1996, the summer of 1996, [the Penn State President] called a few people in his office to talk about the World Campus. He had received an e-mail from one of our campus executive officers saying we've got a lot of things going on at Penn State, a lot of changes we're making. While we're making these changes, why not talk about an online campus of the university?

It is unclear whether the new president sensed the advantages of moving quickly early in his tenure to launch what some may have considered a politically risky venture. As one administrator explained:

I think it was a timing issue. We had talked about . . . [an] online campus as early as 1994, and there was a sense the university wasn't ready for it. By 1996 things had changed. We had a new president, a new vision. . . . He was ready for information technology. Didn't phase him. Western Governor's University had begun to be talked about and there was a sense that hey, there was movement here in this field and acceptance at the political level, so I think with all those things going on, and a young President who had visions for Penn State as a land grant university . . . so [the President] called some people into his office, in July of 1996, and said let's start talking about this, and we wrote a concept paper, and on the strength of that concept paper, in September of '96, in his State of the University address, he noted that one of the activities for the upcoming year would be to explore the feasibility of the World Campus.

In November of 1996, the President formed a University wide team to examine the feasibility of such a venture. The study team presented the report in March 1996, recommending that the University move ahead with the World Campus and offered recommendations for the organization's mission and goals. The representation of the planning committee and independent interviews seem to confirm that once planning was underway, the committee sought input from a variety of constituencies from across the campus. The World Campus concept did receive approval from the Penn State Faculty Senate and Graduate Council, which was a significant milestone in the estimation of some, since these campus groups would be intimately involved in making the program viable (particularly the faculty). In May of 1997 the World Campus leadership team submitted a proposal to the Sloan Foundation requesting funds to capitalize the World Campus. By July, staffing and development were underway. Development involved working with the deans and department chairs to understand which programs might be most appropriate for the World Campus. Marketing studies followed the discussions with the deans. Through a winnowing process by which the deans' views and marketing research outcomes were examined, 15-20 courses were selected to form the basis of five programs. These initial "signature" programs were underwritten by the Sloan Foundation grant.

With the selection of courses, the preparation of technology-mediated curriculum began in earnest. By November 1997, the World Campus Web site was operational, displaying for the first time the mission, focus and curricular offerings that Penn State intended to make available to its worldwide audience. As the authors of the World Campus Annual Update (1998) noted, once the World Campus staff began to interact with the rest of the University community, several challenges arose. Creating new or diverting internal funds for World Campus course development raised the potential for conflicts over funding with academic units who might be considering similar initiatives. Variations in faculty release time policies made negotiation with schools and colleges more time consuming. Policy disconnects and questions that had not been addressed prior to the launch of World Campus became apparent in several ways. New questions were raised regarding academic approval policies, the role that World Campus should play as a central unit responsible for technology-based courses, integration of registration and student services functions, pricing and revenue sharing and credit assignment and unit rewards for participation.

Despite the excitement that was voiced my many of the persons that I interviewed, some members of the Penn State community were suspicious of World Campus because they viewed it as top-down process initiated by the Penn State President and top administrators with insufficient input from faculty. It was what one informant labeled "very hierarchical." According to this informant, the initiative was touted as a new service for students, but motivations were more likely to build the reputation of the University and improve its financial strength. While the dual notions of motive are hardly incompatible, the process of introducing World Campus did seem to be directed from above.

The future of World Campus and the degree to which it sees itself as a leader in the field of distance education and outreach is captured in the following statement, which portends extensive growth and permeation of World Campus approaches within the academic community of Penn State.

> The difference between Penn State's World Campus and the distance education initiatives of other universities lies in scope, organization, and institutional commitment. No single US institution or organization is currently delivering as broad and varied a spectrum of educational activities as Penn State is preparing to offer—20 to 30 academic programs (degree, certificate, and noncredit professional education) encompassing more than 300 courses by the year 2002. Most programs, developed and taught on-load by senior faculty, ensure that its impact is felt throughout the academic environment. The World Campus envisions providing a comprehensive, University-wide administrative matrix for scanning the national and global environment and developing programs where constituents' needs and Penn State's academic strengths converge.

In the next section, I examine Penn State World Campus based on the dimensions of the operational framework discussed in chapter 2.

ANALYSIS OF THE PENN STATE UNIVERSITY WORLD CAMPUS

Extraorganizational Conditions Influencing the Organizational Form and Administrative Patterns of the Penn State University World Campus

The variables discussed in this section examine a broad set of environmental influences on the organizational form and administrative patterns of the World Campus. The analysis focused on the competitive and institutional environments reflected in four areas—uncertainty, dependence, normative and cognitive factors. Imprinting (the degree to which the World Campus has acquired characteristics at its founding that are retained in its current organizational form) and incorporation (the extent to which the organization comes to reflect salient features of its environment over time) were not observed in this analysis. I believe this is due principally to the relatively brief history of this organization, as compared with other organizations in this study.

Uncertainty

Complexity: The degree of similarity in the organizations with which World Campus relates may be differentiated by the set of external and internal relationships it maintains. Its external relationships have taken two forms: those that affect the overall organization; and those that are program specific. One senior administrator explained the distinctions:

> We call them general partners. It's partners who are interested in the enterprise generally. The Sloan Foundation, obviously, is very much interested in that. We have had a long-term relationship with AT&T and they're interested in the success of the World Campus because it obviously has business implications for AT&T, but also there's opportunities for research and development and other kinds of things. . . . We also have partnerships on the program level. Each of the programs that we've initiated so far involves a partnership affiliation with a major professional association, a company, or an industry group that has a vested interest in their clientele having access to this program from Penn State, so turf grass management, there's a partnership agreement with the Golf Course Superintendents of America. Chemical dependency counseling, there's an arrangement with the National Association for Drug and Alcohol Counselors.

The need to capitalize the World Campus and develop a strong client base have been major factors influencing the type and nature of external relationships that the organization has pursued. Its focus on philanthropic partnerships, corporate alliances and industry associations are likely to continue at both the general and program level. In the short run, this tendency in relationship building may limit associations with organizations that are not suitable clients.

The degree of complexity that the organization faces is moderated by the manner in which it has structured its organizational processes. Because it does not rely on vendors to supply critical functions in the course development and delivery processes, it is less inclined to have relationships with dissimilar organizations (aside from those mentioned previously). However, sources of internal complexity are evident in the cross-functional teams used to develop World Campus programs. The intricacy of the product suggests that the development team consist of members with varied talents and skills.

Stability—Variability: The World Campus leadership perceive themselves to be operating within an environment in which differentiating their organization and educational products is difficult. Organizations with distinct missions, organizational structures and clientele—such as Western Governors University, California Virtual University, or inner campus initiatives like Penn State world Campus—can be viewed as similar in the public perception. One senior leader expressed the lack of clarity:

> The fact that these are all undifferentiated right now in the public's eye, makes it very difficult for us to, to really describe what we're doing, and to really differentiate ourselves from the pack, and the success or failure, some of those initiatives will be, will be based on factors that really aren't issues for us, and so there, one issue that we deal with in this external environment is this lack of differentiation about this term, virtual university.

Another area in which the organization's leaders perceived change to be taking place was over the nature of competition and collaboration between and among higher education institutions. Competition for students has long been an issue for higher education institutions. However, the ability to deliver educational services to the doorstep of students, as one administrator noted, has intensified greatly the competition that World Campus faces. He explained that a technology-mediated Master's of Business Administration degree, for example, may be delivered to a student from "the British Open University, the Australian institutions, Canadian institutions, a four year religious school, a land grant university, a for-profit institution, a private institution, and they're all saying we'll teach you at home." Collaboration raises similar stability issues. In this new environment, leaders have questioned "to what extent do we want to offer joint degrees, articulated degrees? To what extent do we want to jointly develop courses that each institution then offers itself, or simultaneously offered the same course." World Campus leaders are faced with few established ground rules for structuring relationships that may provide financially beneficial outcomes, which is clearly important for a self-supporting unit.

Threat—Security: The degree of security that the organization faces was often discussed not as an external issue, but rather an internal one. World Campus staff is very sensitive to the changes taking place in the environment of online learning. They are particularly concerned with meeting student expectations and delivering educational services that serve specific market niches. The vulnerability that World Campus faces may be best explained by its ability and willingness to change as an organization, as the comments of one senior leader illustrate:

> There's a lot of angst associated with the risks that we're taking, the fact that we can't look back at an old process and say all right, how can we just move that process into this new environment? We have to create it brand new, and a lot of people don't like that. A lot of people would prefer to have some stability in their lives. We can't afford to have that kind of stability.

Dependence

Munificence—Scarcity: Because the World Campus relies upon a well-developed set of internal relationships, it is not highly reliant upon personnel with functional capacities from outside of Penn State. Exceptions may be found in the relative scarcity of financial resources within its internal environment. As a self-supporting unit, the World Campus was dependent upon external founding from the Sloan Foundation to acquire the start-up capital it needed to launch its operation. Similarly, it is also dependent upon its student customer base in order to sustain its operation.

Normative

Authorization of Structural Features: The organizational form and administrative patterns of the World Campus appear highly determined by the operating policies of the University as a whole. Because the aim of the World Campus is to make no distinction between learners in residence and learners at a distance, the academic units establish most of the academic policies guiding World Campus. The organization is raising critical policy questions, however, that tend to influence the entire University. For example, differential pricing for in-state and out-of-state students may cause the University to rethink such policies. The distinction between in-load and over-load compensation for distance education teaching is another policy issue that the World Campus organization has caused many to debate. A final example is the team concept for program development, which is changing the perception of curricular ownership from one that has been largely faculty-centered to the current system of shared ownership.

Acquisition: The World Campus structural model evolved from discussions (and site visits) of outside organizations that were developing distance-learning capabilities. It also developed as a function of strong internal considerations regarding rational approaches to organizing that would be acceptable to the campus community. Outsourcing of instructional development, for example, was considered but not adopted because of concerns over quality and how the broader academic community at Penn State would interpret such a move. The planners also balanced how decentralized the operation should be, as strong tendencies toward decentralization of functions to the school or college level tends to be the norm at Penn State. One administrator characterized the debate in this way:

> Why can't each college just have a virtual component? . . . There was that kind of debate, where you decentralize all of this at the college level and not have a World Campus the way we've conceptualized this, the 25th campus of Penn State.

The discussion of structures and practices considered more rational in the Penn State environment also raised the issue of how peripheral the World Campus should be as a campus unit. Policies to pay faculty members in-load for teaching their courses through World Campus was one outward sign of an attempt to move distance education from the periphery to the mainstream of academic life. An administrator explained:

> I knew what I was getting into when I came out here, I wanted the challenge. We were peripheral. We weren't in the mainstream. We were kind of a side bar. That's all changing, not to say we're in the mainstream yet, I think some people think we have progressed more than we have. We've still got a long way to go . . . but that's what we're talking about.

Cognitive

Legitimation: World Campus leaders face issues of legitimation from external and internal constituencies. Its alliances with corporations such as AT&T confer to the organization a sense that its educational products (and by implication its manner of delivering products) are valued by external constituents. The exposure that World Campus has attracted places it in a unique position within the State of Pennsylvania and potentially the nation. Penn State's desire to mainstream distance education within the research university context is a bold one. By moving in this direction, it is seen as a leader (clearly a position that the organization cultivates). As a leader, it is in a position of legitimacy, which allows it to speak out on virtual education within the state. Others have recognized this position of legitimacy, which adds to the organization's status as a leader. The comments of a senior administrator reveal the complexities:

> We've . . . tried to position Penn State, potentially as a leader in the higher education community, in this kind of virtual education. I think Western Governors [University] is making an overture to Pennsylvania to join that consortium, and we were suggesting that that isn't the way to go and we were lobbying against that, and I think we were successful in persuading the Governor not to go that route.

However, as this administrator admitted, internal issues of suspicion from other Pennsylvania institutions can undermine World Campus's position as a leading voice within the state. "Now, I think what's getting in the way of that, to be honest with you, is a lack of trust on the part of our sister institutions in what Penn State's up to."

Attempts to gain external legitimacy were not always viewed as positive by persons within the World Campus. Some members saw the World Campus—corporate alliances as being too accommodating to the corporate side of the partnership in order to gain legitimacy. Discussion of legitimacy brought this reaction:

> Who are the educators and who are the potential customers? And because they throw us a couple hundred thousand dollars you know, I've kiddingly said . . . are we going to put AT&T on the football helmets? . . . Our leadership is very good at talking partnerships, but they don't know how to do them because we allow ourselves I think all too often to be taken advantage of, because we're educators, we're not business persons. We don't know how to maneuver in that environment.

Internal recognition of the value that World Campus brings to the University community remains a continuing challenge for its leaders. Within the academic departments of Penn State, deans, department chairs and faculty can have difficulty seeing the value of their unit for advancing the curricular goals of their program. Similarly, individual faculty members may see the World Campus as a legitimate outlet for their creative energizes, but find insufficient reward in comparison with their scholarly endeavors. And though some faculty may eagerly seek to participate they may find no market of students for their courses.

Institutionally Shared Beliefs: Like many postsecondary education organizations, Penn State World Campus is watchful of Federal policies that constrain or enhance the promulgation of distance education. One senior leader identified the Higher Education Reauthorization Act as a critical piece of legislation, which in its current form places limitations on the delivery of courses and market for students that World Campus seeks.

Certainly, policy externally is important to us. The rewrite of the Higher Education Authorization bill could have dramatic positive implications for the World Campus and other similar ventures. It could also . . . I doubt if it could dampen things more than the current bill has (laugh), but the failure of the Federal government to meet the expectations of lifelong learners and their needs, would leave a barrier that needs to be removed.

World Campus leaders are also influenced by business sector trends, particularly in areas such as electronic commerce, marketing and information technology. One administrator described several areas where externally defined (business) practices were being closely monitored and potentially integrated within World Campus.

We're learning from business in terms of how they do electronic commerce, and advertising online. . . . We've got a sales force that we call our client development arm. We've got a marketing research group. . . . The same would hold true for technology, we're benchmarking pretty closely with technology companies, and trying to stay as current as we can on new and emerging technologies and trying to have kind of a research and development thrust in that area.

Interorganizational Conditions Influencing the Organizational Form and Administrative Patterns of the Penn State University World Campus

Analysis in this section examines the relationships that the World Campus has with organizations within the external environment that may shape its organizational form and administrative patterns.

Uncertainty

Interconnectedness—Isolation: The World Campus has few, if any, external linkages to entities whose activities influence its product development or other academic processes. This is not to say that the organization is isolated, but rather that it has a good deal of discretion in how it develops and delivers its programs. Nor is it isolated in terms of its customer base—be it corporate client or individual student. It does have a loose association with the Internet Service Providers that provide students with Internet connections, but these relationships may be fleeting since they are tied to student enrollment.

Concentration—Dispersion: The resources that the World Campus requires for effective operation (e.g., content, technology expertise and equipment, support services, etc.) are highly concentrated in the University infrastructure.

Dependence

Coordination—Non-coordination: The World Campus does not face a group of external entities whose actions are coordinated. Penn State does not report to a board of any sort, which leaves World Campus as a unit of the University with very few coordinating mechanisms. As one senior leader explained:

> We'd like Penn State to work with the state system of higher education and the community college network, and . . . private institutions . . . there'd have to be some coordinating superstructure for that, and the state really doesn't want to invest in that, so they're really taking a kind of hands-off attitude. We've been trying to just develop our capability here and maybe exchange courseware with CIC [Committee on Institutional Cooperation] institutions.

An exception is the CIC, a group of the Big Ten athletic conference schools and the University of Chicago, which have an informal agreement to collaborate and share information and practices that may benefit the member institutions. An initiative to promote and exchange distance learning courses from members' institutions was begun in fall 1998.

Interorganizational Power: The notion of interorganizational power as a means to exert influence over external organizations or individuals in order to control resources did not emerge as a significant theme in this study. However, when one reorients that question to consider the internal nature of power, a different and telling view emerges. The delicate relationships that World Campus maintains with the academic departments and faculty place it in a position of being highly reliant upon the faculty for content. This is not surprising. Yet, as the World Campus staff has discovered there are subtle nuances in the power relationships that the organization maintains with the faculty. The "readiness" of an academic department, as one administrator described it, is based on numerous factors—the reputation of a particular faculty member, his or her availability, research or other commitments, internal department politics associated with teaching a World Campus course, among others. Faculty members with respected reputations and market demand for their courses are highly sought after by the World Campus staff. These faculty members possess a disproportionate balance of power in the course development process. Some recognize this and choose to exercise that power, while others do not. Less respected faculty members (e.g., those not possessing tenure or not on a tenure track) may possess less power over the course development process. The nature of intraorganizational power dynamics was expressed in this discussion of the course development process. A staff member noted:

The shining stars are more difficult to work with, but we have to look at the long-term and the long-term view is that they're a safer bet, they're probably a better payoff, they're a better investment for us. . . . And the market will develop. . . . Versus we have some others who have been great [meeting course production deadlines] . . . because the dynamic of the relationship has totally changed . . . either they're not tenured, they're not tenure line . . . they're not perceived as having clout or real sway in their department. They're not especially recognized in their field or their area of discipline. Sure they're easy to work with. Why? Because they need us.

Normative

Inducement Strategies: Incentives for making changes in organizational form or administrative patterns were not revealed to be externally directed strategies, but rather an ongoing process of defining mutual benefit between external partners and World Campus leaders. There is a co-mingling of ideas that defines key relationships with external partners. The Sloan grant, for example, brings the nature of the external—internal relationship and associated incentive strategies into high relief.

> With Sloan, they literally helped shape the initiative, so from the beginning when we were talking about World Campus, we'd had enough experience with Sloan that we knew what their goals were and they were very simpatico with ours. . . . We were evolving a study group's ideas and sharing them constantly with Sloan . . . because our particular person, [program representative] was out in the world and checking out what others were doing and he was saying yeah, you're on target, or maybe you need to go here, so we really used him to help guide the dialogue and really shape what we thought this philosophically would be as well as practically.

Another perspective for understanding the interactions of World Campus and its external partners is highlighted by the prevalence of mutual strategy setting as a function of long-standing relationships. The informants I spoke with did not see external partners as offering new strategies to help shape the organization. Instead, most felt that the World Campus programs and the organizational form and administrative patterns that support these programs were merely building upon relationships that were already quite mature. One senior leader explained:

> I think it's played itself out more in terms of already existing relationships that then got built on, and of course that's part of your larger context or your environment, sort of in peoples heads and it's already there, and your tendency would be to go in that direction. We've had a long-standing relationship with AT&T and then as AT&T broke up with AT&T Lucent, then that

developed with Lucent as well, and so there was a natural partnership waiting to happen in this particular effort as well.

Imposition of Organizational Form: The World Campus faces few coercive efforts to legitimately change its organizational form or administrative patterns. As discussion of inducement strategies pointed out, the relationships with external entities capable of creating incentives for change are typically mutually beneficial and not directed by an external partner. Clearly, some shaping of curricular content or assessment and evaluation criteria does occur. AT&T and Lucent Technologies, for example, work with World Campus representatives to create meaningful curriculum for its employees. This arrangement is negotiated, not directed by AT&T or Lucent. Likewise, the Sloan Foundation works with World Campus staff to create effective evaluation criteria for its sponsored programs. World Campus staff provides Sloan with important feedback and revisions on how to evaluate the program more effectively.

Intraorganizational Conditions Influencing the Organizational Form and Administrative Patterns of the Penn State University World Campus

The organizational form and administrative patterns of the World Campus were influenced by several factors derived from the organization's history and other issues related to the organization's internal management environment. The findings suggest that World Campus has been influenced also by relationships with key internal constituencies.

Faculty Work Patterns and Relationships: A prominent theme influencing the internal processes of the World Campus are the relationships the organization develops and maintains with the program's faculty members. One senior leader described the influence of the World Campus on working relationships with faculty in this way:

> Faculty in a traditional campus environment are used to being individual entrepreneurs in terms of how they think about their courses. . . . This [World Campus] requires them to work in a team environment . . . to meet deadlines imposed by other people, that are sometimes well in advance of how they normally think about these things. That is not an easy change for a faculty member to make . . . one of the issues we're facing right now is the whole question of faculty workload, faculty empowerment, moving faculty into a team environment.

The change needed to transform the internal environment at Penn State in order to nurture these new work patterns is evolving. For example, discussion of in-load versus over-load payment for faculty, faculty contracts and responsibilities, and the creation of a separate World Campus faculty continue to be issues that serve as an ongoing source of debate among World Campus leaders and staff. Faculty members sign a contract that outlines the conditions associated with participating in a World Campus program. The contract explains items such as the type of program to be taught (e.g., master's degree, certificate) and roles and responsibilities (e.g., which courses, which semesters, and department release time for World Campus activities). As one staff member explained:

> It's a process of buying out faculty time . . . a quarter percentage of their time is typically the formula we work with and usually two semesters prior to the release of a new course we expect them to have 25 percent of their time dedicated to working with us to develop the content.

Language and historical perspectives of faculty work also influence the nature of relationships that World Campus staff members develop when working with faculty members. Market oriented language and new perspectives on faculty work, such as viewing a course as a product, have at times been a source of cultural misunderstanding between faculty and World Campus staff. As one administrator pointed out:

> At the heart of all of this . . . is really this cultural shift for a faculty member to be engaged with us because it changes what it means to work. . . . They're [faculty] working under a certain set of assumptions and historical perspectives that are just informed by hundreds of years of experience. [Mock conversation with faculty member] Now, we're coming in and saying well, okay, now take that product and I say product, what product? Well, you know, your course. That's not a product, that's my course. You must be confused. You must be thinking about the shoe salesman...no, we're talking about your course. . .when we use the word marketing, we're using a business term here. When we use the word client development, we're using a business term. When we talk about going out and creating a need in the market, these are all languages around running an entrepreneurial business.

Intraorganizational Relations: The perception that the World Campus organization creates among other campuses and campus units is a critical influence on the form and processes it continues to define and redefine. For example, in reports and in conversations with World Campus leaders, overtures are made to ensure that other units do not view World Campus offerings as threats to their own programs. Potential conflicts may occur when World Campus program development plans conflict with plans that an academic department at the University Park campus has to offer its own distance learning programs. Conflict in intraorganizational relations may also occur when a World Campus program has too much of a University Park

feel as viewed by one of the other Penn State campuses. As one administrator explained, it is a constant process of reassuring other units:

> The conflict around World Campus occurs because it represents a threat to
> some groups. Whether it should or not, it does. The President says to us,
> something we take very seriously, World Campus has to be self-supporting,
> can't take any students from other parts of the university, isn't going to raid
> our campuses. And of course they're very threatened by this, and they're all
> threatened because if we take students and they don't get them, they lose
> money. . . . I think our strategy is as old politicians who go around, and we
> talk to them as soon as possible and you keep talking to try to help them
> understand what our strategy is, what our mission is, and that we aren't a
> threat to them, even though they think we are.

The Tension of Market Demands and Internal Constraints: The focus
of development for World Campus educational products is linked to a clear
notion of the market that the organization wishes to serve. As one senior
leader explained:

> We don't really anticipate that we're going to go out there and replicate the
> whole university. We're going to be focusing on three levels really, post-bac-
> calaureate degrees, professional master's degrees, and professional post-bac-
> calaureate certificates. . . . If we were to go out with a program that is dupli-
> cated at every university in the country, there would be no particular reason
> for students to come to Penn State.

The focus upon a narrowly defined segment of the adult learner population provides advantages for Penn State because it can conduct market
research that is very targeted and presumably more accurate. It can also
serve to create profiles that influence the type and nature of the learning
communities that students find most beneficial.

While World Campus leaders expressed a strong belief that the market
should determine programs that are selected for development, this orientation is also balanced by a focus on selecting the most prominent, well-
respected programs for which there are faculty willing to teach. The balance between market demand and finding the internal capacity to fill those
market demands remains a constant tension. An administrator described
the tension in this way:

> The struggle, the tension that we're experiencing is that when the World
> Campus was to first go out last January, we used the language a lot that said
> we're going out with our premier programs. . . . We have some really high
> visibility programs here, Engineering, Business, Medicine . . . now we have
> the challenge of working with those programs and then saying well, we can
> market their programs to a clientele, so that's kind of how we started. It

quickly became evident that working with some of these premier programs wasn't going to be easy. They had different agendas, different priorities, they had a whole different set of constraints.

This same administrator went on to explain that the subtleties of matching the needs of the market with the desires of an academic department can be difficult and can dissolve quickly or after protracted discussion. Difficulties can emerge over issues such as the willingness to offer a degree program versus a certificate program, or a more immediate issue like the inability to generate enough revenue from a program to make it self-sustaining.

Presence of an Organizational Champion: The formation of the World Campus organization has received a great deal of support from the Penn State President. Many World Campus staff members pointed to the President's energy as a major factor contributing to the creation of the organization. The current Vice President for Outreach and Cooperative Extension is also credited with taking an active role in structuring the relationships with academic deans and department chairs that paved the way for program development. These key leaders in conjunction with the senior leadership of World Campus were also viewed as initiating a top-down approach to organizational formation.

The Penn State University Modus Operandi: The final intraorganizational theme that emerged from the analysis is comprised of two subthemes that are defined by the cultural context of Penn State University. Some readers may see these themes as emblematic of many research universities, however informants described the themes as unique to the context of Penn State. The first theme addresses the nature of outsourcing for the World Campus and the organization's seeming lack of desire to outsource any operational functions. One perspective was that Penn State had tried outsourcing in the past (it was considered for some aspects of the World Campus and was not selected as an organizing model) and had not had a good experience. One administrator noted that such experiences had contributed to "a certain culture at Penn State that I would call kind of building your own—building your own systems, building your own technology solutions." The approach of using resources within the Penn State University structure was seen by one senior leader as a way to assure that high quality standards would be met.

The second theme emerging from the Penn State context is that of a highly decentralized operating environment. The environment constantly pits the value of centralized organizing, seen in central administrative organizations like World Campus, with more decentralized operations in the Schools and Colleges. The debate is an old one. One administrator described what a decentralized approach means for his portion of the operation and the ongoing challenges it poses:

> They [faculty] had probably reluctance or lack of trust in working with a central unit that would manage the course development and manage the registration and collect the fees and then work with some kind of income sharing arrangement. A lot of discussion around that, and probably not the degree of organizational confidence and trust in the central World Campus outreach organization as I'd like there to be, but you know, that's really typical. Colleges always think they can do it better on their own, and more efficiently and effectively on their own.

The Nature of the Organization

The organizational form and administrative patterns of the Penn State University World Campus are examined in the following sections, corresponding to the outline presented within the conceptual frameowk.

The Organizational Form of the Penn State University World Campus

Strategy

Intraorganizational Strategy: In order to shield the organization from potential threats in its environment, the leadership team has adopted a strategy of flexibility and continuing innovation, particularly in terms of technology selection. Innovation in educational products and technology systems is perceived by members of the management team as a hedge against the rapid changes taking place in society. As one senior leader explained, the Internet was not a viable, widely accessible educational tool just five years ago; locking the World Campus into a particular technology would stifle innovation. His comments on buffering the organization from threats in the environment focused on the internal choices that he and others would make. He pointed out:

> The biggest threat to the World Campus right now is we would limit our vision, and settle down into a system that's inflexible. . . . Worst thing we could do is to say we are doing this technology. We are defined as X, as the Web. . . . It is very early for us to say that's going to be our technology. We have seen what's happened when institutions have organized themselves around satellite. That's all we're going to do is satellite. They're not players, so the worst thing we can do is get a loyalty to a particular technology and lose our flexibility in terms of being able to meet student needs. . . . To me, the biggest threat to us is that is complacency with our own innovation.

Similar language is consistent in the earliest planning documents, which stated that "Competition is increasing dramatically. . .Not to move aggressively. . .could put the University at a long-term disadvantage in terms of developing new constituencies and new sources of revenue." Educating internal constituencies on the benefits of constant innovation in the instructional process by presenting a convincing message has been an associated task faced by members of the World Campus staff. In a culture that some informants saw as risk averse, the call for innovation and flexibility to protect the University from detrimental external events provides an ongoing challenge.

Interorganizational Strategy: World Campus activities and policies intended to alter the nature of the organization's environment have focused on relationship building and linking internal capacity and external demand for educational services. For example, one senior staff member discussed the organization's need to develop policies that would allow it to assess the value of engaging in external partnerships. These core principles, as they were termed, would help the organization decide which partners or clients would be most amenable to new initiatives or joint activities. The policy would also help World Campus define for itself the nature and type of changes that it ought to attempt within its environment. She discussed the policy in this way:

> You can't have an effective partnership unless you understand the needs of the partner and you can clearly communicate to the partner your needs . . . we need to have a core set of partnering principles, and then tailor those for different situations, for example our client development will tailor those for corporate partnerships. . . . I think as an organization, we need to have a core of that type of principle that doesn't change . . . a bottom line. There's a point beyond which you will not compromise, or whatever.

Linking the internal capacity of Penn State—its academic programs, technology resources and student support services—with the needs of a specific market of adult students has been a prominent strategic issue for the organization. The approach is based ideally upon building a subtle understanding of the market for World Campus courses prior to developing an academic program or, at the very least, developing marketing data in conjunction with relationship building with an academic unit. Faculty willingness to participate in World Campus programs plays a major role in shaping the World Campus' ability to influence changes in its external environment. A member of the strategic management group explained the strategy that he saw emerging:

The first thought is not are we creating a campus? If so, what disciplines do we want to offer? If we offer disciplines, what courses, sub-disciplines or degree programs are we going to offer? Rather, the first approach has been what faculty are interested in teaching? Let's do a market survey. Is there a market for what they want to teach? If they want to teach these courses and there's a market, will people be willing to pay what it costs to make this self-sustaining?

Resource Strategy: In keeping with the interorganizational strategy of a strong market orientation and responsiveness to Penn State academic units, the World Campus planning group investigated three financial models. These included an independent nonprofit organization, an auxiliary organization and a centralized organization structure. The World Campus Study Team recommended that the organization operate as a centralized unit or cost center within the existing budget structure for distance education. A report to the Penn State community (Ryan, 1997) explains that the World Campus will "require multiple sources of support. These include: University resources; Sloan Foundation funding for asynchronous learning network elements; Corporate support; Customer support for individual programs; [and] Tuition income from World Campus programs." World Campus leaders tended to be quite protective of information regarding the figures on revenue from each of the aforementioned sources and the costs associated with their programs.

It is important to note that the academic units are not responsible for funding the course development costs for their World Campus academic programs. The World Campus has relied primarily upon its $1.3 million grant from the Sloan Foundation to support course development. World Campus tuition and fees are set based on the perceived market value and development costs and, therefore, are determined on a program-by-program basis. Costs associated with library and information technology infrastructure are treated as a cost item within the University-wide technology infrastructure. Given the organization's goal of becoming a self-supporting unit that will not only recover its costs but also return income to the cooperating academic department, it is unclear from the available information if or when the World Campus will be able to accomplish this goal.

Structure

Centralization: The perception of the degree to which members of lower organizational levels participate in decision making varies with ones level in the organization. Senior leaders tended to emphasize the matrix structure of the organization as a means to build consensus in the decision making environment. He explained:

very few people around that table report to the same person, and very few of them report to me . . . some of my own staff supervise people who administratively report to someone else outside of our organization entirely. Our marketing people report to the same group, to a different Associate Vice President. Our instructional designers report to the Computer and Information System's unit, which reports to a completely different Vice President, and completely different administrative chain. . . . Organizationally we're a matrix, we're a network, so a decision making process has to be consensual. There's very little formal authority to do this. (Laughter).

Other members of the organization at lower levels expressed a different opinion. One administrator commented on the decision making process in this way:

It starts off very hierarchical . . . Dean to Vice President have a conversation at a reception and get the idea and then we . . . go through this formal process, almost kind of a common sense summit meeting where you go to a corporate partner site and bring top people, but by the time it filters down to my level, which is the implementation, the hands-on, the 'gonna and gotta' get it done person, it becomes a lot less formal and it becomes a lot more nebulous because you know, decisions and commitments that are made at a very high level often times don't take into account a lot of the day-to-day realities. Operational issues of what we can get done, what we can ask people to do, what people will in turn do.

Formalization: The World Campus is moving toward a more formalized operational structure. That is, procedures and processes are being documented and reviewed in order to make the means and ends of the work within the organization more explicit. The course development process—from marketing through delivery and assessment—is being thoroughly examined and displayed in a series of elaborate flowcharts. These flowcharts are intended to ensure that members of the organization understand connections between functions, the educational product is meeting constituent needs and maximum efficiency is achieved in the course development process.

Complexity: The full range of functions encompassing the academic instructional process is represented in the structure of the World Campus organization. A matrix model is used in which units from varied parts of campus are integrated to create the organization's educational products and services. World Campus staff work with colleagues in Penn State's academic departments, Center for Academic Computing, Center for the Study of Higher Education and Outreach and Cooperative Extension marketing unit to form the World Campus operating structure. The day-to-day challenges and overall advantages of integrating a diverse set of functions within the matrix model brought this observation from one member of the management team:

> Being a matrix organization, I have to have influence over a lot of people over in Keller Building [offices of other functional units], directors in different units over there. I have absolutely no authority over anybody, so it's a challenging way to make things happen. A lot of relationship building, and that doesn't happen really fast, and you just can't mandate it you know, 'you will build a good relationship with that person.' You have to put in time and effort, and sometimes do some fixing up when things go wrong. [However,] I think it increases commitment and buy in through out the organization.

Configuration: All functional areas of the World Campus operate within the superstructure of the Penn State University system. In its current stage of development, organizational functions are provided primarily by the University Park campus. Marketing, content development, instructional delivery systems, course development, student support services, and evaluation functions are co-located on the main campus of Penn State. However, the vision of a much more distributed though perhaps, not necessarily more differentiated organizational structure was advanced by one senior administrator. He noted:

> [The World Campus is a] University wide delivery system where any of our campus colleges could offer a program . . . to a national or international audience, so we might have particular expertise at our Erie Campus . . . or a particular engineering technology that doesn't exist at University Park. And the faculty who have expertise . . . in delivering some of those things in a World Campus type format . . . we would work with those faculty in that college. . . . The distance might be a challenge but in today's environment it shouldn't be. If we can deliver education at a distance, we should be able to develop it where people aren't necessarily sitting side-by-side.

Process

Design and Management of Technology and Tasks: The design and management of the technology and tasks of World Campus is best seen in the program development process, a complex integration of the organization's functional areas. The process integrates marketing, negotiation with academic departments, course development (including integration of technology-based course management tools), student services (e.g., application, registration, and student advising), course management, and evaluation and assessment. The process strikes a careful balance between the deadlines indirectly tied to market expectations and the internal constraints faced by faculty and staff who are developing the program. A key management task, according to one senior leader, has been trying to move management decisions down to the operational level. Still, the faculty members who work with World Campus staff have their own deadlines, which as some members of the staff have discovered can supersede World Campus expectations. Contracts, artifacts of the process, outline expectations yet have no binding force. As one staff member pointed out regarding this critical juncture of the process:

> We're largely perceived as an outside entity, even though we don't think of ourselves that way, that's how we're perceived by faculty and for us to come in an try to lay it out on paper as a contract . . . we all recognize that we have very limited power to enforce such a contract, although we do them and it's important to do them . . . it guides us, but it doesn't rule us in that you know, things change. Things change on our end and we also, likewise need the same flexibility to tell the faculty well . . . we thought we'd offer this course, but you know, the market's not there. The enrollments aren't there you know? We need to look at adapting.

While individual faculty may expect World Campus managers to understand the demands of their teaching, research and service schedules, World Campus leaders hoped the faculty would understand the market forces they faced. The demands of the market for relevant content, as the previous quote illustrates, offer no abiding rules for structuring the process of program development.

The process relies heavily upon the program manager to coordinate the varied parts of the program development process. As one member of the Strategic Management Group contends, the responsibilities of the program manager are out of sync with the authority placed in persons in that position. For example, do program mangers have the clout to stop or alter projects? He pointed out that this is a problematic aspect of the program development process:

> At this point, the reality of it is they don't have the authority. The program manager can no more tell the faculty this course ain't gonna happen without getting the blessing of [senior leaders], than a frog. (laugh) There's no way this person is going to have the authority in the foreseeable future to make, to perform what would reasonably be a function of their position. . .How did a program manager get to be in that position of authority? Well, I think because this has largely been a management decision process . . . so the program manager always looks like the person to give the responsibility, you know? Who's in the position to see the aspects of instructional designs and faculty interaction and content development, and market and that's pretty much everything right now, but it won't be [in the future].

The evaluation of organizational processes proceeds from two perspectives and is an assigned task for two members of the Strategic Management Group, emphasizing the contribution of evaluation for the continuing improvement of organizational processes. The first aspect of evaluation focuses on the internal workings of the organization—linkages between functional areas, means of increasing communication, eliminating redundancy, etc. The second evaluation perspective, which is under contract with the Center for Higher Education, examines the influences of the internal processes on the faculty and the students in World Campus programs—the outcomes and effectiveness for those persons in teaching and learning.

Political Process: The process by which organizational conflict is resolved within the World Campus is just beginning to exhibit discernible patterns, according to some of the persons that I interviewed. Hard and fast rules have not been established within the organization. However, it is not the case that organizational leaders have ignored conflict; rather they are keenly aware that they must create or modify organizational policies as new sources of conflict emerge. As one leader explained:

> Initially it's a question of turf, control over decision making, control over resources, and ultimately trust. . . . For a long time, there was a lot of anxiety about what everybody else is doing. I know I'm doing my job but what about all these other people here . . . are they doing their job? And the cross unit communication became very important just in terms of letting people know that in fact, people were doing their jobs credibly. . . . Now I think there's a sense of conflict over empowerment. . .communication up and down in a system. . . . Do I have to say yes to protect myself? Will my supervisor defend me?

One staff member brought a different perspective to the issue of empowerment by suggesting that conflict arose and was resolved by often automatically elevating operational concerns to the upper levels of the organization. Thus, day-to-day operational issues were thrust into the domain of senior leaders, instead of being dealt with at lower (and perhaps more appropriate levels). During my visit, the leadership team and other staff members were wrestling with this conflict and attempting to come to a resolution.

The Administrative Patterns of the Penn State University World Campus

Normative Structure

Values: Few informants expressed the values of the organization as tersely or as effectively as one staff member who contended that "the only value is the quality of education." The focus on quality is an often repeated value that takes several shades of meaning within the World Campus. For some, the quality of education is measured in student satisfaction and learning quality, which many are quick to defend, as the comments of one administrator reveal:

> I think the thing that ties people most together is service to students, and it's interesting in meetings how often you'll hear somebody say, and this at first will sound a little strange, they'll say well somebody has to speak for the student.

Another member of the organization who separated quality into two distinct aspects—the nature of the product and its marketability, explained:

> I think one of the most important values is to deliver a very high quality product and for them that quality is defined in terms of a couple of terms. I guess instructional design elements, are appropriate design elements present? Are they using good tools to convey content? I think from the marketing standpoint, is this a marketable, is this successfully marketed, is there a market first of all? Did we correctly assess the potential market? Then once a course is out there, did it find a market? . . . And finally from the marketing standpoint, would there be repeat customers if you will? Is there a continuing market?

The other core value repeatedly expressed by members of the organization was that of providing access to educational services. One administrator stated "the idea of providing access to others, to those who may not otherwise have opportunities is an important value of ours." While another administrator seemed troubled by what he viewed as an over-emphasis on corporate clients to the detriment of students for whom access to Penn State's courses would be truly enriching. The point is made in the context of altruism and the bottomline:

> More and more it seems as if the only thing that counts or the primary emphasis is the bottom line. In other words, colleges saying we would be willing to work with you and provide approval to your organization to offer our baccalaureate degree if and only if we're convinced that the revenue sharing plan put into effect is really going to enrich our coffers significantly, and what is absent from the discussions compared to the early days. . .is any kind of altruistic sense of why we're doing this. . . . I know we have to become more and more like a business all the time, but. . .it seems to me very much a cold, free enterprise, capitalistic motive that seems to be cited for why we're doing this.

Norms: The generalized rules governing behavior in this organization are guided by the standards set for the university as a whole. Many expectations are emerging as unique problems arise and must be addressed. For example, the realization that a program development deadline would be missed forced World Campus leaders to consider how to handle the situation and consider policies for how the process should be approached should it happen in the future. As one administrator explained, "We're a real meeting culture, and we get together and we suggest that people put issues on the table and exhibit their frustrations or concerns that they have." Meetings often serve as the focal point or organizing mechanism for identifying issues that may later be addressed by more generalized rules or process revisions.

Role Expectations: Role expectations according to some members of the staff were self-imposed, rather than conveyed through managers or policy manuals. Several student services staff members pointed to standards such as a 48 business hour deadline for responding to student inquiries. Like the norms of the organization, role expectations for this relatively young organization are emerging. Role expectations have emerged as a result of standards set by associated operations, such as the distance education or continuing education units. The student services area is a good example, since its processes have merged with the World Campus. Role expectations are also created or revised as novel situations occur that call for evaluations of current roles and decisions concerning how a specific position might be improved. It is clear from the conversations with informants that the role expectations of the program manager position are likely to be revised.

Behavioral Structure

Activities: The activities of organization members are related to the functional expertise they provide. For this organization, the principal work activities are those of managing and developing programs, not managing external relationships related to essential organizational functions. World Campus employees bring particular expertise to the organizational matrix—each representative is an expert in his or her field. The staff members that are direct reports to the World Campus are primarily managers who oversee, build relationships, and develop strategies and policies for the organization. However, the majority of World Campus staff has other responsibilities. For example, the marketing group provides services to the Continuing Education unit, as well as other units within Outreach and Cooperative Extension.

Interactions: Because World Campus staff members are co-located at the University Park campus of Penn State, many of the interactions that take place are face-to-face. Such meetings are often used to engage participants who form the multi-functional teams. Electronic mail is used to augment meetings and clarify and coordinate interactions. Contact with students is increasingly by electronic mail. It has had an influence on the pace of interactions within the organization. One staff member remarked that, "the whole pace of operation it seems can be really picked up once people figure out they can apply online, get their questions answered online. . .trying to set up an appointment with an advisor or a faculty member, send out that e-mail—within a couple of days you better have an answer!" Intra-campus interactions with faculty and academic departments are also important and frequent interactions. The approach of World Campus leaders has been to treat academic units as partners—sharing revenue and encouraging buy-in through joint planning and development. These interactions are perhaps the most critical since the content for World Campus offerings is solely dependent upon these academic units.

Sentiment: The organization members I spoke with expressed varied feelings toward their work. Many expressed concerns that are not atypical of any workplace—difficulties in communication, challenges of adjusting to change and frustration over increasing workloads. Most, however, felt that the World Campus was a positive step by the University and were pleased to be a part of it, despite the frustrations. The sentiments of one senior leader, though outwardly dramatic, were heartfelt. He explained:

> There are very few generations of people in university life who get to do something dramatically new. . . . That's a nice thought to have. That at the end of the day, the work matters because we really are part of positioning the land grant university for the realities of the next century in terms of who our students are going to be, what's going to face them, what's going to face us economically, competitively as a nation. What's going to face us internationally and how do we create a new kind of global community. We're part of that and to me that justifies all the hassle (laugh) of doing this work.

CONCLUSION

The Penn State University World Campus is an illustration of a publicly supported, virtual campus specializing in professional certificates and undergraduate and post-baccalaureate degree programs via the Internet and other technologies. Established in 1996 and enrolling its first students in 1997, the World Campus is a new model of outreach in the land grant tradition. World Campus is an internal network, with a matrix organizational structure. It uses the expertise and talent of academic and administrative units of the University Park campus to create cross-functional teams that provide all aspects of the instructional experience for remote students.

It views its mission as that of a centralized unit that will foster technology-mediated outreach for the University's most prominent programs, while building learning communities with the vigor of any found on a residential campus. As the beneficiary of a Sloan Foundation grant, it has placed itself in the forefront of asynchronous course delivery. External relationships with corporations and associations help to define the market for the World Campus's educational services. While within the University, some view the organization as an outsider or source of competition. The organization's relationship with its content providers—Penn State faculty—may well determine the degree of success that the World Campus is likely to achieve.

The World Campus case provides leaders with an organizational example that draws on much that is familiar about the higher education enterprise as we know it today. The organizational design adopted by the World Campus retains all of the University's resources within a common umbrella. No external partners or vendors are present within the organization's functional areas. This design is intended to provide a check on the quality of the organization and its programs, while providing suitable flexibility for innovation. Their model is familiar in that it remains largely centered on the expertise of the faculty member, which most believe is essential for course quality and adherence to the cultural norms of the institution. By keeping control of all aspects of the organization within the confines of Penn State, the organization's leaders believe that the quality of the overall academic experience will be improved. Correspondingly, the World Campus brand name will be well positioned since it is clearly an extension of a well-known university.

The World Campus organizational design will be an important experiment in postsecondary education. As other public institutions experiment with distance learning organizations in an attempt to remove many of the perceived and real restrictions evident within their institution's current policies and structures, the World Campus design approach and strategies will be held up for comparison. How and how well the World Campus will continue to drive innovation, grow revenue and define itself in the marketplace will be important indicators for anyone interested in virtual postsecondary education organizations.

CHAPTER 8

Cross Case Comparisons

T HE ANALYSES PRESENTED IN THIS CHAPTER PARALLEL THE STRUCTURE established by the study's research questions, a method recommended by Eisenhardt (1989). The first analytic dimension presents the themes found by comparing internal with stable network structures. Because each of these organizations uses remote, technology-mediated delivery for its educational services and products, the second comparison analyzes the technology delivery mode be it either synchronous or asynchronous as points of differentiation. The third set compares distinctions of product type (niche-focused or broad market) to clarify questions about the contribution of the educational products created by these organizations. The fourth analytic set examines the nature of values across these organizations by considering inter-group differences based on the relative strength or weakness of organizational linkages to business and industry. In the final set of analyses, the inter-group differences structure is used to consider the divergence and origins of purpose embodied by these organizations.

ANALYZING THE INTER-GROUP DIFFERENCES IN STRUCTURAL FORM

The initial analysis involved examining within group similarities in two groups as differentiated by network structure. Two comparative groupings were established based on prevalence as internal (UNET and World Campus) or stable (CECC, CMIL and NTU) network structures. In the main, dynamic networks were not reflected as characteristics of these organizations and, therefore, were not included. Some characteristics of dynamic networks were evident in the partner relationships of NTU's

ATMP short courses, but stable network qualities were more prominent. Inter-group difference patterns (see Table 8.1) are explained in detail in this section.

The Internal Network

The thematic differences captured in the cross case analysis indicate that organizations with internal network forms exhibit a tendency to use changes in internal processes and relationships as a means to reduce uncertainty encountered within their environment over issues such as competition or technology changes. This might include policy changes regarding compensation for faculty, new reporting relationships or process revisions. They see increasing competition for students within their external environment caused by advancements in instructional and information technologies. The degree of security they possess is often based upon an ability, not to shape external expectations, but rather to alter the internal operation to more effectively meet market demands. This may point to why these organizations have fewer external relationships with organizations that are dissimilar to one another.

Internal networks also tend to rely on resources found within their internal organizational environment, but such reliance can limit the organization's choices regarding functional expertise or other resources because it is limited to a more finite resource pool (or may have to hire from the outside). These organizations can also face a rather lean environment for financial resources as well. The selection of organizational structures and policies are often determined by the existing operating policies and structures set by the larger organizational structure in which the organization is embedded. This tendency may minimize the likelihood that structural models adopted by the organization run counter to the expectations set by the academic community as a whole. Although once established, these organizations often become the source of novel questions and problems that seem not to fit comfortably within existing policies or procedures of the larger organizing unit.

Legitimacy for these internal network organizations was derived from the recognition they received from external funders. In addition, learner satisfaction with the educational product was perceived as a source of credibility. There was also the tendency among these organizations to couple their legitimacy in terms of their relationship with the larger unit in which they were embedded. For these organizations, the internal connotations of legitimacy are very important. For example, the World Campus was very conscious of its placement within the University Park campus. Leaders were concerned about the perception that they were peripheral to the campus and what this might convey about the seriousness of their operation to the academic community. UNET saw its status diminished when the System's faculty rejected the separate campus proposal.

The connections that internal networks exhibit in dealing with external entities often take shape through interactions over program choices. However, this structure tends to de-emphasize any role for external entities in the actual course or program development process, which often involves faculty, instructional designers or others. These organizations face few coordinated external groups. Trust building is essential for these organizations, but this takes time and is often viewed in terms of personal ties with the community or potential clients and seems to reflect few transitory relationships. Relationships with external (and often internal) constituents indicate a negotiated rather than controlling relationship with partners or constituents. Each organization felt constrained by current Federal policies on financial aid that require institutions to have at least 50% residential enrollment, although this policy had few direct consequences on organizations in this group. These organizations did not voice concern over accreditation standards, as they had strong ties to a larger system which provided the support and credibility needed for accreditation of their programs.

These internal network organizations also saw themselves as drawing the attention of other campus units, who felt that the new programs and manner of operating might create competition for the established programs. Few viewed these new organizations as benign additions to the campus community. UNET may be the most provocative case, since the reaction it drew because of its plans to create a separate campus embroiled the System President and others in controversy. A common theme among every organization in this study was the presence of an organizational champion or champions who supported the creation and development of the unit. Each internal organizational also exhibited signs of tension in balancing its desire to serve students, typically couched in terms of meeting the demands of the market, with the desire to serve internal constituents like faculty who faced their own pressures to meet deadlines often unrelated to distance learning activities.

The Stable Network

The stable network organizations represented in this study appeared to have more elaborate contacts and relationships with dissimilar organizations within their external environment. The network of relationships suggests greater organizational complexity than the internal network forms. However, to a greater or lesser extent, each found these external relationships mediated by its relationship to the larger unit in which it was embedded. While this was not demonstrated in the NTU case, the other organizations found great benefit in affiliations with organizations such as UC—

Berkeley Extension (CMIL) or the other system campuses (CECC). In CMIL's case its credibility was clearly linked to UC—Berkeley's reputation as a strong research institution, which influenced its ability to secure grant money. And for CECC, its affiliation as a System college gives it leverage to seek course content from the other System campuses. All of these organizations were keenly aware of the influence of information technologies in breaking down historical barriers separating regional, national and international product markets. Responses to these environmental changes, unlike internal networks, were typically found in the development of extensive relationships with external entities, particularly as they pertained to the course development and delivery process. Outsourcing of functions is the most striking example. The perceived level of security that each organization experienced was often discussed in terms of the strength of its relationships with specific client groups, such as corporations or businesses.

Each of the stable network organizations was inclined to see its content as the most critical resource, as did the internal networks, but in the stable networks the content providers were viewed as an outsourced function, which most leaders felt gave them the flexibility to match market expectations more quickly than if they "owned" the instructors outright. For each of these organizations, the linkages in their network were of extreme importance, yet each evolved in slightly different ways. Each organization saw its legitimacy linked to demonstrating the value of their educational products in the eyes of their customers, although each had varied ways of assessing that influence due in part to the different types of educational products offered by each organization. The internal legitimacy of each organization was typically not a prominent concern (CMIL did differ on this point). Each seemed to view their reputation as an issue tied to the products and their impact, although each was aware that their partners (as opposed to larger unit affiliation in internal networks) could be sources of legitimacy for them. For example, NTU officials often spoke of the quality of content coming from the finest Engineering programs in the country. CECC touted the innovation of companies like RealEducation and Jones Education Company and what that meant for their programs. Aside from CMIL, the other two organizations were more likely to de-couple their credibility from the parent unit and link it more to their partners. One might expect this at NTU, which has no higher unit structure, but it also seemed to be the case at CECC. As such, stable networks saw innovation flow to them through their partners, a type of organizational learning, in which new technologies or instructional practices come to be institutionalized in the educational products or organizational structure. For example, CMIL found the templates used by AOL to be useful initially for creating courses, but revised those templates in the next generation products that they decided to develop on their own. NTU blended the organizational structure of its academic partners with that of its corporate partners to achieve a hybrid model that is responsive to accreditors while also facilitating client development.

Table 8.1: Comparison of Extra, Inter, and Intraorganizational Differences in Internal and Stable Network Forums

Internal Networks (UNET and World Campus)	Stable Networks (CECC, NTU and CMIL)
Focus on internal processes and relationships to reduce uncertainty in the environment.	Focus on external relationships to reduce uncertainty in the environment.
Degree of security based on ability to change internal processes to meet external demands	Degree of security tied to relationship with clients. Attempt to build capacity quickly enough to meet external demands.
Selection of structural models that are acceptable to academic community.	Selection of structural models deemed to be most effective in the marketplace. External models used as sources for practices and structures seen as more modern or appropriate, such as outsourcing.
Legitimacy measured by satisfaction with educational product and grant funding. Internal legitimacy with academic units is important. Legitimacy tied to relationship with parent organization. (CMIL may belong here on this dimension.)	Legitimacy linked to value of products by customers. Internal legitimacy of unit often not questioned. Unit reputation more of a stand alone issue. De-coupled from parent unit.
Relationships with external entities not associated with program development process.	Relationships with external entities tied to program development process.
Instructors retain greater control over course development process.	Structures provide a source of control over curriculum (e.g., standardization, contract instructors, lack of tenure) and by implication the course development process.
Not overly sensitive to accreditation standards. (CMIL may belong here on this dimension.)	Greater tendency to view accreditation standards as important.

The stable network organizations are highly interconnected with several organizations or individuals that provide some key aspect of their program/course development process. Interactions are built on trust relationships and not control relationships, which makes the milieu one of negotiation by the parties involved. Clearly, mutual benefit must be present. Yet, each of these organizations has developed structures that create an aspect of control, at least in some sphere of the course development process. For example, structures such as CECC's standardization of curriculum, CMIL's reliance on contracted instructors, or NTU's lack of tenure tend to frame interactions in ways that give the organization discretion over key processes. These organizations also had a greater tendency to view accreditation standards as important (CMIL was not overly concerned, however). NTU and CECC, the most structurally non-traditional of this group, responded in different ways to the accreditation issue. For NTU, which had received accreditation twice, it was of profound importance to look like a traditional academic institution. For CECC, the approach was to sit down with representatives from their accrediting agency and try to shape new standards for non-traditional organizations prior to an accreditation visit. A leader or leaders who advanced and supported the organization had influenced each organization in this group significantly, which was a general similarity in every organization in this study. Another prominent theme, expressed in slightly different ways by each organization, was a concern over the reputation and "brand" image that they were portraying in the marketplace. Within CMIL and NTU, the marketing function tended to be more pronounced than at CECC.

ANALYZING INTER-GROUP DIFFERENCES BASED ON TECHNOLOGY DELIVERY MODE

The second analysis consisted of examining within group similarities in which organizations were grouped according to their predominant delivery technology, either synchronous or asynchronous. Synchronous delivery involves technology-mediated interaction between instructor and learner that is conducted in real time, while asynchronous technology-mediated delivery emphasizes a break in time between when the instructor delivers instructional material and when the learner interacts with that material. This distinction is made, in part, for convenience as each institution has some aspect of their technology delivery system rooted in either form. Inter-group differences are summarized in Table 8.2.

Synchronous Technology Delivery Mode

Organizations in this category show a tendency toward educational products that are consistent with a clearly defined organizational mission or historical affiliation of units providing content. For organizations that emphasize synchronous delivery, responsiveness to incorporating new technologies is of high importance. This is seen as a major focus of interest within their external environment. These organizations also tend to reflect support roles developed around specific technology, such as community-based personnel, for example, whose responsibilities are linked to effective functioning of the technology system. The strength of the partnerships that develop around the technology is particularly critical for these organizations. As such, technology systems (instructional television at UNET and satellite at NTU) provide a key structural determinant carried over from the organization's founding. Synchronous organizations have close ties to learners, either through a community presence or by virtue of close working relationships with corporate representatives. The relationships tend to be long-standing and emphasize mutual benefits and close, trusting working relationships among individuals. Such ties were evident in the satellite failure at NTU and the cultural enrichment and community partnerships that UNET offers to many communities in Maine. It is an interesting phenomenon that for organizations so focused on incorporating new technologies (e.g., Web-based instruction), that it is actually older technologies (e.g., ITV or satellite) that remain the workhorses of these organizations. An explanation may be found in the personalization or advocacy that emerges among the staff once systems have been in place for some time. An alternative explanation might be that these organizations are less willing to make changes in systems that have been successful in the past. Yet another may be that since these organizations are quite savvy technologically, they are likely to change to newer systems only at a point when it is most advantageous.

Table 8.2 Comparison of Extra, Inter, and Intraorganizational Differences by technology Delivery Type

Synchronous (UNET and NTU)	Asynchronous (CECC, CMIL, World Campus)
Some constraint of product line types because of organizational mission or historical affiliation of units providing content.	Evolving notion of product lines based on ability to understand the product market.
Strong emphasis on support roles, especially for the technology areas.	Less emphasis on support roles. Technology may allow learner to take more active role in setting technology specifications.
Instructional television and satellite delivery - technologies incorporated from the founding of these organizations - are determinants of the current organizational structure and patterns.	Few previous instructional technology systems to influence newly developed organizational structure or work patterns.
Technology structures determine work routines, organizational structures, and personal attachment to particular types of technology delivery systems. Produces some advocates for the existing system.	While the technology choices influence work routines and structures, there was little observable attachment to one system over another, so long as educational objectives were being met.

Asynchronous Technology Delivery Mode

Those organizations whose principal delivery mode is asynchronous delivery tend to view newer technologies as a strategic advantage to meet the needs they see arising in the marketplace. Technology is viewed as a means to eliminate historical market boundaries amid an environment that is perceived to be increasingly competitive. All are concerned about their ability to acquire the necessary talent to meet market demands more quickly. Quite unlike those organizations that rely on synchronous delivery, however, these organizations have less elaborate support structures around their technology systems. The technological systems tend to place more responsibility on the learners and less on a support staff who are responsible for maintaining the technology. These organizations appear to have fewer structural determinants around their technology systems, which may influence the structure of work routines.

Among this group of organizations can be found few previous instructional technology systems to influence the organizational structure or work patterns. In part, the program development process seems to determine the technology system selection, which was not the case in the synchronous group. Some members of this group also tend to benefit from a "coat-tails" influence due to partners that can provide access to current innovations in instructional technology. They seem to benefit most from contact with organizations that are unlike themselves, which may facilitate organizational learning opportunities and foster new ways of doing business in an electronic medium.

ANALYZING THE INTER-GROUP DIFFERENCES BETWEEN NICHE AND BROADER MARKET PRODUCTS

The third analysis set examined within group similarities among organizations whose products reflected a more specialized audience (niche market products) and those that reflected a broader audience (more generalist programs). Organizations such as CMIL, NTU and World Campus offer programs that are defined by service to a particular (usually professional) audience, while UNET and CECC offer more broad-based programs such as associate's, bachelor's or master's degrees (although there are clearly specific majors represented). Inter-group differences are summarized in Table 8.3.

Niche Market Products

Organizations that develop niche oriented educational products demonstrate organizational structures that place much emphasis on understanding markets and translating that understanding into specific products. They do this through a vetting process that attempts to link the marketing function (which is usually a distinct functional area) and the academic content providers. Product lines that pass the vetting process and are developed tend to be those with a clear audience and for which suitable instructor support exists. These organizations are conscious of their ability to make a profit (or at least break even) on the products that they develop. They are more likely to assess the competition in the marketplace prior to making a decision to launch a new program than those organizations with broader market products. Similarly, they are quite concerned about how their product will be differentiated from other products in the marketplace. Often, this can mean relying on the academic reputation of the institution (or partner institutions for NTU) in order to contrast their product lines from other providers.

Organizations in this group are quite deliberate in creating processes by which the academic quality may be assured in the products they develop. For example, the approval process for CMIL courses, though considered by many in the organization to be bureaucratic, does tend to ensure that a recognized authority—the Berkeley Academic Senate—verifies the quality of their programs. Significant external entities (e.g., community groups, associations, corporations) influence and aid these organizations in defining the types of programs that they should offer. These relationships vary in their intensity and influence, although each organization does express a deep belief in their desire to serve their constituents—be they in the local community or around the world.

Broader Market Products

For CECC and UNET, those organizations with broader offerings, the push and pull of market forces exhibit a less distinct structural nature within the organization. Matching the demands of the market with available organizational capacity is not as systematic a process as one would encounter in the niche product organizations. The process is much more free flowing with amenable instructors, market opportunities and new program ideas combining in unique ways to generate new products or deliver existing products. For example, each of these organizations have engaged in or are considering alliances with institutions from other states in order to broaden the types of educational products they may offer. While making a profit on such courses is clearly important, the ability to match the needs of students in their target markets appears to be the primary concern rather than profit.

Table 8.3 Comparison of Extra, Inter, and Intraorganizational Differences by Product Type

Niche Market Products (CMIL, NTU and World Campus)	Broader Market Products (CECC and UNET)
Have vetting process for linking market opportunities to internal capacity.	Less developed vetting process for matching market opportunities to internal capacity.
See competition and product differentiation as very important for identifying the most lucrative products to develop.	View partnerships with out-of-state institutions as important for offering a wider variety of products.
Have structures or processes for ensuring that high quality reputation is conveyed in product (e.g., course approval process, academic structure accreditation, "signature programs")	More likely to view products in terms of convenience, accessibility and concern for student economic advancement as basis for reputation and quality.
Significant partnerships help to define the terms of specialized program offerings.	Less distinct external impetus for organizations to consider offering very customized educational products for a specific company or industry.
Well developed marketing function with targeted market research capabilities.	Less prominent (or no) marketing function.

Organizations in this group tend to speak of their products in ways that emphasize the product's accessibility and convenience. Notions of quality are understood to rest on a course or program's ability to improve the economic status of the learner. Both organizations expressed concern over competition, but differed in their orientation based upon structural particularities. UNET's re-organization shifted the focus of responding to competition from a direct responsibility to that of facilitator for campus units, while CECC is largely externally focused with direct responsibility to offer new programs. It is not surprising that these organizations lack contracts with corporations or other entities to develop industry or company-specific educational products since they receive little pressure to do so. While such influences are minimal, each organization is far from isolated. Each maintains contacts with key constituencies that provide advice of a general nature to the organization pertaining to broader trends they should consider for improving their educational products.

ANALYZING ORGANIZATIONAL VALUES ACROSS CASES

In this section I examine the predominant values of each organization, as stated by organizational actors, expressed in organizational documents and observed during the site visits. The values of these organizations were content analyzed. Inter-group differences were then examined by dividing organizations according to the strength or weakness of their ties with business and industry (see Table 8.4). While every organization has some linkage to business or industry, those organizations with stronger ties (NTU and CECC) rely very directly on business as their principal clients or to provide critical organizational functions. Organizations such as CMIL, UNET and World Campus do have clear linkages, but these linkages are far less mission critical than in the other organizations. The distinction is primarily one of degree and methodological convenience.

Strong Ties to Business and Industry

CECC and NTU, the organizations with the strongest ties to business and industry, are likely to place a high value on collaboration among partners as well as on their internal interactions. CECC, for instance, saw collaboration as the only viable alternative for an organization that had few financial resources. These organizations were also likely to mention quality of educational offerings as a key value, particularly pertaining to responsiveness to students and content that meets the needs of learners. These organizations tend to demonstrate few overt conflicts over the values orientation of the organization. Most informants seemed quite committed to the values of their particular organization. This theme was an interesting one since CECC and NTU are the least traditional and most heterogeneous in terms of alliances of the organizations included in this study.

Weaker Ties to Business and Industry

Those organizations with weaker business ties expressed many of the same values as the group with stronger business ties, yet did so in slightly different ways. For this group, collaboration was also an important organizational value, but took the form of serving students as opposed to a vehicle for creating an operating advantage. These organizations were quite sensitive to student needs and were proud of the access that their programs generated. However, members of these organizations tended to express much more conflict over the values they saw as pervasive within the organization. For CMIL, this meant a conflict over how standardized an educational product should be without a loss of quality. For UNET, internal conflicts were apparent over how students would be served following the reorganization and if leadership in the distance learning area nationally was a position and status worth subjugating. Members of the World Campus were conflicted over the degree and scope of interactions with business and industry organizations and what their presence and funding meant for the academic standards of the institution. The level of values conflict seemed somewhat at odds with the homogenous nature of these organizations and their more traditional organization structures as compared with the organizations with closer business ties.

Table 8.4 Comparison of Organizational Values Differences Based on Strength or Weakness of Ties to Business/Industry.

Strong Ties (CECC and NTU)	Weaker Ties (CMIL, UNET and World Campus)
• Collaboration very important, particularly to facilitate lean operating style.	• Collaboration very important for serving students.
• High value on responsiveness to student particularly in meeting content needs.	• High value on responding to students and facilitating access to learning resources.
• Fewer internal conflicts over value choices.	• Greater internal conflicts over value choices.

ANALYZING THE INTER-GROUP DIFFERENCES IN ORGANIZATIONAL PURPOSE

The fifth set of analyses examined within group similarities among organizations whose purposes were differentiated according to how long the organization had been in existence. Comparisons were made by separating the organizations into two groups—those in existence for more than five years (CMIL, UNET and NTU) and those in existence for less than five years (CECC and World Campus). Inter-group differences are summarized in Table 8.5.

Organizations in Existence for More Than Five Years

Older organizations exhibited some evidence that historical relationships with their larger organizing units (or Board in NTU's case) were influential in determining the organization's purpose. This can set terms by which the focal organization deals with its partners or other campus units. The purpose of these organizations is often to act as a focal point for collaboration. In doing so, they can vary in their likelihood of accomplishing their mission, overcoming past mistakes and building on successes. In the case of UNET, for example, controversy over the development of a stand-alone virtual organization may hinder the accomplishment of some aspects of its mission for quite some time and was clearly an impetus for changes in the organization's purpose. NTU's experience in the Asia-Pacific region, while in the short run problematic, proved a valuable learning experience as the organization spun-off the NTUC organization. The organizations in this group did not tend to view themselves as organizations whose purpose was to infuse change in the environment of higher education or within their particular organization structures. Each saw itself as a leader, either programmatically, technologically or both, but that leadership tended to stop short of an expressed mission to drive new ideas or changes into other organizations. For numerous reasons, each of these organizations has been restructured in some manner. The influence of restructuring has differed in each organization: reinforcing the organization's purpose at NTU; expanding its purpose at CMIL; and seemingly clouding its purpose within UNET.

Organizations in Existence for Fewer Than Five Years

For the newer organizations in this study, collaboration is a very critical organizational purpose intended by the organization's founders. Both CECC and World Campus are currently engaged in determining how best to carry out this organizational mission. The collaborative intentions are often at odds with another organizational purpose—creating change. These organizations are imbued with a belief that they are agents of change for the larger organizations within which they are situated. Both CECC and World Campus have demonstrated this by quite intentionally incorporating organizational forms and engendering new (internal and external) relationships that have pushed other campus units into new territory. This, at times, has raised suspicions among the campus units, which has undermined the collaborative purpose of these organizations.

Table 8.5 Comparison of Extra, Inter, and Intraorganizational Difference in Organizational Purpose by Period in Existence

Greater than 5 Years (UNET, CMIL and NTU)	Less than 5 Years (CECC and World Campus)
• Are intended to be focal points for collaboration within larger organizing system (NTU not a clear fit on this dimension), but past practices and history may slow or enhance collaboration based on the ability to integrate lessons learned from past experience.	• Are intended to be focal points for collaboration. Still collecting experience on more effective collaboration approaches.
• These organizations see themselves as innovative leaders, but not as intentional change agents.	• Constituted to foster changes within the existing system.
• Have undergone some form of organizational restructuring, although the effects have differed.	• New organizational approach.

SUMMARY

The cross-case analyses in this chapter were intended to explicate key differences and similarities regarding the organizations in this study. The analysis has paralleled the structure established by the research questions. In doing this, I have attempted to make plain both the distinctions and associations that are essential to reaching an understanding of these organizations. I have tried to do this by examining not only organizational form and administrative patterns, but also by analyzing the products, values, purposes and potential for success that these organizations exhibit. These contrasts and similarities lay the groundwork for the following chapter in which I present the key findings of this research study.

CHAPTER 9

How Virtual Postsecondary Educational Organizations Function within a Knowledge Industry Environment

T HE CENTRAL GOAL OF THIS STUDY AND THE FOCUS OF THIS CHAPTER IS TO advance an understanding of how the virtual postsecondary educational organizations included in this study function. Differentiating the organizations in this study was facilitated by contrasting organizations in a systematic way through discrete analytic lenses and by conducting content analysis of specific cases. These lenses or analytic structures, which were tailored to correspond to the research questions, provide insights for distinguishing within group similarities, intergroup differences and distinctive patterns between and among cases. The outcomes of this analytic method juxtapose the essential qualities that distinguish the operational dynamics of these organization types as seen in varied ways, including differences in products, values and purposes.

While these analytic techniques are a useful means to surface the central findings, it is also important to enfold relevant literature that can sharpen our understanding of these organizations. My justifications for doing so are threefold: First, my intent is to encourage and anticipate the shape of investigation and debate at a time when the sophistication and prevalence of these organizations within the postsecondary education or Knowledge Industry environment are more pronounced. Second, the findings provide an initial conceptual step toward theory development (though not a theory in and of itself) at a time when little theoretical or empirical evidence exists on these organizations. While the implications for researchers often depends on the evolution of other empirical studies, the influence on administrators who are subject to rapidly changing environmental contexts may be more immediate, since in the absence of tested experience, these findings may become a proxy to guide management actions. Finally, this chapter provides an opportunity to integrate the findings of this study with diverse literatures from postsecondary education, organizational behavior and organizational sociology. The synthesis can provide awareness of overlapping interests to researchers in diverse fields.

UNDERSTANDING VIRTUAL POSTSECONDARY EDUCATIONAL ORGANIZATIONS—THE FOUR PROBLEMS THESE ORGANIZATIONS MUST SOLVE

Major theme groupings arise from the cross-case analysis that informs the findings of this study. The key findings are best understood as problems that each organization must resolve in order to sustain its operation. The influences that shape the organization's response to each problem provide a basis for understanding the operational dynamics of each institution. The support and explanations for these findings provide an integrated response to the question of how virtual postsecondary education organizations operate in relation to values, products/services and organizational purpose. The issue of organizational success factors is addressed in a separate section of this chapter.

Problem One: Matching Market Opportunities to Organizational Capacity

The first major operational concern of virtual postsecondary educational organizations is their ability to match opportunities present in its environment with the capacity (e.g., instructional content) that the organization possesses or may possess by engaging in partnerships (e.g., outsourcing). Several key themes emerge that reveal the major influences that shape how these organizations solve such a problem.

The analysis suggests that organizations may be differentiated in their ability to match market opportunities to organizational capacity according to their competence in identifying a market for their educational products and understanding the needs of learners in those markets. Two principal factors influence an organization's ability to do this: First, the historical purpose or mission of the organization can create barriers as well as incentives to develop specific markets. The degree to which an organization has the flexibility to reshape its purpose, as in the case of CECC's discussion of an alliance with a four-year institution, will influence its definition of market. The purpose will also help to determine how aggressively the organization pursues information about who comprises its market, who are its significant competitors, and find answers to similar market oriented questions. For example, contrast the flexibility that NTU possesses in pursuing market opportunities, as compared with UNET whose purpose tends to limit how assertive it can be in the marketplace. Understanding of the market is often linked to a more developed market research function (though this may not always suggest better quality information). Organizations do vary in the importance they place on their marketing function.

Second, an organization's ability to understand its market may be influenced by the strength of ties to organizations or groups whose expertise can be used to shape particular product lines (e.g., degree or certificate programs). Organizations vary in their relationships with corporate entities, associations and other communities of learners. The variance in relationships based on trust, previous social contact or desired approval from these groups can shape the target market and associated products. As DiMaggio's (1992) study of the Museum of Modern Art (MOMA) found, organizers' proximity to external individuals in the social network based on past experiences was influential in providing information and reliability about potential new relationships. Consider, however, that the organizations in this study lack the longevity and history of an organization like MOMA with its network of more elaborate and diverse social ties. In more experimental organizations such as these, the network of social contacts that managers bring to their positions are likely to play a larger role (at least initially) than any that are newly constructed. In addition, organizations with short histories have not laid the groundwork of institutional attachment that an older organization may have. For instance, respect and support of an organization like MOMA is likely to continue even when senior leaders change, while support may be much more fragile for organizations with shorter histories and less "institutional relationship capital" to draw upon. This may be mediated to some degree by affiliation with larger institutional entities as in the cases of CMIL or World Campus where ties to external social entities are likely to be more long-standing.

Three mediating factors appear to influence an organization's ability to link market opportunities to organizational capacity. To a greater or lesser extent, an individual or individuals who championed the organization's cause affected each organization. The advocate can play a very important role in identifying particular educational services that should be developed, developing contacts in the organization's environment and conveying the importance of a particular set of educational products and services to persons within the organization. These leaders typically sought to lead their organizations in significant transformational changes (Burns, 1978). Indeed most are still in the midst of realizing those changes. The cultural shift embodied in significant change initiatives for organizations within very traditional instructional environments can be frustrating. The organizational champion can become a focal point for critics who see this leader and his or her cause as inseparable. Recall how personalized the exchanges became between administrative leaders and faculty leaders during the attempts to develop a virtual university in Maine.

A second factor is the degree to which the features of the instructional technology system, often put in place at the organization's founding, match the expectations of the market and the expectations of those within the organization. Learners may come to value features such as interactivity or the latest, most innovative technologies that come to be viewed as efficacious, but may not correspond to the current internal capacity of the technology system. For example, instructional television and satellite delivery methods used by UNET and NTU tend to downplay some aspects of immediate interactivity between student and instructor and among students. The choices these two organizations have made differed: UNET has begun to migrate their technology by advancing Web development in order to serve their campus units and consider new markets for students; NTU has sought new markets using variations of the same technology, but delivering it to users in different ways such as through their home computers. The match can also be influenced by the behavioral attachments that support staff develop about the effectiveness of the technology. Some can become advocates for a particular delivery system, which can slow the development of new technologies. This finding is consistent with Orlikowski's (1992) view of technology as continually socially and physically constructed. In this sense, technology has a socially transforming quality as personal attachments to delivery systems shape the administrative patterns of the organization, which in turn reinforce particular structures and procedures around the technology. For instance, I had a long conversation with a staff member of UNET who explained that he saw little reason to change from the current microwave system to asynchronous transfer mode technology since the current technology could handle any task that new instructional systems would present. He developed comprehensive reports showing the performance of the older technology and was proud of how dedicated his technicians were in keeping the older system up and running. He felt that there was much more capacity to be gotten out of the older system if someone would listen to his case.

The final mediating factor is the degree to which market information and information concerning internal capacity pass through a more or less elaborate vetting process. In other words, how formal is the decision making structure for linking external and internal information and how inclusive or centralized is this process? Differences in formality and centrality may inhibit or facilitate a beneficial match. Matching information through the vetting process is complicated in some contexts, like that of World Campus, since decisions made at the top may be based on different expectations that are actually present in campus units. As several studies have found (e.g., Arrow, 1974; Blau and Scott, 1962; Vroom, 1969; Williamson, 1975), effectiveness of decision making structures vary in accordance with the complexity of the information processing task. For organizations such as these that are often still investigating the most effective ways of vetting information, information processing tasks may vary by program or project and need to be adjusted frequently. This suggests that more elaborate vetting processes may correspond to more elaborate information processing needs within the organization. As the complexity of the information processing task rises or falls with a particular project, vetting may need to be contracted or expanded through adjustments in more or less formal or centralized decision making processes.

Three key factors influence an organization's understanding of its organizational capacity and ability to mobilize that capacity to meet the market opportunities. The first influence is the extent to which the organization (here meaning both partners in a stable network form and units in an internal network form) is seeking to generate revenue as a priority. Organizations differ in their willingness to develop products intended to generate the greatest return on investment or rather to see educational products and services as meeting an obligation to a particular audience and achieve a reasonable profit. Clearly, every organization is concerned about generating sufficient revenue, but organizations will differ in regard to its importance. Consider how this point may change even within one organization over time as in the case of NTU, which has moved to a for-profit status for some aspects of its operation. The conflict that may result within the organization over the question of how much revenue is sufficient can impair an organization's ability to match markets with internal capacity. The notion of revenue in a few of these organizations raised fundamental questions over who the academic enterprise was meant to serve, especially in more traditional environments such as Penn State or UNET.

A second factor is the organization's ability to understand the pressures and demands placed on its content providers and then develop specific responses (seen in the design phase) to overcome those pressures and demands. Since content is usually seen as the most important organizational resource, the ability to fold content providers expertise with market demands is essential. In the vetting process, a content providers status, motivations, and ability to meet deadlines often surface as significant issues that must be balanced against the potential rewards in the market. Often this may entail discovering the particular cultural aspects of the academic discipline (Birnbaum, 1988). The cultural aspect is highly significant since receptiveness to technology or belief in a market orientation may differ by not only by content provider, but also by discipline. Conversely, the market may also dictate how saleable the content of a specific discipline may be, despite the amenability of a particular content provider to prepare a course or program.

A third factor is the extent to which the organization is perceived to be a source of competition for other units or content suppliers. Often, since these organizations were constituted to be change agents within a system or campus structure and develop new educational products and services, they may be perceived as intruding on another unit's market. The examples of this vary by organization depending upon such factors as the structural arrangement, cultural expectations or level of trust between the units. At CMIL, historical arrangements between Extension units limit effective partnering, which can make new initiatives that cross geographic boundaries seem threatening. At NTU, Engineering departments from various institutions may choose to partner with NTU or not based on how advantageous they find the arrangement to be compared with offering their own courses without NTU. Certain departments will not partner with NTU because they are convinced that the quality of their offerings and ability to go it alone will generate greater rewards and enrollments. The degree to which this results in cool relations with some content providers can undermine development of organizational capacity and ultimately, reduce the chance of matching market opportunities.

Problem Two: Designing Systems that Connect Market Opportunities to Organizational Capacity

Once the issue of matching markets and capacity has been solved, the next major operational concern of virtual postsecondary educational organizations pertains to how these organizations design systems that allow them to sense and interpret their markets and structure functional areas to produce their educational products.

The first key dimension influencing design considerations for the system is the degree to which organizations are embedded within existing structures. Stand-alone operations, periphery and utility units carry with them intrinsic structural codes that convey appropriate communication flows and control relationships. The original placement of the organization within the larger organizing structure and founding technology systems have a direct influence on design structures available to solve the market—organizational capacity matching problem. For example, the structural placement of CECC as a systemwide institution conveys a different level of importance (and impartiality) than if the institution were under the governance of just one of the system's community colleges. This may imply that key elements of the structure of these organizations are determined early in their histories and are not easily changed (Stinchcombe, 1965). Matkin (1997) addresses the issue of organizational placement in his study of continuing education and technology transfer activities. He found that the organization's position relative to the university core provides distinct advantages and weaknesses depending upon such dynamics as faculty role, degree of control, degree of buffering, integration with partners and the community and internal factors related to the organization's capacity to perform critical organizational functions. For several of these organizations proximity to the core of their larger organizing structure provides important recognition that what they do is important to the entire campus or system community. However, as Matkin rightly points out, organizations that are too closely managed by the core of the institution may have difficulty building effective relationships with external constituencies.

A second factor influencing the design problem of these organizations is the degree to which financial aid and accreditation policies are viewed as important to the organization. Federal student aid policies that prevent financial aid disbursements to students attending institutions in which distance learning enrollments exceed 50% limit some of these institutions in their ability to design educational systems. CECC, for instance, must affiliate its associate's degree programs with particular institutions since students will not receive financial aid if the degree is offered under the auspices of CECC alone. Similarly, expectations of accrediting agencies can shape product development processes that may have very little in common with approaches that are most effective for meeting market demands for rapidly evolving technology-based products. For example, most institutions must use traditional measures of class hours and seat time to categorize their products, although this is beginning to change with the advent of competency based systems such as those being introduced by Western Governors University. On the other hand, organizations will vary as to the importance they place on seeking accreditation or financial aid policies that are based on the belief that operating in accordance with such policies grants them more credibility or opens potential learner markets. This finding is in agreement with the position of some institutional theorists (e.g., DiMaggio and Powell, 1989; Meyer and Rowen, 1977; Scott, 1992) who recognize the role of external organizations and cultural expectations in creating structural organizational changes in the focal organization. The organizations in this study appear to be influenced differentially by both coercive and mimetic isomorphic forces. Coercive forces are found in the form of accreditation standards and financial aid policies. Mimetic forces appear to the degree that specific organizations internalize organizational models and systems found in other organizations within their environment. The age of the organization and willingness to create nontraditional educational structures works differently in each organization. Consider for example NTU's strong adherence to the academic department structure, yet willingness to employ a sales force to enhance its market presence. This organization needs the support of accreditors, yet understands that it must match the sophistication of training organizations in its marketing strategies.

The third influence is the autonomy and discretion that leaders posses to design a system that reflects or differs from the values expressed by particular constituents. For example, academic community values, corporate client values and individual learner values may at times be conflicting. At CMIL, the expectations of the Sloan Foundation for creating asynchronous learning courses were not always clearly understood by faculty committees whose role it was to approve the courses that CMIL would offer. Finding a balance among these interests can influence system design and perceptions of the success of the system in meeting learner needs effectively, particularly in areas where rapid prototyping and distribution is important for making popular topic areas available in a timely way.

A fourth factor influencing design is the degree to which external relationships come to be incorporated within the system's functional areas and their degree of importance to the operation. The differences may lie in an organization's decision to manage a series of outsourced relationships as opposed to directly managing the process or task. For some of these organizations this is a choice, while others are constrained by the practices of a larger organizing structure. Mowshowitz (1997) has used the term "metamanagement" to denote the way in which virtual organizations are managed, which may help to explain the distinction made here. The incorporation of external relationships differs somewhat from its application to the matching problem in that the influence of relationships in the design phase can directly affect processes as partnerships are built into the system. A rational-actor approach would suggest that managers select partners based upon their ability to contribute to the operation in a way that is far superior to other potential partners. In this view, partners are screened and then the best partner is selected based on the focal organization's ability to control the relationship to its benefit. This is the view adopted by Mowshowitz (1994, 1997), particularly in regard to his explanation of switching—the dynamic assignment of available services to requests for services in virtual organizations. This view implies that knowledge products are commodities that may be developed most efficiently by effective switching (Chellappa, Barua, and Whinston, 1997). Manager actions and resulting systems observed in this study appeared to be much less rational than the switching concept would imply. For those organizations that do include partners in their systems, geographic proximity, past relations and experiences based on trust are the principal drivers. For CECC, an organization that believes in the commodifying of knowledge and uses extensive outsourcing, limited funding and the opportunity to create co-ventures with Denver area firms were the most important considerations. Various studies and observations of for-profit organizations attest to the presence of trust or good relations as a context for relationships in network organizations (see for example, Dore, 1983; Handy, 1995; Perrow, 1993; Powell, 1990). However, since most of these organizations do not operate in a for-profit mode, the suggestion is that they may in fact value similar modes of operation as network organizations in the for-profit arena.

The next influence on design is the technology system that the organization selects to solve the matching problem. As has been discussed, legacy technology systems can influence the matching process. However, in the design phase, information technology has a more limited operational focus. Systems selected to deliver the technology are often done so because they are believed to enhance student learning. For instance, the World Campus intends to use several types of instructional delivery systems to provide the most appropriate learning tools. However, in meeting this worthy objective, managers can unknowingly design systems that need greater levels of technical support or focus much more of the technology management aspect of the instructional process than on the student. For example, consider the differences in responsibility that a student would encounter at UNET when a malfunction occurs in a classroom-based instructional television course versus a Web-based course. In each case, the system that has been designed (intentionally or as a result of existing technology) is based on a solution to the matching problem; but when malfunctions in the system take place, the learner feels substantially different burdens. The selection of the operational technology is typically also a large portion of the costs associated with designing the system. Because of the cost issue, organizations can differ markedly in their ability to update technology and reconsider the design problem in a timely manner.

Problem Three: Managing the System

The third major functional consideration of virtual postsecondary educational organizations is the manner in which organizational leaders control and stabilize the system that they have designed and foster new innovations from that system.

Control and stability came to be seen as central tasks of managers in administrating the system. These had several nuances. First, and perhaps most centrally, the course and program development process and managers' ability to control aspects of the process were critical influences for solving the management problem. The means by which control was exercised by managers varied. For example, CMIL and NTU used contractual measures to ensure that outsourced partners would meet their obligations, while World Campus and UNET simply kept key functions internal to the organization for control purposes. Because of actors' power within the system varied and historical policies varied as well, managers were constantly in a position of balancing competing interests. Emerson (1962) described power as relational, situational and rhetorical—a function of social relation, locale and articulation, not merely individual qualities. These classifications may provide some perspective on variability in power relations in these organizations as managers move between internal and external contexts and experience differential power relationships. For example, leaders of CECC benefited from an historical policy of curriculum standardization to control the make up of courses entering the system, while simultaneously exercised little control over how quickly a content provider (faculty member) developed a course. The influence of powerful actors (relative to the manager) and historical policies were also critical for shaping other components of the managing solution. The degree of acceptance of non-organic models, such as outsourcing of functions or switching between function providers, shaped managers' alternatives. Consider the decision by World Campus to keep critical functions in-house after examining potential outsourcing partners when it was determined that the campus community would not respond well to outsourcing. Another factor related to control and stability within these organizations concerned the approach used by managers to reduce environmental uncertainty. Managers used different approaches in rationalizing the system that they had designed. While not mutually exclusive, some organizations like NTU and CECC tended to stress external relationship building (e.g., with clients, potential functional partners, advisors) as opposed to internal relationship building (e.g., convincing academic units to develop distance learning courses) as their principal strategy for rationalizing the system, as was the case with the other institutions in this study.

In managing the system, these organizations were influenced to a large degree by the role of an organizational champion. In every organization, a key leader was evident who sustained the momentum of the organization and encouraged innovation. To varying degrees, aspects of the management problem were addressed by a concern about innovation under varied degrees of operational choice. Managing the system often was seen as a process of continuously finding new ways to innovate in order to stay ahead of the competition, build internal relations, serve students more effectively, serve new markets of learners, or react to campus needs. For example, CECC is structured in a way that permits the organization's managers to create alliances without having to follow many formal procedures. This finding shows affinity to the organizational types advanced by Hrebiniak and Joyce (1985) in their explanation of autonomy and innovation under conditions of high and low determinism and choice. Their integration of strategic choice and environmental determinism may help to describe variances in managerial action in these organizations in accordance with managers' understanding of perceived external and internal constraints and available strategic choices. Determinism and choice can vary in these organizations in relation to an organization's purpose and goals. At UNET, service to campus units creates conditions of constrained choice and greater determinism. UNET must respond to the campuses as individual entities that possess varied demands and expectations, which may limit the organization's ability to develop economies of scale or common processes. At NTU, managers exercise greater choice often because technological innovation and leadership in engineering education are ingrained organizational purposes. For each of these organizations, innovation was often reified in the use of new instructional technologies, which were viewed as a tangible sign of improvement.

Another factor gleaned from the analysis was that managers varied in their ability to innovate based on their facility in learning from their alliances and partnerships—the learning "coat-tails" effect. That is, organizations came to approach managing the system and redesigning the system (over time), by learning from the expertise (or limitations) of their alliance partners. CMIL, for instance, was able to gain knowledge of course templates from their relationship with AOL. This association provided CMIL with the knowledge necessary to construct their own version of course templates that are used in their second generation online courses. This finding is consistent with the work of network scholars who contend that network forms of organizing "foster learning because they preserve greater diversity of search routines than hierarchies and they convey richer, more complex information than the market" (Podolny and Page, 1998, p. 62). For the organizations in this study with stable network forms, the opportunities for organizational learning may be more frequent since they are likely to exhibit more unfamiliar practices through their relationships.

Finally, organizations differed in their approach to collaboration. The role of collaboration influenced solution of the management problem by causing managers to frame collaboration as an efficiency seeking approach or a change-agent strategy—at times concurrently. For CECC, collaboration was used to both acquire the resources necessary to operate (since its allocation was insufficient to function at full capacity) and also to link the organizational capacity of the community colleges within the System. Collaboration, therefore, had an external as well as internal focus. The manner in which the desire for collaboration by the focal organization was perceived by external and internal units tended to affect levels of intraorganizational competition, highlight variances and similarities in organizational values, influence grant funding and, as previously stated, influence organizational learning. Collaboration between NTU and its partner institutions tended to align the values of each organization around a single focus -the learner of the sponsoring firm. However, alliances with corporations tended to sharpen the distinctions over values and service within World Campus. These differences may be attributed to how collaboration was nurtured and the underlying reasons behind the collaboration. The differences in collaborative response in these organizations may be linked to collaboration as an operational necessity. As organizations realize how important collaboration is to their success, they try to create conditions that emphasize mutual benefit to each partner. Given the distinctions in organizational maturity, those organizations with more experience in finding common ground or understanding the types of partners that are most advantageous may derive the most value.

Problem Four: Establishing Legitimacy of the System and its Products

The final operational dimension of virtual postsecondary educational organizations involves the organization's ability to create educational products that are valued and credible to learners (external constituency) and also the degree to which a system designed by the organization is viewed as legitimate by external and internal constituencies. The legitimacy dimension interacts with the management dimension to the degree that developing credibility is important for fostering innovation or minimizing uncertainty. Similarly, the management dimension influences the legitimacy dimension to the degree that managers' actions are assessed to be motivated by a need to gain credibility. This distinction is made in order to provide greater conceptual clarity.

The analysis suggests that organizations are most influenced by three factors in their ability to create legitimacy for their products. First, legitimacy is influenced by the distinctiveness of the organization's educational products in the marketplace as projected through its marketing. Distinctiveness is used here to denote quality within a specific context. For example, each of these organizations varies in terms of the status of their courses and offerings. The status of a Penn State program or UC—Extension program differs from that of CECC, for example. Quality in this sense is niche dependent. CECC has distinctiveness within the community college market, but little quite naturally in the professional graduate certificate market. Distinctiveness is often a difficult influence to assess, since the market for distance learning educational products and services is emerging. Many managers spoke of their "brand" by using terms that learners might consider to evaluate the product. These included such characteristics as convenience, accessibility, quality, interactivity, learner financial return and cultural growth. For organizations operating within an emerging market and industry such as these, brand distinctions suggest that comparable product substitutes may not exist in this early stage. First to market advantage that several of these firms enjoy may in fact translate into brand distinctiveness that makes them leaders in their respective market niches.

Second, legitimacy of the product was influenced by the institution's system of organizing. For example, a stable network form like NTU or CECC relies on multiple content providers. World Campus relies on one—itself—and has a well recognized brand in the Penn State University name. Yet, interestingly, all of the organizations in the study were concerned about the distinctiveness of their products in the marketplace. One possible explanation is that the product may become more or less distinctive (and potentially viewed as more credible initially by learners) by virtue of the focal organization's ties to higher status entities—the legitimizing "coat-tails" effect. The structures that the higher status unit may put in place such as course approval processes may be considered somewhat bureaucratic, however. CMIL is a clear example. Several studies conducted in the for-profit arena (e.g., Baum and Oliver, 1992; Podolny and Phillips, 1996; Stuart et al., 1997) have found that legitimacy accrues to the focal organization by associating with a higher status entity.

Stuart et al. (1997) have shown however, that the advantages of such ties tend to diminish as the focal organization ages. For educational organizations with more pronounced institutional environments and less developed task environments, the association with higher status entities may signal a valuable strategy for conforming with symbolic norms and expectations in the environment—as NTU's alignment with traditional academic departments attests. But in addition to this, and building on my previous point, this potential status advantage is only valuable to the degree that the organization's marketing function exploits the status relationship by creating identifiable symbols about the relationship rather than simply identifying that the relationship exists. This may involve comparing and clearly demonstrating the advantages of the focal organization's educational products over a competitor's products (if one exists) in order to sharpen the distinction, which may open administrators to charges that they value financial return over collegiality. In each organization, it appears that marketing the advantages of the higher status relationship was an evolving process.

Third, levels of learner satisfaction influence the legitimacy of the products. This is obvious, but the point is made to bring attention to the fact that students convey legitimacy by enrolling in courses and are not likely to re-enroll if they are not satisfied with their learning experience. The speed of Internet development and other forms of media and the increasing presence of for-profit educational providers suggests that learners will have many avenues to pursue their educational goals. For the organizations in this study, the opportunity to attract new learners and retain others may be only a limited window of opportunity.

Influences on the legitimacy of the system are naturally related to the products it creates. However, three distinct factors emerged that influence the system's legitimacy. First, the legitimacy of the system is influenced by the degree to which the organization is seen as a competitor and an agent of change by other units. For several organizations, this has meant incorporating a strategy that emphasizes the system as a revenue stream for campus units. CECC, for example, has used this strategy effectively as a means of building partnerships with content providers at other institutions. Organizations that emphasize the innovations of their system can run the risk of being seen as illegitimate by organizations who operate within its larger organizing structure. These units may view the focal organization's system as a competitor to their own or become uncomfortable with the nature or pace of change. This was clearly at the heart of the UNET controversy as the virtual campus initiative was viewed to be a threat to faculty members at the system campuses.

A second and related factor, which can complicate the first, is the focal unit's relationship within a larger organizing structure. While a stand-alone institution like NTU is not concerned by this, the other organizations in the study were interested in assessing their relationship within the larger structure. Specifically, the place that the organization holds within the larger organizational structure conveys the perception that the organization is central or marginal to the larger organizational unit. By association, the system that the organization develops can be viewed as marginal since the focal organization is not a key player in the larger system. The importance of the World Campus within the larger Penn State campus would have been marginalized, for instance, if the unit not had the reporting structure and support from Penn State's President that it received. Third, external recognition conveys legitimacy. Interestingly, the key factors that can make legitimacy a concern in an internal organizational context may be viewed quite differently by external entities. The very system that is threatening or recognized as marginal to internal constituencies can be viewed by external associations and grant funders as highly legitimate since innovation or the desire to break away from more traditional structures is highly valued. Consider that CMIL (in conjunction with UC—Berkeley Extension) received a grant from the Sloan Foundation to develop asynchronous online courses. This opportunity actually brought much more scrutiny of the organization's courses from the Berkeley Faculty Senate when they were brought before that body for approval than had CMIL's previous independent study courses.

THE ADAPTATION CYCLE OF VIRTUAL POSTSECONDARY EDUCATIONAL ORGANIZATIONS

Differentiations in organization form and administrative patterns emphasized in the original operational framework (see Chapter 2) focus on the combined influences of extraorganizational, interorganizational and intraorganizational factors that shape management actions. The extent to which managers internalize these influences through their interactions with various internal and external organizational actors give rise to the differences found in organizational form and administrative patterns. The original framework suggested (implicitly) that the nature of influences exhibited in extra, inter, and intraorganizational conditions create forms and patterns that are somewhat static. The impression is that managers recognize forces that influence strategy or processes; organizational forms and patterns are established and become accepted practice. This was rarely the case. Clearly, the influence of environment (internal and external) upon organizational form and patterns evolves continuously, but at different rates and emphasizing somewhat different characteristics in each organization. The temporal dynamic of these organizations is simply not represented in the original framework.

The original framework, drawn from resource dependence theory, sees organizational managers as rational actors (Institutional theory is also used and is discussed separately in this chapter). The rational actor view assumes that managers not only make informed decisions based on an understanding of external and internal factors, but also that they possess the ability and willingness to carry out those decisions. In the resource dependence perspective, managers are active in searching for opportunities and threats within their environments in order to develop exchange relationships that will maximize the acquisition of necessary resources, while minimizing associated dependencies (Pfeffer and Salancik, 1978). It is assumed that actors will use several strategies (e.g., buffering, bridging, etc.) to lessen these dependencies. However, control in respect to external and internal entities in this study was revealed to de-emphasize the power to constrain or direct action. Control or agency may be better seen and understood as a function of social ties (e.g., geographic proximity of entities, historical relations, realization of mutual benefit, trust) that shape managers' decision making about organizational form and patterns. Ties connect actors through one or more relations, described in such ways as information sharing, social interaction or attendance at the same meeting or conference (Garton, Haythornthwaite and Wellman, 1997). A new framework might incorporate a view that understands actors in terms of what DiMaggio (1992) has called the "practical-actor conception of action" (p. 138), which emphasizes the ongoing choices made, often unknowingly, within existing social and relational structures.

The original framework also included factors derived from institutional theory. Institutional theory indicates that rationalized myths created by complex social networks, collective organization within the environment and the leadership of local organizations become embedded within organizations in order to gain legitimacy, define the value of structural elements and maintain organizational stability (Meyer and Rowen, 1977). Since postsecondary educational organizations are subject to laws and other social and cultural pressures for conformity, an understanding of the institutional environment was deemed critical in influencing manager actions and ultimately organizational form and administrative patterns. Using this perspective, actors come to believe in the rational value of certain myths, although these myths may not be objectively verified. The findings indicate that these organizations vary in their isomorphism with environmental institutions in terms of how they respond to or are influenced by Federal policies, accreditation standards, and such myths as competition, collaboration, innovation, convenience and flexibility. These myths reinforce structures and shape relations internally and externally. In particular, acceptance of myths intended to create legitimacy find their way into how organizational actors mold the organizational system and select and present educational products to potential customers.

CONTRIBUTIONS TO THE LITERATURE OF HIGHER EDUCATION AND ORGANIZATIONAL BEHAVIOR

By synthesizing the findings of this study with both supporting and disconfirming literature about those findings, a novel conceptual framework emerges that refines the original operational framework and makes a unique contribution to higher education and organizational behavior literatures. The new framework (see Figure 9.1) is consistent with observations made by Miles and Snow (1978) and Miles, Snow, Meyer and Coleman (1978) concerning the adaptive cycle of organizations. However, the model advanced here differs from the assumptions of those scholars in several respects. First, since these organizations are embedded in an environmental context that emphasizes both a task (competitive) and institutional context, management action must incorporate considerable understanding of not only competitive pressures, but also pressures for conformity as well. Second, the network organizational form must be seen as a tool that may create a complex organizational dynamic capable of enhancing organizational learning and status, which was beyond the scope of earlier research on adaptation. Third, the role of the practical-actor in the solution of key adaptive problems is central to understanding differences in virtual postsecondary educational organizations. Since the pioneering work of these early adaptation scholars, much has been reinterpreted about the role of management action, especially in light of organizational sociology and network organizational forms, which inform our understanding of management action in relation to social networks in postsecondary education organizations. Finally, the factors influencing the structure of adaptive solutions (summarized in Table 9.1) suggest that the interplay of for and non-profit orientations in extant theory strengthens support for the factors advanced. However, caution must be exercised to the degree that applications of this framework beyond similar organizational types presented in this study will tend to degrade the generalizability of the adaptive framework.

Figure 9.1: The Adaptation Cycle of Virtual Postsecondary Educational Organizations

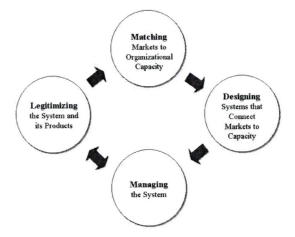

A Footnote: Success Through Understanding, Renewal and Relationships

The findings of this study suggest that successful organizations are those that possess a more textured understanding of their place within the market, their learners and their internal capacity. It seems that organizations that have more highly developed marketing research functions are better able to understand the market and the place of the organization's products within it. The degree to which organizations can create educational experiences that integrate new information on what the learner wants and incorporate experts' views as to what the learner needs may separate the successful from the less successful organization. As the study has revealed, the denser the relationships (and potentially more diverse) the focal organization has with entities within its environment, the more effective it may be in understanding the market and its options in designing effective systems. Denser is used here to mean not only more relationships, but also deeper relationships in terms of their social and trust engendering qualities. Such relationships have been shown to lead to enhanced revenue gathering potential (e.g., grants).

Those organizations that have the greater chance for success are also more likely to create systems that provide understanding about the value of their organization in juxtaposition with organizations offering similar products. Brand and reputation are starting points, but real understanding is likely to be found by demonstrating the benefits of an organization's educational products six or twelve months after the completion of a course, for example. Those organiza-

Table 9.1: Factors Influencing Adaptive Problem Solving

Problem 1: Matching	Problem 2: Designing	Problem 3: Managing	Problem 4: Legitimizing
Identify market and understand needs of learner	Embeddedness within existing structures	Control of course/program development process	*PRODUCT*
Role of organizational champion	Importance of financial aid and accreditation policies	Power differentials vis-à-vis managers	Distinctiveness of product
Founding technology system	Leader discretion/autonomy	Historical policies	System of organizing
Elaboration of vetting process	Degree to which external relationships play functional role	Approach to reducing environmental uncertainty (internal vs. external)	Ties to higher status organization (coat-tails effect–legitimizing)
Orientation to revenue	Technology type selected	Role of organizational champion	Marketing exploitation of status
Understanding of content providors		Innovation orientation (coat-tails effect–learning)	Learner satisfaction
Focal organization's image as a competitor		Approach to collaboration (efficiency, change agent)	*SYSTEM*
			Approach to collaboration (competitor, agent of change)
			Location in larger organizational system
			External recognition

tions with the most elaborate feedback systems for understanding and incorporating this information into products will be most successful and quite likely, more legitimate in the estimation of their learners. An understanding of internal capacity, management choices and system design options appears to be highly influenced by the organization's historical associations, policies and past decisions. Gaining understanding in this context can be highly politicized, arbitrary or subject to the personal qualities (positive or negative) that internal actors attach to the organization's leaders. It is obvious that organizations embedded in structures in which understanding is constrained or poorly appreciated are likely to be less successful in a Knowledge Industry context. It would seem that organizations that can de-emphasize the influence of internal actors in the system (without a debilitating of loss of legitimacy) might achieve greater success.

A useful perspective for shedding light on the nature of understanding in these organizations may be to consider them as information processing systems (Galbraith, 1977) or interpretation systems (Daft and Weick, 1984). These perspectives may provide an organizing structure to delineate managers' actions in these organizations and how the influence of previous experiences enhances or constrains an organization's ability to use information (understand) effectively. Additional research is also needed to discern how an organization's information environment (as distinct from task and institutional) influences virtual postsecondary educational organizations and how these organization types respond to their environments based on such factors as the information load, complexity and turbulence of environmental information (Huber and Daft, 1987).

The ability to renew the system by effectively solving (and continuing to solve) adaptation cycle problems will also divide the successful from the less successful organizations. Renewal is used here to denote the ongoing cycle of adaptation that an organization experiences. Those organizations that are able to put understanding into practice will have the greater advantage in renewal. This issue has two components: a temporal component—how quickly should the cycle be renewed; and a learning component—how effectively did we incorporate the knowledge that we understand to be beneficial. Organizations that are able to maximize learning opportunities provided by associations with partners who have something to teach them will gain an advantage—the learning coattails effect. This assumes that the focal organization must possess some form of internal monitoring or evaluative process to achieve this. Those organizations that are able to do this more efficiently (which may not mean faster) than their competitors have an added advantage.

In theory, the more dynamic the system for matching market opportunities to organizational capacity in the form of switching or outsourcing, for example, the greater the likelihood of finding a match. However, there is a caveat, which draws on a distinction made by Leana and Rousseau (in press). These authors argue that organizations may lose the benefits accrued by outsourcing when knowledge that is contained in the relationship (e.g., firm-specific cultural knowledge) is lost by switching to a new partner. Organizations that are able to differentiate favorable or less favorable instances to switch or outsource will benefit. This may have a differential influence on stable organization forms that rely more heavily on outsourcing, thus creating more risk in the renewal process.

The final perspective on success has been touched on previously, but deserves more treatment. The findings suggest that relationship building in each of these organizations is important. Effective relationships can provide information on and access to markets, offer system design possibilities, convey legitimacy, provide learning opportunities, generate revenue sources and influence product selection and development choices. What defines the successful organization from the less successful, especially over time? The work of Krackhardt (1992) may provide some insight. He argues that strong ties, relationships in which two parties share interaction opportunities, affection and a history of interaction, are more likely to provide a sense of trust that may help people to overcome resistance to change or environmental uncertainty. Weaker ties provide access to information, but not that extra willingness needed to provide help to another. Krackhardt's suggestion goes beyond the notion of mutual benefit or relationship building merely for the purposes of control. Rather, effective relationships, whether intraorganizational or interorganizational, are those in which the pretext of a relationship is trust and perhaps not solely a business dealing. Organizational success may in fact be sustained by those managers, whether internal or external, who understand the importance of creating interaction opportunities, situations to foster genuine understanding, and the realization that trust needs time to take root.

CHAPTER 10

Implications for the Knowledge Industry/Sector

Knowledge seems like kind of a shaky industry . . .

> \- Bruce Vermazen
> Chair, Philosophy Department
> UC- Berkeley

I BEGAN THIS STUDY BY SUGGESTING THAT PETERSON AND DILL'S (1997) application of Porter's model of forces driving industry competition is an effective conceptual approach for understanding changes taking place in postsecondary education and beyond. It is from this model that competition as an ethic for reconsidering organizational form and administrative processes is at its most influential. The specter of competition may convince institutions that are considering virtual delivery and virtual organization that competing effectively is the guiding principle for success in an industry based on the convenience, accessibility, ubiquity and applicability of knowledge. The economic underpinnings of this approach may be troubling to some, indeed the implication is that information (and knowledge by association) is a commodity that can be bought and sold. A potential refinement that emerges from this study involves the use of an industry perspective to explain the environmental context of these organizations. An alternative perspective, which may be useful for examining the practical implications of this research, is to expand the industry dimension to consider what Scott and Meyer (1991) have called a sector. The sector approach builds on the economic perspective by moving beyond designation of a group of organizations that offer substitute products to include organizations with which a focal organization relates, often surfacing organizations that are embedded within other organizations or those whose functions are diversified. Such a reconceptualization may shift the discussion from one focused upon economics and the task environment of organizations to one that also considers institutional aspects of an organization's environment. My hope in studying these organizations has been to neither fan the fires of criticism nor unduly extol their virtues, but rather to offer, as a good pragmatist might, a summary of the lessons that might be learned if one pays careful attention to these organizations and their differences.

In the next segment of this chapter I will attempt to portray the findings of this study in a practical perspective by suggesting points for effective administration of these organizations and discussing potential implications for key actors comprising the Knowledge Industry/Sector. I will conclude by offering some thoughts about the potential limitations of this study, while also presenting several ideas for future research on virtual postsecondary educational organizations.

VIRTUAL POSTSECONDARY EDUCATIONAL ORGANIZATIONS: CHANGING THE RULES OF THE GAME

Researchers and practitioners who use the adaptation model to understand how virtual postsecondary educational organizations function are likely to view the task of organizing as an ongoing endeavor that is influenced by constant changes in relationships, market forces, internal capacity, power differentials, organizational learning and status enhancing alliances. However, the task of organizing is at the same time an endeavor that is influenced by an institution's historical roots such as inherited structures and policies, founding technology systems, and the organization's position within a larger organizing system. The key administrative recommendations offered in the next section of this chapter confirm the push and pull of constant change and the press of competitive forces. The recommendations affirm the experimental nature of these organization types and reinforce their importance in the context of an emerging industry that has yet to establish rules of leadership. These findings are intended for leaders from traditional colleges and universities as well as other postsecondary education institutions who are considering or currently managing virtual postsecondary educational organizations.

The Unsettled Organization

Virtual postsecondary educational organizations may be interesting places to work, but they are not necessarily comfortable places to work. Because the adaptation process can occur at multiple levels within the organization, it is possible that various subunits of an organization can be at different stages depending upon the project in which organization members are engaged. For example, as shifts in the market or changes in organizational capacity cause the two to fall out of alignment, a new cycle of organizational adaptation begins that may unsettle previous policies or work processes. Organization members need to understand that virtual postsecondary educational organizations are rarely in states of equilibrium if they are functioning optimally. The unsettled and ambiguous state is a natural, rather than unnatural condition. Small changes needed to realign internal capacity with external requirements and expectations call for leaders to create new positions, refine work processes, test new technologies, make new alliances, etc. with regularity.

Creation of the Organization Happens from the Top-Down, but Cues for Refinements in the Organization Flow from the Bottom-Up

The organizational histories of the institutions in this study attest to the fact that senior level organizational champions were the primary forces behind the creation of these organizations. The vision and founding characteristics stressed by key individuals have left significant impressions on each organization. As the organization grows, operational level changes become increasingly more important. The inability of a key content provider to get a course finished in time, for example, has significant ripple effects throughout the organization. Refinements in process and practice flow from the operational level, which are closest to the learner, instructor or front-line support person. Often necessary operational refinements cannot be anticipated from the top-down. Organizations that can effectively communicate operational level information to key decision makers will outperform those that do not.

Redefined Macro and Micro-level Boundaries

Unlike their traditional higher education counterparts, virtual postsecondary educational organizations offer educational products that do not fit neatly into regional distinctions that often guide marketing and enrollment management decision making. Remotely delivered educational products in these organizations may draw students from across the United States and abroad. The service mission of an institution like CECC extends the "community" of community college beyond local confines. Thus, these organizations are likely to be seen as sources of competition by other institutions with which they may be allied. Similarly, because markets can evolve with the sophistication and reach of the organization's delivery technology, new competitors are not easy to identify.

In micro-level work processes, boundary distinctions are also redefined. The team-oriented approach to curriculum development that many of these organizations employ can break down distinctions over status and intellectual property ownership. Instructor, content developer, program manager, instructional developer and numerous others share in the creation of the educational product. As such, a course shifts from purely the instructor's domain to a team of individuals with different views of the process. Making explicit the terms of the development team's relationships can ease conflict and improve the process.

Look to Partnerships and Alliances for New Ideas and Added Credibility

For each virtual postsecondary educational organization in this study, partnerships played a significant but varied role in their operation. Partnerships played essential functional roles at NTU and CECC since outsourcing relationships were central to their operational model. External relationships offer for some organizations an opportunity to develop new expertise that is critical to improving products and processes. Key alliances also help to develop and define product markets and products, so that these organizations are able to benefit from the credibility of partner associations. Internal alliances are also beneficial. Affiliation with "brand name" institutions, in the case of World Campus and CMIL, brought additional credibility to the educational products each organization developed. Effective organizations see partnerships as portals to new information and enhanced legitimacy.

Select Different Change Drivers depending upon the Organizational Structure in Use

The selection of internal as opposed to stable network forms drives the strategy for changes that virtual postsecondary educational organizations may employ. For organizations choosing internal network forms, change is initiated by improving their internal processes to better align market opportunities with organizational capacity. This may mean developing extensive process maps, for example, as a way to drive efficiency into internal processes. Organizations that choose a stable network structure will rely on strategy improvements to align markets with organizational capacity. These organizations tend to emphasize improvements in external linkages with partners or customers as the principal means of driving change within their organization. While organizations in this study used both approaches, most seemed to focus on one or the other to facilitate change.

The More Innovative the Organization Becomes Structurally, Potentially, the Less Distinct its Identity Will Be in the Marketplace

This point seems paradoxical since innovation should bring organizational distinction. However, for these organizations the more innovative the organizational structures (e.g., the development of stable network forms) the less distinctive the focal organization can become in the estimation of the learner. Consider NTU, a stable network organization that relies on alliances with top engineering schools to provide its content. While the learner may readily recognize all or most of its member institutions, the NTU name is often not distinctive outside of some engineering circles. The distinction that should come from association with top-flight schools and the accompanying enrollments one might expect for access to a mix of such advanced courses may be supplanted when the focal organization is of lower status than its functional parts. This may be overcome by marketing that conveys the specific advantages that a blend of institutions offers, rather than promoting the fact that such alliances exist. Learners are likely to be attracted to the short and long term educational and career advantages that such an alliance can demonstrate.

Organizations Must Create New Markets rather than Relying upon Shifts from Other Types of Enrollments

As an administrator at CMIL noted, their goal is not to transfer an independent study student to an online program, but rather they need to attract new students to online offerings. The revenue models of these organizations necessitate new enrollments to cover the costs of program development. Several of the organizations in this study are active in exploring the potential of international student markets, corporate initiatives and new product models. These approaches often lead them into uncharted waters, which requires the staff to develop new organizational expertise and understanding of the learners they will serve.

Content is the Most Critical Resource—Content Providers Hold the Key

Since the principal role of these organization types is to deliver instruction, the content that is delivered is of critical importance. Matching the expectations of learners while ensuring suitable organizational capacity to deliver education usually revolves around the availability of high quality content. Organizations that contract with content providers through an outsourcing arrangement may have more flexibility in this regard. However, outsourcing content is often unacceptable in many organizations because the highest quality or most sought after content providers are already within the system. How an organization manages its content may call for revisions in organizational policies regarding release time and payment of content providers. It may also demand more flexibility in bringing new content providers into the system in order to meet the expectations of the market. Any revisions in content provider policies must include parallel changes in processes that verify the content to be of a high quality.

Consider Different Product Management Strategies Depending upon the Audience You Are Trying To Reach

Organizations in this study tended to focus primarily on products and services for specific markets (such as certificate programs or specialized degree programs) or broader products (such as associate's or bachelor's degrees). The product management strategy differed significantly based on the distinction in market. For example, recognition of academic reputation in their products is very important in those organizations that create niche products. Niche product organizations tend to have more complex quality checks (even to be point of being bureaucratic). However for those organizations with a broader market product strategy, recognition of convenience in their products was very important. These organizations tended to have less complex quality screening procedures. For virtual postsecondary educational organizations the converse may also be true, organizations with strong reputation orientations should decide to develop niche market products, while organizations with strong convenience orientations should choose to develop broader market products.

Success Can Be Achieved without the Latest Technology, but an Organization Must Work Hard to Know Learners' and Instructors' Needs and Understand when the Technology in Use Is No Longer Sufficient for Effective Instruction within its Market

Few of the organizations in this study believed that a single technology-mediated instructional delivery model would allow them to compete effectively in the market for very long. Considerations were first and foremost on delivering effective instruction. This does not mean that they were constantly employing the latest technologies, however. Organizations can achieve success so long as learning outcomes are being met to the satisfaction of learner and instructor. This means that organizations must listen closely to their learners and their instructors to monitor the effectiveness of their courses. Nonetheless, virtual postsecondary educational organization leaders must also be watchful for changes in their market. In an emergent industry with few brand leaders, learners may have come to value particular technologies over another when content and price are relatively equal considerations.

Because of Technology-Mediated Delivery, Learners' Expectations about Technology-Mediated Administration Will Be Raised

Student services administrators know well the expectations placed on them in virtual postsecondary educational organizations. They are expected to operate at Internet speed—emails answered quickly and completely, all information readily accessible online. Technology-mediated delivery of educational content can contain an implicit expectation that administrative services will operate in a similar manner and at similar speeds as delivery. Effective organizations match delivery and administrative expectations by viewing these systems as complementary processes. The best organizations will realize that integrated systems may work best when students play a significant role in self-managing aspects of the administrative process, as is increasingly the case with the instructional process.

Outsourcing Instructional Technology Systems May Be Too Risky

For the vast majority of organizations in this study, the instructional technology system is a function that is so critical that outsourcing is simply too risky. As a key component that defines a virtual postsecondary educational organization, the technology delivery system is a core competency that must remain within the organization if organizational success is to be achieved. It does not mean, however, that outsourcing should not be considered. CECC has had very good experiences with its technology partners. The relationship has freed the organization's managers from hiring technical staff to manage the system, which has kept head count low and costs down.

IMPLICATIONS FOR KEY ACTORS

Government Leaders and Other Policy Makers

The external environment of virtual postsecondary educational organizations is influenced to a great degree by the rules, policies and expectations of federal and state government and other policy making bodies such as accreditation agencies. The influence of these organizations is likely to continue so long as the current laws and expectations remain in place. For many of these institution's leaders, policy making bodies were lagging in their ability to address the concerns that their organizations were raising. The result was often a feeling of constraint in the options leaders had available in designing their system. The problem may be that these organizations and their products are difficult to categorize since most might be conceived as some blend of education and electronic commerce. They are commodities crossing state lines, yet subject to the same guarantees of quality as should be expected by a residential student in a classroom. The implication is that virtual postsecondary educational organizations need product validation and support for students that these institutional bodies can provide.

A related issue concerns policies at the state level. In particular, roles that states may take in this arena to encourage, discourage or shape the development of these kinds of organizations. First, it is clear that for state-affiliated organizations knowledge as a commodity is an important standpoint. As institutions cross traditional geographic boundaries with their products, institutional missions are often affected. Consider the national and global enrollments of a community college like CECC. Clearly, community has a different meaning than the one to which most have become accustomed. State government leaders must realize that these organizations are economic development instruments, with knowledge as the principal export commodity. Second, and related to the first point, if one sees virtual postsecondary educational organizations in terms of economic development, then the actions a particular state may take become immediately joined to other industry or sector actors. By highlighting the constraints placed on these organizations by the Federal government's financial aid polices, for example, one may argue that the Federal government is restraining trade in the states. Overcoming these restraints may position entities from government, non-profits and for-profit organizations that could benefit from expansion of educational trade into a new coalition for affecting change.

Academic Leaders and Administrators

I address the implications of this research to two types of academic leaders and administrators—those who are considering virtual postsecondary educational organizations and those who are already embedded within them. For those administrators considering virtual postsecondary educational organizations, this research raises numerous issues for consideration. In fact, the organizational histories of each organization may prove to be the most valuable planning tool for deciphering the pitfalls and advantages of organizational actions. The adaptation cycle may also be useful as a strategic planning tool, particularly for considering the implications of legitimacy, which are explicitly considered.

For administrators of virtual postsecondary educational organizations within embedded institutions, the adaptive cycle may be used to continually reconsider the influences of certain "givens" in the organization. Periodic review of the adaptive cycle of their organizations may cause administrators to question why things are as they are and consider new strategies for understanding, renewal and relationship building. In addition, understanding the adaptive cycle and its influences may raise questions about which aspects of the organizational system need more attention. What the adaptive cycle does not provide are answers to questions of how to adapt more effectively, although the predicted characteristics for success may provide some insights.

For both situations, the findings of this study may cause leaders and administrators to look at their organization less in relation to its formal organization chart, but as a dynamic set of relationships. The influence of those relationships—their strength and nature—provides a new map of the organization and its influence. It may also help to direct strategic action by identifying key actors who are critical to success in solving the adaptation cycle problems. The net effect may be to move practical actors in the direction of rational action or reflective decision making.

Faculty Members

In the previous chapter I noted: "It would seem that organizations that can de-emphasize the influence of internal actors in the system (without a debilitating loss of legitimacy) may achieve greater success." While internal actors are considered here to be both faculty and administrators, actions by groups representing faculty such as the American Association of University Professors, may view the faculty aspect of "internal actors" with less than benign interest. My approach in making the statement is a straightforward one—those organizations that can minimize internal political conflict while maintaining legitimacy are in a better position to succeed than those organizations that do not. The statement raises a fundamental issue for faculty. How will content providers play a role in shaping the organizational system beyond that of merely being viewed as an input to the system or a nominal check on quality? The answer may lie in understanding what I see as tension within the academic environment within some of these institutions.

One may view the make up of the academic community in a polarized way as consisting of two politically motivated groups—those who want a customer or market-centered perspective (often held by administrative leaders) versus a faculty-centered view (often but not always held by faculty and instructors). The Customer/Market-centered mind believes the system exists to give students what they want by responding very quickly to the will of the market. The Faculty-centered mind believes the system exists to serve the faculty member or instructor as the central actor in the educational process.

As the minds collide, a key question for faculty members or instructors (of either mind) to ask is: how will my perspective be included? This includes asking questions about compensation, incentives, quality control, competing demands and full versus adjunct appointments. By raising these questions, I contend that a tacit negotiation begins that may resolve itself into a middle ground in which the learner-centered perspective may emerge. Borrowing from the language of Penn State's World Campus, the fusion of views gives rise to a learning community. The Learner-centered view recognizes that this is a highly negotiated environment with but one focus—to understand and provide what the learner needs, not necessarily just what the learner wants or what an instructor is willing to provide. The question assumes that many different constituencies will play a role. It remains to be seen what role faculty and instructors will play in this negotiated environment.

Entrepreneurs and Venture Capitalists

The implications of this research for some entrepreneurs will be to solve the problems associated with the adaptive cycle. This may include providing marketing systems, technology services with extensive data mining capability or even act as a partner who is intended to enhance status (one might easily imagine a top management consulting firm offering an executive certificate in conjunction with a top business school or several business schools that would be available to a wide audience). The degree to which outsourcing becomes a more widespread organizational practice may help to determine how quickly entrepreneurs could enter the educational marketplace.

For venture capitalists the adaptive cycle is yet another tool for examining the strength of an organization based on very specific questions about the organizations' proposed solutions to four critical problems. Organizations that are worthy of investment capital must typically demonstrate a viable revenue stream to support and grow the operation. However, the findings of this study suggest that "relationship capital" may be a very critical (though subjective) characteristic determining whether a virtual postsecondary educational organization is a viable investment. The adaptive cycle provides two important windows for considering relationships; through the learning and legitimizing coat-tails effects . Investors might inquire as to the nature of relationships as an additional strategy for considering an investment. One may infer that the long-term capital investment strategy for these organizations is one in which a profit or a self-sustaining revenue position is highly unlikely in the first few years. Assessment of a suitable exit strategy for these organizations is potentially similar to many Internet start-up companies, which, though potentially highly valued, are not profitable in their first several years. Using NTU as an example, the blending of for and not-for-profit organizations may create new revenue sources, but this also exposes the organization to greater risk and possible survival issues if investor's return on investment is not met.

POTENTIAL LIMITATIONS OF THE STUDY

This study is limited to the extent that the original typology used to select the cases represents an accurate image of the organizational types existing within the Knowledge Industry. In a dynamic environment, such as the one experienced by these organizations, new organizational permutations are evolving at a rapid pace. The selection of the cases in this study was done to represent distinct types, all of which deliver technology-mediated distance education and possess either internal or stable network organizational characteristics as delineated in the selection framework. However, the evolving nature of these organizations can make it difficult to specify an overall population. Variance was reduced by restricting the cases to those in which differences in characteristics were most transparent (in spite of difficulties in getting institutions to cooperate) and which were consistent with the selection framework.

A second potential limitation involves the likelihood that the adaptation cycle model resulting from this study is too idiosyncratic. The findings of this study attempt to create understanding of differences across these organizations in a way that is novel by providing evidence of non-obvious relationships that have emerged through the analysis. The method was employed to ensure that the findings were empirically valid and testable. By incorporating diverse literatures, the adaptation cycle model may perhaps be applied more broadly, but it remains essentially a conceptual approach that is particular to this organizational phenomenon.

FUTURE DIRECTIONS AND THE SIGNIFICANCE OF THIS RESEARCH

Much remains to be accomplished. Immediate contributions can be made by those scholars bold enough to define systematically and categorically the population of organizations comprising the Knowledge Industry and for the most ambitious, the population of organizations comprising the Knowledge Sector. No methodology has emerged to extract information about the new ventures, embedded units or cross-institutional alliances that may provide the population level data that could be so interesting to scholars in numerous disciplines. And as the organizations fail, it would be important to gain understanding about their rate of failure from a population level. From an organization level, clearly, much is yet to be explored. The focus upon differences and adaptation in this study provides an initial contribution. However, moving from a theoretical base to analyze the empirical or using the empirical to create generalizable theory are each viable and necessary alternatives. Finally, a major hurdle to theoretical and empirical study remains the emerging mixture of non-and for-profit entities that differ substantially in the degree of access they will provide to researchers. Building trust relationships over time and drawing on lessons from colleagues in the for-profit sector may provide essential clues for resolving this challenge.

Educational research poses a twofold responsibility—explore questions of theoretical and empirical import to the field, while considering the utility of research for practical application. The outcomes of this study are critically important for reasons that are time sensitive and empirically and theoretically relevant. A theoretically derived model is essential since the synthesis and integration of empirical findings, assertions of generalizability, and direction of future research may be undermined without such research. Timely and relevant research is needed to guide the actions of those designing and managing organizations as well. This is especially relevant in fields such has higher education, which have historically emphasized the importance of practice as a research outcome.

Specifically, the contribution of this research is that it places these organizations in an educational environment that is both competitive and institutional; understanding that technology has extended the knowledge services of multiple competitors in a medium that breaks down the geographic boundaries of residential education. However, it also recognizes that the status and legitimacy of these organizations is still very much in question and therefore, has explored the manner in which the management team responds to this organizational imperative. This study examined how organizational forms firmly rooted in the emerging Knowledge Industry may differ according to their approach to solving four adaptive problems: 1.) Matching market opportunities to organizational capacity; 2.) Designing systems that connect market opportunities to organizational capacity; 3.) Managing the system; and 4.) Legitimizing the system and its products. In so doing, I have tried to offer insights as to the success that these organizations may achieve based on their ability to adapt effectively.

Typology of Postsecondary Education Organizational Forms Supporting Virtual Educational Delivery within the United States

	Private sector sponsored				Public sector sponsored			
Descriptive Variable and Form	**Business/ Corporate**	**Stand-alone Proprietary Institution**	**Proprietary, Public and/or Private Higher Education Institution - Corporate-sector Alliance**	**Public or Private Higher Education Institution Continuing Education**	**Public Higher Education System Utility**	**Virtual Campus within a Public Higher Institution or System**	**Statewide Consortium of Public and/or Private Higher Education Institutions**	**Multi-State Consortium of Public and Private Higher Education Institutions**
Current Examples	Dell University, Oracle University, Intel University, Novell Education Division	University of Phoenix (On-line Campus), Intenational University, Magellan University, Knowledge Universe	Michigan Virtual Automotive College, National Technological University	NYU Virtual College, New School DIAL program, U-California Ext. Center for Media and Independent Learning	Network for Education and Technology Services (U-Maine System)	Pennsylvania State University World Campus (Institution), Colorado Electronic Community College (System)	Minnesota Virtual University, California Virtual University	Western Governors University, The Community College Distance Learning Network
Educational Product or Service	Training Modules, management education	Degrees, certificates, short courses, training modules	Facilitate development, delivery and marketing of degrees (customized) certificates, short courses	Degrees, certificates, short courses	Facilitate delivery, development, marketing of degrees (customized), certificates, short courses	Facilitate development, delivery, marketing of degrees (customized), certificates, short courses	Degrees, certificates, short courses	Degrees, certificates, short courses (most under consideration)
Principal Clientele	Corporate Employees	Working adults and corporate clients	Working adults, Contracted educational clients	Woking adults	Branch Campuses, educational partners, and a wide variety of students	Working adults	Residents of the state and potentially a global audience as well	Residents of multiple states and potentially international students as well
Organizational Mission	Provide education and training for employees in order to enhance business competitiveness	Provide access to distance/time independent educational experiences	Provide access to distance/time independent educational experiences to corporate partners and/or niche audiences	Provide access to distance/time independent educational experiences	Facilitate the educational outreach missions of individual campuses	Provide access to distance/time independent educational experiences	Facilitate the educational outreach missions of public and private higher education institutions within the state	Facilitate the educational outreach missions of individual institutions and their partners and offer degree or certificate programs in some instances

Bibliography

Acker, S. R. (1995). Space, collaboration, and the credible city: Academic work in the virtual university. *Journal of Computer Mediated Communication.* Available: http://cwis.usc.edu/dept/annenberg/journal.html, 1–11.

Aldrich, H. E. (1979). *Organizations and environments.* Englewood Cliffs, NJ: Prentice-Hall.

Alexander, M. (1997). Getting to grips with the virtual organization. *Long Range Planning, 30*(1), 122–124.

Arrow, K.J. (1974). *The limits of organization.* New York, NY: W.W. Norton & Co., Inc.

Baker, W. E. (1992). The network organization in theory and practice. In N. Nohria, & R.C. Eccles (Eds.), *Networks and organizations* (pp. 397–429). Boston: Harvard Business School Press.

Baker, W. J. & Gloster, A. S. (1994). Moving towards the virtual university: A vision of technology in higher education. *Cause-Effect, 17*(2).

Baldwin, L.V. (1997, July). *The national technological university: A pioneering "virtual university."* Paper presented at the Tokyo Institute of Technology, Tokyo, Japan.

Baum, J.A.C. & Oliver, C. (1992). Institutional embeddedness and the dynamics of organizational populations. *American Sociological Review, 57,* 540–59.

Birnbaum, R. (1988). *How colleges work. The cybernetics of academic organization and leadership.* San Francisco, CA: Jossey-Bass Publishers.

Blau, P. M., & Scott, W. R. (1962). *Formal organizations.* San Francisco: Chandler.

Blau, J. R., & Others. (1994). *The expansion of two-year colleges: Tests of institutional and political economy theories in a dynamic model* (ED368399).

Brand, M. (1995, Fall). The wise use of technology. *Educational Record*, 39–45.

Brown, J. S. & Duguid, P. (1995). *Universities in the digital age.* Palo Alto, CA: Xerox Corporation.

Burns, J.M. (1978). *Leadership.* New York: Harper & Row.

Cameron, K. S. (1991). Organizational adaptation and higher education. In M. W. Peterson (Ed.), *Organization and governance in higher education* (pp. 284–299). Needham Heights, MA: Ginn Press.

Chellappa, R., Barua, A. & Whinston, A.B. (1997). An electronic infrastructure for a virtual university. *Communications of the ACM, 40(9),* 56–58.

Chesbrough, H. W. & Teece, D.J. (1996, January/February). When is virtual virtuous? Organizing for innovation. *Harvard Business Review, 74,* 65–71.

Child, J. (1972). Organizational structure, environment and performance: The role of strategic choice. *Sociology, 6,* 1–22.

Clark, B. R. (1991). The organizational saga in higher education. In M. W. Peterson (Ed.), *Organization and governance in higher education* (pp. 46–52). Needham Heights, MA: Ginn Press.

Daft, R. L. & Weick, K.E. (1984). Toward a model of organizations as interpretation systems. *Academy of Management Review, 9(2),* 284–295.

Davidow, W. H. & Malone., M.S. (1992). *The virtual corporation.* New York: HarperBusiness.

Davis, T. R. V. & Darling, B.L. (1995, Summer). How virtual corporations mange the performance of contractors: The super bakery case. *Organizational Dynamics, 24,* 70–75.

Dill, W. R. (1958). Environment as an influence on managerial autonomy. *Administrative Science Quarterly, 2,* 409–443.

DiMaggio, P. J. (1983). State expansion and organizational fields. In R. H. Hall & R. E. Quinn (Eds.), *Organizational theory and public policy* (pp. 147–161). Beverly Hills, CA: Sage Publications.

DiMaggio, P. J. (1992). Nadel's paradox revisited: Relational and cultural aspects of organizational structure. In N. Nohria, & R.C. Eccles (Eds.), *Networks and organizations* (pp. 118–142). Boston: Harvard Business School Press.

DiMaggio, P. J. & Powell, W. W. (1983). The iron cage revisited: Institutional isomorphism and collective rationality in organizational fields. *American Sociological Review, 48,* 147–160.

Dolence, M. G. & Norris, D. M. (1995). *Transforming higher education*. Ann Arbor, MI: Society for College and University Planning.

Dore, R. (1983). Goodwill and the spirit of market capitalism. *British Journal of Sociology, 34*, 459–482.

Dowling, J. & Pfeffer, J. (1975). Organizational legitimacy: Social values and organizational behavior. *Pacific Sociological Review, 18*, 122–136.

Eisenhardt, K. M. (1989). Building theories from case study research. *Academy of Management Review, 14(4)*, 532–550.

Emerson, R. M. (1962). Power-dependence relations. *American Sociological Review, 27*, 31–40.

Faucheux, C. (1997). How virtual organizing is transforming management science. *Communications of the ACM, 40(9)*, 50–55

Galbraith, J. (1977). *Organization design*. Reading, MA: Addison-Wesley.

Garton, L., Haythornthwaite, C. & Wellman, B. (1997). Studying online social networks. *Journal of Computer-Mediated Communication, 3(1)*. (Online). Available: *http://www.ascusc.org/jcmc/vol3/issue1/garton.html*. (January 8, 2002).

Grenier, R. & Metes, G. (1995). *Going virtual: Moving your organization into the 21st century*. Upper Saddle River, NJ: Prentice Hall.

Handy, C. (1995, May/June). Trust and the virtual organization. *Harvard Business Review, 73*, 40–50.

Holmberg, B. (1989). *Theory and practice of distance education* (2nd ed.). New York: Routledge.

Homans, G. C. (1950). *The human group*. New York: Harcourt.

Hrebiniak, L. G. & Joyce, W. F. (1985). Organizational adaptation: Strategic choice and environmental determinism. *Administrative Science Quarterly, 30(3)*, 336–349.

Huber, G. P. & Daft, R.L. (1987). The information environments of organizations. In F. M. Jablin, L.L. Putnam, K.H. Roberts, & L.W. Porter (Eds.), *Handbook of Organizational Communication*. (130–164), Newbury Park, CA: Sage Publications.

Hurst, F. (1998). So you want to start a virtual university? *On the Horizon, 6(4)*, 1–8.

Ives, B. & Jarvenpaa, S. L. (1996). Will the internet revolutionize business education and research? *Sloan Management Review, 37(3)*, 33–41.

Johnstone, S. M. & Krauth, B. (1996, March/April). Some principles of good practice for the virtual university. *Change*, 38–41.

Jones, D. P. (1995). *Higher education and high technology: A case for joint action* (Report No. HE 029 147). Boulder, CO: National Center for Education Management Systems. (ERIC Document Reproduction Service No. ED 400 721).

Jurkovich, R. (1974). A core typology of organizational environments. *Administrative Science Quarterly, 19*, 380–394.

Kamens, D.H. (1977). Legitimizing myths and educational organization: The relationship between organizational ideology and formal structure. *American Sociological Review (42)*2, 208–219.

Katz, D. & Kahn, R. (1978). *The social psychology of organizations.* New York: John Wiley & Sons.

Kauffman, R. (1996, Summer). Assessing the virtual university. *Adult Assessment Forum*, 13–16.

Keller, G. (1993). Strategic planning in a competitive environment. In R.H. Glover & M.V. Krotseng (Ed.), *Developing executive information systems for higher education (New Directions for Institutional Research, 77,* pp. 9–15). San Francisco: Jossey-Bass Publishers.

Kimberly, J. R. (1975). Environmental constraints and organizational structure: A comparative analysis of rehabilitation organizations. *Administrative Science Quarterly, 20*, 1–9.

Krackhardt, D. (1992). The strength of strong ties: The importance of philos in organizations. In N. Nohria, & R.C. Eccles (Eds.), *Networks and organizations* (pp. 216–239). Boston: Harvard Business School Press.

Lawrence, P. R. & Lorsch, J. W. (1967). *Organization and environment.* Boston: Graduate School of Business Administration, Harvard University.

Leana, C. & Rousseau, D. (in press). Relational wealth: A new model for employment in 21st century. Oxford University Press.

Lee, J. (1993). The evolution of organizational adaptation in Korea. *Journal of Asian Business, 9*(4), 72–89.

Lenzner, R. & Johnson, S.S. (1997). Seeing things as they are. *Forbes, 159*(5), 122–128.

March, J. G. (1987). Old colleges, new technology. In S. K. & L. Sproull (Eds.), *Computing and change on campus* (pp. 16–27). Cambridge: Cambridge University Press.

Matkin, G. W. (1997). Organizing university economic development: Lessons from continuing education and technology transfer. In J. P. Pappas (Ed.), *The university's role in economic development: From research to outreach* (pp. 27–41). San Francisco: Jossey-Bass Publishers.

McKelvey, B. (1982). *Organizational systematics.* Berkeley: University of California Press.

Meyer, J. W. & Rowan, B. (1977). Institutional organizations: Formal structure as myth and ceremony. *American Journal of Sociology, 83*, 340–363.

Meyer, J. W., Scott, W. R. & Deal, T . E. (1981). Institutional and technical sources of organizational structure. In H. D. Stein (Ed.), *Organization and human services* (pp. 151–178). Philadelphia: Temple University Press.

Meyer, J. W. & Scott, W. R. (1983). *Organizational environments: Ritual and rationality.* Beverly Hills, CA: Sage Publications.

Miles, R. E. & Snow, C. C. (1978). *Organizational strategy, structure, and process.* New York: McGraw-Hill Book Company.

Miles, R. & Snow, C. (1986). Organizations: New concepts for new forms. *California Management Review, 28*(3), 62–73.

Miles, R. E., Snow, C. C., Meyer, A. D., & Coleman, H. J. (1978, July). Organizational strategy , structure, and process. *Academy of Management Review,* 546–562.

Miles, R. H. (1980). *Macro organizational behavior.* Glenview, IL: Scott, Foresman and Company.

Mowshowitz, A. (1994). Virtual organization: A vision of management in the information age. *Information and Society, 10*(4), 267–288.

Mowshowitz, A. (1997, September). Virtual organization. *Communications of the ACM, 40*(9), 30–37.

NRENAISSANCE Committee, et al. (1994). *Realizing the information future.* Washington, DC: National Academy Press.

O'Leary, D. E., Kuokka, D., & Plant, R. (1997). Artificial intelligence and virtual organizations. *Communications of the ACM, 40*(1), 52–59.

Orlikowski, W. J. (1992, August). The duality of technology: Rethinking the concept of technology in organizations. *Organization Science, 3*(3), 398–427.

Penn State Outreach and Cooperative Extension. (1998, January). *Strategic plan update.* State College: Penn State University.

Perrin, D. G. (1997). New knowledge society and higher education. *ED Journal, 11*(3), 12–20.

Perrow, C. (1993). Small firm networks. In R. Swedberg (Ed.), *Explorations in economic sociology* (pp. 277–402). New York: Russell Sage Found.

Peterson, M. W. & Dill, D. D. (1997). Redefining the postsecondary Knowledge Industry: New challenges, a new paradigm and new planning perspectives. In M.W. Peterson, D.D. Dill, L.A. Mets, & Associates (Eds.), *Planning and management for a changing environment: A handbook on redesigning postsecondary institutions.* San Francisco: Jossey-Bass, Inc.

Pfeffer, J. & Salancik, G. R. (1978). *The external control of organizations.* New York: Harper & Row, Publishers.

Podolny, J.M. & Page, K.L. (1998). Network forms of organization. *Annual Review of Sociology, 24,* 57–76.

Podolny, J.M. & Phillips, D.J. (1996). The dynamics of organizational status. *Industrial and Corporate Change, 5,* 453–72.

Powell, W. W. (1990). Neither market nor hierarchy: Network forms of organizations. In B. M. Staw & L. L. Cummings (Eds.), *Research in organizational behavior, 12* (pp. 295–336). Greenwich, CT: JAI Press..

Rockhill, K. (1983). *Academic excellence and public policy: A history of university extension in California.* New Brunswick, NJ: Transaction Books.

Rossman, P. (1992). *The emerging worldwide electronic university.* Westport, CT: Greenwood Press.

Rucker, T. (1998, August-September). Accrediting virtual classes is key to remaining competitive. *Community College Journal, 69*(1), 36–40.

Ryan, J. H. (1997). *The world campus a report for discussion by the university community.* State College, PA: The Pennsylvania State University.

Schank, R. C. (1998). Horses for courses. *Communications of the ACM, 41*(7), 23–25.

Scott, W. R. & Meyer, J. W. (1988). Environmental linkages and organizational complexity: Public and private schools. In H.M. Levin & T. James (Ed.), *Comparing public and private schools* (pp. 128–160). New York: Falmer Press.

Scott, W. R. & Meyer, J. W. (1991). The organization of societal sectors: Propositions and early evidence. In W.W. Powell & P. J. DiMaggio (Eds.), *The new institutionalism in organizational analysis* (pp. 108–140). Chicago: The University of Chicago Press.

Scott, W. R. (1991). Unpacking institutional arguments. In W.W. Powell & P. J. DiMaggio (Eds.), *The new institutionalism in organizational analysis* (pp. 164–182). Chicago: The University of Chicago Press.

Scott, W. R. (1992). *Organizations rational, natural, and open systems.* Englewood Cliffs, NJ: Prentice Hall.

Singh, J. V., House, R. J., & Tucker, D. J. (1986). Organizational change and organizational mortality. *Administrative Science Quarterly, 31*, 587–611.

Snow, C.C., Miles, R. E., & Coleman, H. J. (1992). Managing 21st century network organizations. *Organizational Dynamics, 20*(3), 5–20.

Stake, R. K. (1994). Case studies. In N.K. Denzin & Y.S. Lincoln (Ed.), *Handbook of qualitative research* (pp. 236–247). Thousand Oaks, CA: Sage Publications.

Stinchcombe, A. L. (1965). Social structure and organizations. In J. G. March (Ed.), *Handbook of organizations* (pp. 142–193). Chicago: Rand McNally.

Stuart, T. E. , Hoang, H., & Hybels, R. (1997). *Interorganizational endorsements and the performance of entrepreneurial ventures.* Unpublished manuscript, University of Chicago Graduate School of Business.

Tapscott, D. & Caston, A. (1993). *Paradigm shift: The new promise of information technology.* New York: McGraw-Hill, Inc.

Thompson, J. (1967). *Organizations in action.* New York: McGraw-Hill.

Tolbert, P. S. & Zucker, L. G. (1983). Institutional sources of change in the formal structure of organizations: The diffusion of civil service reforms, 1880–1935. *Administrative Science Quarterly, 23,* 22–39.

Tolbert, P. (1985). Institutional environments and resource dependence: Sources of administrative structure in institutions of higher education. *Administrative Science Quarterly, 30* (1), 1–13.

Van Dusen, G.C. (1997). *The Virtual Campus : Technology and Reform in Higher Education.* Washington, DC. Ashe-Eric Higher Education Report, Vol. 25, No. 5.

Verdin, J. R. & Clark, T. A. (1991). *Distance education.* San Francisco: Jossey-Bass, Inc.

Voss, H. (1996, July/August). Virtual organizations: The future is now. *Strategy & Leadership, 24,* 12–16.

Vroom, V. H. (1969). Industrial social psychology. In G. Lindzey & E. Aronson (Eds.), *The handbook of social psychology: Vol. 5* (2nd ed., pp. 196–268). Reading, MA: Addison-Wesley.

Ward, D. (1994, January/February). Technology and the changing boundaries of higher education. *Educom Review,* 23–27.

Weiss, R. S. (1994). *Learning from strangers.* New York: The Free Press.

Williamson, O. E. (1975). *Markets and hierarchies: Analysis and antitrust implications.* New York: Free Press.

Zucker, L. G. (1977). The role of institutionalization in cultural persistence. *American Sociological Review, 42,* 726–743.

Index